# FURNITURE RESTORATION
## —— AND REPAIR ——

### F O R   B E G I N N E R S

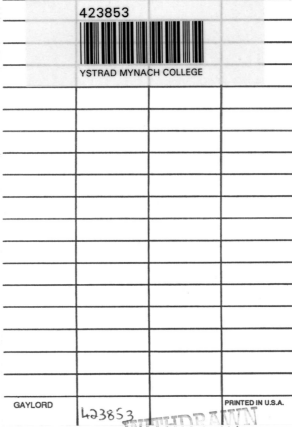

# FURNITURE RESTORATION AND REPAIR —

## FOR BEGINNERS

### KEVIN JAN BONNER

GUILD OF MASTER CRAFTSMAN PUBLICATIONS

First published 1994 by
Guild of Master Craftsman Publications Ltd,
166 High Street, Lewes,
East Sussex BN7 1XU
Reprinted 1997

© Kevin Bonner 1994

ISBN 0 946819 64 5

Photographs by Kevin Bonner, except where
credited otherwise.

**Back Cover photograph by Daniel Salaman.**

Illustrations on pages 13, 64, 71, 78, 79, 80, 81, 93, 95,
116, 120, 127, 153, 155 and 184 by Tim Benké.

Illustrations on pages 9, 23, 30, 51, 102, 134, 104, 148,
151, 152 and 160 by Rob Wheele.

Designed by Lawrance Design

Printed and bound in Singapore under the
supervision of
MRM Graphics, Winslow,
Buckinghamshire, UK

Typeset by Central Southern Typesetters,
Eastbourne, East Sussex

DEDICATION
*For Debbie*

# ACKNOWLEDGEMENTS

*I would like to thank the following for their help in the writing
of this book: Ben, Tom, Jo and Sam for lending a hand; Alice
for her unfaltering aesthetic judgement; all of my past students
– you taught me all I know; and Debbie, without whom nothing
would have been possible.*

*I am grateful to the following for their cooperation in lending
photographs: TRADA Technology Ltd; Arco Ltd; Stanley
Tools; Robert Bosch Ltd; Liberon Waxes Ltd; Cuprinol;
Hamilton Acorn Ltd; ICI Paints Ltd; Rustin's Ltd; John
Boddy Timber Ltd and John Boddy's Fine Wood & Tool Store
Ltd; Craft Supplies Ltd; David James; Peter Legg;
Buckinghamshire College; Eddy Wilson; Campbell Norman-
Smith; Steven Leyland; the trustees of the Wallace Collection;
the Geffrye Museum; Ian Hosker; Binks-Bullows Ltd;
Rentokil Ltd; Do It All Ltd.*

*Apologies to Uncle George and anyone who goes by the name
of Bodger.*

# CONTENTS

# INTRODUCTION

*So here it is at last: from Chippendale to chipboard, how to fix a wobbly chair or a scratched table top; how to French polish, apply a wax finish or remove white ring marks. Absolutely no experience is required and every process is taken step by easy step. Every question is answered and no knowledge is presumed. All you will need to repair and restore any piece of wooden furniture, from the most shambolic to the almost perfect, is this book and just a little bit of enthusiasm.*

Every house in the land, from the smallest flat to the grandest palace, contains furniture. Whatever the present condition, sooner or later, it will need care and repair. If you are looking for an enjoyable and rewarding hobby, look no further than your own tables and chairs. With very few materials and little equipment needed, furniture restoring is an ideal way of becoming involved in an interesting and profitable craft.

If you are setting up home, or on a limited budget, you can use the information in this book when buying second-hand furniture, and turn a piece of junk into a highly prized asset. If you only use this book once in your lifetime, you will easily recoup the cover price.

The information in this guide is the result of listening, learning and responding to the needs and questions of the fellow enthusiasts that have attended my furniture restoration classes over the years. The language will be kept as free as possible from technical terms and 'jargon'.

A B O V E : **This is a good example of what not to restore; the replacement of missing parts is always difficult and expensive.**

Everything in this book is well within the capabilities of someone who has no experience of craftwork or D.I.Y. If you have never picked up a paintbrush before, do not fret. In my experience you are just as well qualified as anyone else to learn how to restore furniture.

Although the manner in which the information conveyed in this book is directed at the absolute beginner, this should not repel more experienced readers. This book contains information that is in common use by the seasoned professional. Whatever your level of experience, if you are looking for an easy-to-follow explanation of some of the more complicated procedures found in furniture restoration, such as French polishing, staining or ebonizing, this book is for you. All of the methods, preparations and information detailed in its pages are also applicable to antique furniture.

Much that is privy to the professional furniture restorer is simple information. That information is passed on in the following chapters, enabling you to decide which procedures are best for your particular project. I shall take you through the essential steps of furniture restoration: stripping, fixing, staining and finishing.

We shall cover all the common finishing techniques and assess their properties. These include ease and speed of application, flammability, toxicity, durability, resistance to water and alcohol, and odour whilst applying. This will enable you to judge for yourself which finish suits your particular project and circumstances.

There are certain crafts allied to furniture restoration that I have not covered. Either they are better served by a separate book (e.g. upholstery), or they are beyond the capabilities of the absolute beginner (e.g. cabinetmaking). Cabinetmaking for the absolute beginner is a contradiction in terms. Most cabinetmaking techniques would involve an outlay for tools and equipment far beyond the needs of the weekend furniture restorer.

## TOOLS AND EQUIPMENT

One of the really nice things about furniture restoration is that the tools and equipment needed are minimal, inexpensive and are usually to be found in the average home.

Most of the materials I suggest you use are available from the local D.I.Y. shop. If you experience any problems obtaining supplies, or are interested in bulk purchases, I have included a list of manufacturers (*see* page 188) who will send you a list of local stockists. Many of them also operate mail order services.

I shall presume that you are working in a space set aside at home, in a small workshop, garage or outside in the garden. I shall also presume that the furniture to be restored is intact and not in need of a new leg, a replacement drawer, or of large sections recarved in the neogothic tradition.

If your chosen project is missing vital parts, I suggest you enlist the help of a weekend cabinetmaker. However, in my experience this should not be necessary; there is enough 100 per cent intact furniture around to keep you busy until you have completely worn out the pages of this book.

During my years of teaching furniture restoration to absolute beginners, I have observed that certain problems seem to recur more frequently than others. Over the next few pages I shall offer solutions to some of the more common problems faced by those new to the craft.

## GOING WITH THE FLOW (OR TAKING THE EASY WAY OUT)

One of the odd things about this craft that I have noticed is that it tends to bring out the heroic in certain people. Now I realize that in times of national emergency, when mountains need shifting, flooded rivers need swimming or the dog needs a walk, this trait can have its benefits; if you are the sort of person who revels in a crisis and excels in times of stress, please ignore the rest of this section.

However, if you enjoy a quiet life and are content with your lot then the following may come as a relief: if you find yourself saddled with an impossible task (and sometimes you won't realize this until you are part way through the project), there may be an alternative approach you haven't thought of, turning your problem into an opportunity. I call this going with the flow.

For example, say the cabinet you are restoring has been covered in unsightly black ink stains, it is far quicker, better and less stressful to ebonize or paint it rather than spend months trying to remove the blemishes so that you can French polish it.

Likewise, if you find an old table in a garage that has been contaminated with engine oil or some such murky substance, rather than spend weeks scrubbing it with petrol to remove the oil, why not take the opportunity to try out an oil finish. If you have had to fill sections of your project with copious amounts of filler, think about trying a painted finish rather than spending weeks trying to patch in the correct colour. Allow the furniture to speak to you. It will often tell you the best type of finish for it.

## THINK AHEAD

Often my over-enthusiastic students will charge relentlessly on with a project without stopping to think about the function of the finished piece. There is an old music hall joke which is worth telling in this context:

First man: 'Did you know that if you wear that hat all the time you will go bald?'
Second man: 'If I wear this hat all the time no one will know that I am bald.'

It loses a lot when put into print, but the basic idea is sound. If you have a nasty and difficult-to-remove blemish in the middle of the coffee table then how about putting a tablecloth and a vase of dried flowers over the blemish and be done with it.

The logical extension of this is taking 'going with the flow' to a catatonic state, which is not what I am advocating and is of course the antithesis of this book. But it does illustrate a very important point: consider the use you are going to put the furniture to before investing your precious time restoring it. If you intend it as a gift for the Prince of Wales, a different approach is called for than if you are using it to cover the damp patch in the spare bedroom. Think ahead.

## BLEMISH INTO AN EYESORE

The other thing to be wary of is turning a small, charming and perfectly acceptable blemish into an eyesore. This is a common practice with beginners who lack furniture in need of serious restoration. They will try and remove minor scratches and wind up with something that stands out like a boil on a nose and have science fiction writers knocking on their door to look at that strange and nauseous disfigurement to their otherwise beautiful coffee table.

If you are an absolute beginner, start off with something that needs stripping completely. It is the small things that often turn into disasters, as they need the most skill and experience.

## OLD FURNITURE, NEW FINISH

When furniture of a certain age is restored and refinished, there is often a visual contradiction between its old, almost antique wood and the brand new finish that looks as if it has just been delivered from the showroom. If you identify this problem with your projects you may wish to consider using some of the distressing methods described in Chapter 23.

## CRAFTSPERSON'S DILEMMA

There is a malady I have become aware of which I have christened the craftsperson's dilemma. It is a very common condition affecting about four out of 10 of my students, as well as numerous professional craftspeople. The symptoms will appear quite suddenly and without warning. A student will enter the class with a beautifully restored chair, or something similar. From their back pocket they will produce a magnifying glass and ask me to peer at a microscopic scratch on the underside of the chair and ask me the best way to remove it. Now then, unless you throw some pretty wild parties, nobody, but nobody, will see these blemishes; that is, except the person who has spent the last month lovingly restoring it.

This is known as the craftsperson's dilemma: you have spent the best weeks of your life on this project, stripping, staining, fixing and then lovingly refinishing. The furniture has almost been exuded from your skin and then reconstituted by you; now you are having problems letting go. You do not know when to stop. You stare at length at the project looking for mistakes and blemishes so that you can make it just a little more perfect. Perfectly good restorations have been ruined by people tinkering with them in this way. In extreme cases craftspeople have been known to strip the finish off and start all over again.

I am aware of the symptoms and I can sympathize, as I am a fellow reformed sufferer. I used to lose a fortune standing at exhibitions and pointing out to anyone who admired my work the imperfections that only I could see. A potential customer would come to my stand with chequebook open and pay me a compliment on the craftsmanship or some such trivia, while writing out the cheque. Then I would chip in with, 'Yes you are quite right, but have you seen under here where I scratched it this morning as I was getting it out of the van?' The chequebook would be neatly folded away while the ex-cheque writer would peer disdainfully at a miniscule blemish that could in all probability be removed by huffing on it and polishing with a sleeve.

But I am better now; these days I take a photograph of the project before I sell it and show it to whoever will look. Then slowly, I find, you can start to let go, and pass all of your love and affection on to the next project. But beware, it can be a recurring problem.

There is a trick I have learnt that has helped me to cope with this problem: I take one step back, take my glasses off and stare at the blemish to see if it is still apparent. If it disappears, from then onwards the blemish is referred to as character. If it can still be seen, then it will have to be dealt with. Now I fully understand that for some of you with worse eyesight than mine, or who wear contact lenses, this is not an ideal way of assessing the seriousness of blemishes, but I think you get the drift of what I am saying and can make up a test of your own.

## UNCLE GEORGE

Another problem that plagues the absolute beginner is what over the years has become termed 'Uncle George'. The problem that Uncle George has come to personify is bad advice.

All you have to do is to announce in a crowded place that you are restoring some furniture and you will be able to write a book on the advice you will receive from Uncle Georges.

Often this advice is totally useless, if not downright dangerous, and you can rest assured that it will take the constitution of a foot-in-the-door salesperson on an incentive bonus to resist not saying sweetly to the Uncle George, 'Thank you, I'll give it a try'.

Often the advice is proffered with a leering, knowing look accompanied by an avuncular wink and is whispered in your ear as though he were telling you the number of a safe deposit box in Fort Knox.

Resist, resist is all I can advise. If you have tried all the remedies in this book and all else fails, then try Uncle George's recipe, and good luck to you.

The most important advice that I give to all of my students is this: some time during your endeavours in furniture restoration you will make a mistake; do not fret, you are in good company – failure is just one of the lessons on the road to success.

NOW SHOWING! STRANGE + NAUSEOUS DISFIGUREMENT OF COFFEE TABLE

# CHAPTER 1

# ABOUT WOOD

PHOTO COURTESY OF JOHN BODDY TIMBER LTD.

*Few things in our lives are permanent. No sooner do we get used to the strangeness of the newfangled than we are throwing it out. In such a climate it is comforting to consider that we have in our daily lives a material that has been a constant feature in mankind's evolution from the cave to the highrise office block.*

## MAN'S RELATIONSHIP WITH WOOD

From swinging through the canopy to engaging in high-level discussions in timber-panelled board-rooms, wood and the constructions made from it have been prevalent in every culture since pre-history. Wood has a direct connection to our most distant ancestors, and as such is more than just a pleasant and useful material; it is the design equivalent of air and water.

Our great grandparents understood the peculiarities and particular uses of different woods, but late twentieth-century society has lost touch with much of the knowledge that was once a common part of daily life. I hope that by reviving some of the knowledge of the basic structure and nature of wood it will make it easier for you to grasp some of the principles involved in working with and restoring the material.

If you have never worked with wood before, this information may appear academic, but you will soon see its importance when you start working with the material. It would be useful for you to take a closer look at some of the wood you have around your home, using it as a teaching aid to make comparisons and observations.

**Fig 1.1** A B O V E : **Sawing a prime ash log on a bandmill.**

# THE COMPOSITION OF WOOD

The most important fact to understand about wood is the way that it is constructed. The best way to comprehend the construction of wood is to imagine it as a tight bundle of straws, glued together. The living tree uses these 'straws' to transport liquid and nutrients to its leaves and upper reaches.

When the tree is converted to planks of wood, it is cut so that the straws are oriented along the length of the plank of wood (*see* Fig 1.1). When cut like this the wood is extremely strong. Once the wood is planed and sanded, these straws reveal themselves as the 'grain' of the wood. Depending on the species of the tree and how and where it grew, this grain can vary enormously in its colour and form. It is the nature of the grain that makes the character of the wood.

If you were to cut across the bundle of straws (grain) you would reveal the straw ends. This area of wood is called the 'end grain' (*see* Fig 1.2) and is much more absorbent than other areas of the wood. Everything that is made from solid wood will have areas of end grain and areas of side grain. Consequently, any wooden item will be more absorbent in some places than in others. This is an important consideration when staining and finishing wood (*see* page 114).

There is also a distinction to be made between coarse-grained and fine-grained wood. Few woods are absolutely marble smooth. Most woods will display a discernible texture when sanded smooth. This can vary from almost invisible pinpricks to pits that look like they have been caused by someone throwing a knife at the wood. Coarser grain woods such as ash, oak and elm, are composed of thicker straws. Smoother, fine-grained woods are composed of thin straws, typified by woods such as beech, mahogany and walnut (*see* Figs 1.3, 1.4 and 1.5).

'Figure' is a term used to describe the decorative pattern that the grain makes. This can vary enormously and is dependent on how the wood is cut during its production, what part of the tree the board is obtained from, and the species of tree.

**Fig 1.2** R I G H T : **End grain showing the ring pattern of growth in the wood.**

**Fig 1.4** A B O V E : **A mid-twentieth-century mahogany armchair.**

**Fig 1.3** A B O V E : **A Restoration chair of beech and cane.**

**Fig 1.5** A B O V E : **A hand-made bureau of walnut.**

## SOME BASIC PRINCIPLES

First, wood is hygroscopic – don't worry, it's not contagious. It means that the dry wood used in furniture-making contains a quantity of water. As part of a natural process it will evaporate from the wood and, if the conditions are right, it will also absorb water from the surrounding air.

When the wood absorbs water it swells slightly, and when it dries it shrinks slightly. This means that wood is in a constant state of 'movement', swelling in wet weather and shrinking in dry weather. As the weather changes so does the moisture content of the air and therefore the moisture content of the wood. This is typically characterized by rattling windows in dry summers and sticking doors in wet winters. It is important to be aware of this movement when working with solid wood.

An allied principle of this is, wood only moves (expands and contracts) to any great degree in one dimension: across the grain. Thus a large table top will move across the grain of the wood, i.e. the width of the table, but not along the length (see Fig 1.6). This process is going on in your furniture all the time, and if it hasn't been built to compensate for these natural forces it can be weakened and eventually destroyed by them.

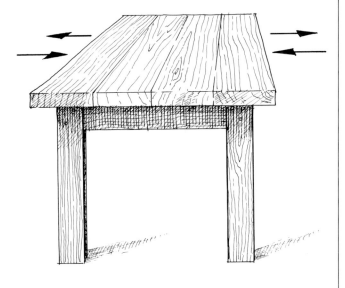

**Fig 1.6** A B O V E : **The expansion and contraction of a table top across its width.**

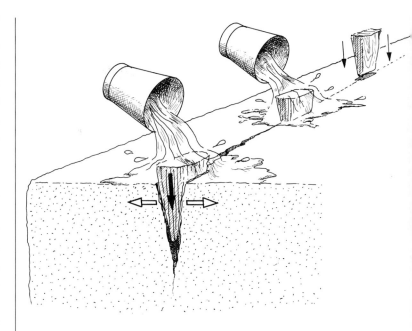

**Fig 1.7** A B O V E : **The Egyptian method of rock quarrying. By wedging dry wood into place, then soaking it, the expanding wood could be used to break away slabs of stone.**

The design of panelled doors is a good example of the way that designers have tried to cope with the natural expansion and contraction in wood. A much simpler and easier-to-make design would be a door made from boards, planed and then joined edge to edge in much the same way as some table tops are made. However, in times of dampness, expansion of the door would be so great that it would jam in the frame, making it impossible to open. In dry weather the door would rattle and let in draughts. By constructing the door using the 'frame and panel' method the wood can expand and contract with only minimal overall shrinkage and enlargement of the door, and it will last for generations.

As an indication of the forces that can be exerted by the movement of wood, the ancient Egyptians used to quarry stone by cutting wedge-shaped holes in the rock face; they would then hammer in a tightly fitting, bone-dry piece of wood and throw a bucket of water over it. The eventual expansion of the wood would crack the rock (see Fig 1.7).

For centuries, consideration of these natural forces has been incorporated into the design and making of all solid wood furniture . . .

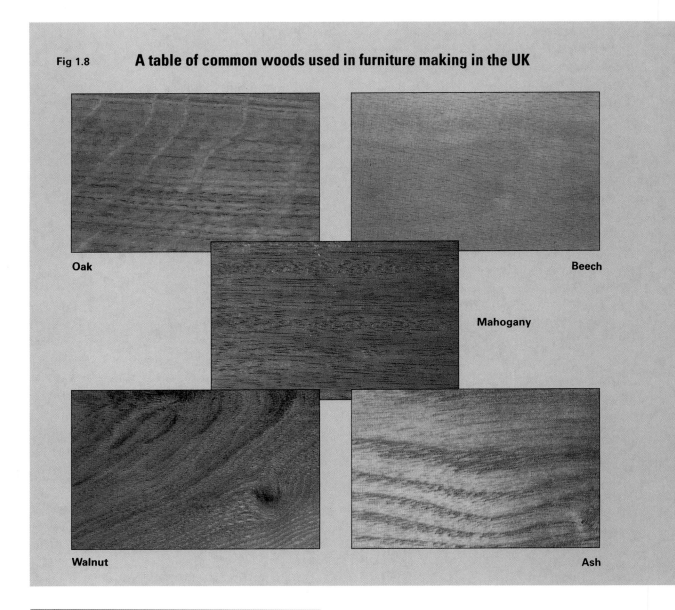

**Fig 1.8** **A table of common woods used in furniture making in the UK**

Oak

Beech

Mahogany

Walnut

Ash

## CENTRAL HEATING

. . . That is until the introduction of central heating. After that, every piece of furniture in the land, constructed using the accrued knowledge of past centuries, was subject to an unnatural, dry, warm atmosphere all year round. Wood in a centrally heated atmosphere no longer swelled in winter and dried out in the summer. It dried out, then dried out some more, and stayed dried out.

Consequently, a lot of good furniture, including many fine antiques, shrank more than the original designers intended, and around the world countless pieces of furniture were ruined. The joints in chairs that had been designed to last for generations shrank, and the glues gave way under the

stress. Cabinets slowly sprung their centuries-old veneer. Table tops suddenly shrank, cracked and warped, and whole sections of oak panelling peeled from the walls like old wallpaper.

One way to overcome the damaging effects of central heating on your furniture is to use humidifiers. These will maintain an even and acceptable moisture content in the air.

At the opposite end of the scale, table tops that are left with water on their surfaces due to rain or spillages, will expand on the top of the wood and will warp and bow under the stress.

Both of these symptoms are commonly seen in furniture restoration workshops. It is important to understand how they occur and the natural processes that wood goes through.

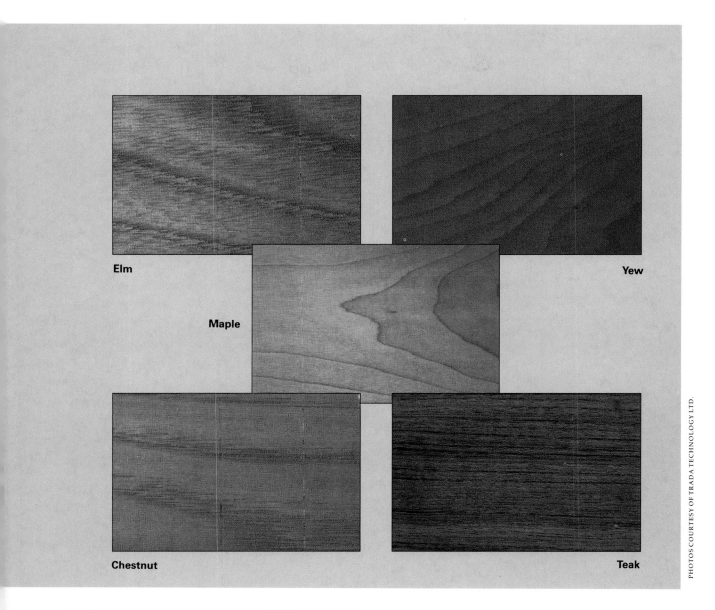

Elm

Yew

Maple

Chestnut

Teak

## DIFFERENT TYPES OF WOOD

There are hundreds of different types of wood used in furniture manufacture. Each has its own particular character, defined by its colour, figure, softness or hardness, oiliness, acidity, grain, density and weight.

Often identifying the type of woods that compose a piece of furniture can be difficult because the natural colour of the wood is altered by the patina, stain or bleach; there may be a colour incorporated into the finish that obscures the wood, or it may just be very dirty.

The best way to learn about woods is slowly, by first-hand experience. With each piece of furniture you work on try to find out the type of wood it is made from. Also, try to discover the names of woods that you find around the house. Soon you will see the same types of wood recurring.

It is not essential to know the type of wood in order to successfully restore it. I have yet to come across a bad restoration due to ignorance of the wood being used. However, the knowledge can be useful, especially when it comes to finishing: oiliness and acidity are features of some woods, and may not be immediately apparent. Some of these characteristics affect finishing techniques, but this will be covered in the relevant chapters.

As you work with wood you will very quickly become aware of its colour, weight, figure and grain structure. These should give you an indication of what the wood is, aided by Fig 1.8.

## MODERN MAN-MADE BOARDS

In the last 100 years great strides have been made in controlling the quirky nature of wood to render it more reliable in its behaviour and therefore more amenable to mass production. This has led to the development of a whole range of man-made timber substitutes (*see* Fig 1.9), many of which can be found in twentieth-century furniture (*see* Figs 1.10 and 1.11). The most successful, such as plywood, chipboard, blockboard and hardboard, are used in much of today's mass-produced furniture as well as in older furniture suitable for restoration.

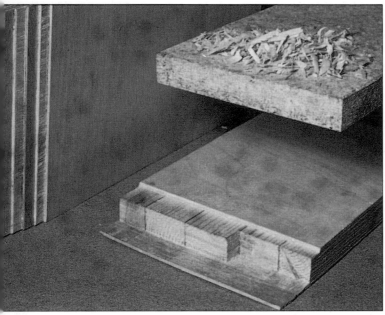

PHOTO COURTESY OF BUCKINGHAMSHIRE COLLEGE.

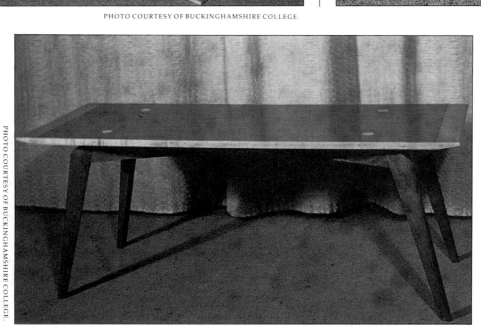

PHOTO COURTESY OF BUCKINGHAMSHIRE COLLEGE.

**Fig 1.10** A B O V E : **A plywood chair.**

**Fig 1.9** A B O V E  L E F T : **Timber substitutes: ply (left), chipboard (above right), and blockboard.**

**Fig 1.11** L E F T : **A chipboard table with walnut veneer.**

# CHAPTER 2

# WHAT TO RESTORE

*The type of furniture that passes through my teaching workshops is myriad. As well as chairs, side tables and writing boxes, it has included toilet seats, game boards, staircase handrails, telephone boxes, plant holders, shoe stretchers, and many larger items that are restored by proxy.*

## FINDING THE RIGHT PROJECT

Most of the furniture restoration projects that are brought to my lessons are much-loved household items that have been lying around the home, attic or garage waiting to have a bit of time and energy spent on them. Once my students have fixed all the miscreant furniture they possess, they look for the next project. This can be found in many places; perhaps the most common supply is friends and relatives.

Without a little forethought and planning you can soon become lumbered with the wrong project for the wrong reasons. Beware! This is a common problem encountered by the absolute beginner; you finish your first project and proudly proclaim to all that will listen your new-found skills. If you find it difficult to say no, before long you will be booked up for the next six months with all sorts of horrendous work, and a telephone that does not stop ringing with irate friends wanting to know when their newly French-polished dining table and eight fully carved chairs are to be returned as they have an important dinner party etc. etc.

This is all very well if you want to set yourself up in business and are organized for it. If not, then you had better have a few well-chosen excuses prepared. Wherever your projects come from, pick and choose them carefully; your time is valuable. Use it wisely.

**Fig 2.1** ABOVE: **A typical first project.**

**Typical first projects**

Fig 2.3

Fig 2.2

## POSSIBLE SOURCES

If you are looking for a specific piece of furniture to restore, there are a number of places you can look. Which places you choose to look will depend largely upon the amount of time and money you have to spend, your personal disposition (not everyone enjoys hanging around corporation rubbish tips), and how quickly you want it.

The following is a list of the possible places where you may find your furniture. The further down this list you go the more expensive the item becomes, but then the quality and the likelihood of it being found there is much greater. At the top of the list the items are cheaper but you will have to spend a lot of time and energy sifting through the dross to pick up a bargain. The hierarchy goes something like this:

- Skips, rubbish bins, rubbish dumps
- Car boot sales, jumble sales
- Market traders, antique bric-à-brac fairs
- Local papers, garage sales, house clearances
- Junk shops
- Smaller auction houses (for household effects)
- Lower-priced antique shops
- Low- to middle-market antique shops
- Antique fairs
- Larger auction houses (antiques and collectibles)
- High-market antique shops

### JUNK SHOPS

The junk shop is the place that I suggest my students frequent to achieve a reasonable balance between cost, time and the chances of finding a suitable project (*see* Fig 2.4).

I do not suggest going to an antique dealer; the furniture on show is often in good condition and not in need of restoration, and is therefore usually of a higher price. However, they are great places to go to get a free education in different finishes, woods, styles, patina and tips on the look of old furniture.

**Fig 2.4** B E L O W : **A junk shop.**

## WHAT TO AVOID

From the absolute beginner's point of view there are certain pieces of furniture that are definitely to be frowned upon. The type of furniture that is ideal for the novice depends on a number of factors but fits a neat profile. Unfortunately we do not live in an ideal world and, more often than not, pieces of furniture choose us.

If you do have a choice, here is a list of don'ts that I have developed over the years from my experiences of teaching and from the mistakes made by my students:

**Fig 2.5** A B O V E : **Barley twist legs. Stripping these can be very time-consuming.**

- Don't start on anything that is of any great value, be it financial or sentimental; there is tons of cheap, unsentimental furniture out there just waiting to be made good and valuable again.

- Don't start on anything that is intricately carved. It can take a long time to strip this sort of project, and it is best to gain experience by working on simpler items.

- Don't start with anything with barley twist legs that need stripping; save it for your third project (*see* Fig 2.5). These can be very difficult to strip.

- Don't try to restore anything larger than you can lift. Until you have mastered the basics, four-poster beds, wardrobes, large sideboards or sets of chairs are not recommended; wait until you have the experience to judge how long the work is to take and whether you want to get that deeply involved.

- Don't buy a piece that needs a major part for it such as a new leg or drawer. Go for items that are 100 per cent intact – unless you have a very good friend who is a cabinetmaker.

- Don't attempt to restore furniture which has a lot of damaged or missing veneer. This is a very common problem, frequently seen in junk shops and the like. My advice is do not become involved. If you are determined to buy a piece suffering from this problem, read Chapter 11 on veneers carefully *before* buying.

If you are interested in a project that includes some upholstery, you may have to remove the upholstery completely, especially if the chair is wobbly. Unless you are a dab hand at upholstery, reconsider. If the chair is not wobbly (it rarely is), you can protect the upholstery with masking tape and old newspapers (*see* page 82 for further information).

If you wish to tackle French polishing, then choose a small coffee table or side table with a flat top and plain uncarved legs. French polish in some form or other is the most frequently occurring finish in junk or antique shops, and it is also the easiest of finishes to remove.

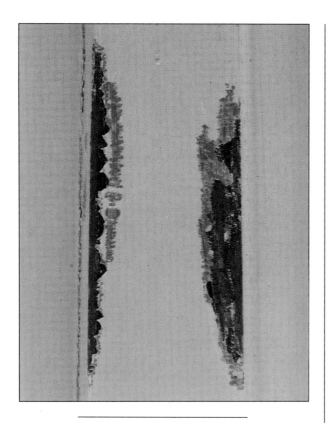

**Fig 2.6** A B O V E : **Paint over French polish, showing the ease of removal.**

The most difficult finish to remove is a properly applied painted finish on an open-grained wood such as oak or elm. This finish consists of primer coat, then undercoat, then top coat. If you want to return it to bare wood, you will have your work cut out. Happily, this finish is often applied over a French polish finish and therefore does not have the same adhesion as paint properly applied to bare wood.

It is essential to test any painted furniture to see if it is going to be easy to strip or not. This can be done with a penknife or similar instrument. Scratch the surface to see if the paint flakes away easily leaving French-polished wood underneath. If it does, you are on to a good thing. Often the paint has been chipped somewhere and you will not need to test it; just observe (*see* Fig 2.6).

If the paint is difficult to scratch off and, when removed, leaves a paint residue in the grain of the wood, think very carefully before you continue. It is probably better to wait until you are a little more experienced before sampling the delights of stripping properly applied paint. I and many of my

students have tried it and I can assure you, it is a life-changing experience. We are all of the same mind: never again!

If you are unlucky enough to inherit something with a properly applied painted finish, lightly sand it down, apply another painted finish over the top and leave it for the next generation of restorers; they may have invented something by then to get it off with ease.

Having said all that, I am continually being amazed at the difficulty of the projects that my students turn up with on the first night. Often they frighten the life out of me in terms of what is involved, yet they frequently go on to restore the furniture to first-class condition.

So if you really want to strip that ornately carved four-poster and French polish it, then don't let me put you off. It is extraordinary what a little enthusiasm and determination can achieve (plus of course an excellent book to guide you).

## WHAT TO BUY

Look out for solid woods. Anything made of solid wood (as opposed to chipboard) that has lasted for 50 years, will last for an eternity. There is a lot of pre-war solid oak furniture around which is extremely well made and low-priced. And it looks exceptional when refinished (*see* Fig 2.7).

**Fig 2.7** A B O V E : **An example of a piece of pre-war solid oak furniture.**

## THINK BEFORE BUYING

It only takes a split millisecond to make the decision to buy, but you could be saddling yourself with months of regret. Before buying, think about your working space and the other practical problems involved in restoring the furniture. Is it to be delivered? Are you to start work on it straight away? If not, where is it to be stored? What is the most likely finish for this project? How long will the project take, and have you got enough time to complete it satisfactorily?

These may seem like unnecessary problems to put in your way, and if you are anything like me and you fall in love with a piece of furniture, all common sense is likely to go out of the window anyway; paltry considerations like how you are going to get that solid oak sideboard on to the number Nine bus fade to insignificance in the face of an unmissable bargain. But at least you have been warned!

## HOW TO BUY IT

One of the most enjoyable aspects of furniture restoration is the fact that with a little experience the hobby will pay for itself and, if you want, make a tidy profit too.

Once you have found a piece of furniture you think you would like to purchase, there are a number of tips that I can pass on to help improve your purchasing power. These have been culled from my experience as a dealer and buyer.

If you can, shop on a weekday. Weekdays are usually slower trade than weekends and you will have more time to talk and haggle, and the trader will be more prepared to make a deal.

Make friends with the dealer, or rather, do not antagonize. Second-hand furniture dealers attend auctions. They know other shops that sell second-hand furniture and will be offered pieces of furniture

Contrary to what many people think, furniture that uses plywood in its construction is not substandard. Many pieces of furniture made this century utilize this material, and as long as the veneers that comprise the plywood are in good condition and are not bubbling up, then you will almost certainly be looking at a very robust and practical piece of furniture; well worth restoring and refinishing.

A simple chair is a very good starting point for the absolute beginner. The less complicated it is, the quicker and easier it will be to strip (*see* Fig 2.8). The other good starting project is a small, flat-topped table. Happily, such items are to be found in hundreds of junk shops worldwide (*see* Fig 2.9).

and attend house clearances on a daily basis. They see a lot of second-hand furniture in their working day. If you speak to them nicely they will often keep an eye out for just the piece you are looking for, at the price you are willing to pay. If they do not have the piece you are looking for, they will almost certainly know where to find it.

Most dealers will be prepared to haggle. This is where you can have a lot of fun if you are willing to engage. The first thing to realize is that the prices a dealer sets are extremely flexible. Often the items in a shop are bought in quite cheaply and all the shopkeeper is looking for is the best price they can get, as quickly as possible. First ask how much the item is. Whatever price the dealer first suggests, it should be countered after a short interlude with the question:

'Is that the best price you can do?'

It is rare in my experience for a dealer not to give some form of discount. Next, you should bring to the dealer's attention that it is not quite what you were looking for. You were looking for something a little smaller, bigger, darker, lighter, taller, shorter etc. (even if it is exactly what you have been searching for all your life). Wait for the response (further discount), then bring to his attention any defects that come to your attention and ask if there is any discount for them. If you can find some woodworm or even the suspicion of woodworm then steadfastly demand a discount just for taking it off his hands (you will of course be armed with the knowledge contained in Chapter 9 concerning the treatment of woodworm).

If you really want to squeeze every drop, go away for half an hour, then come back and look at it again. Walk around it again, muttering something along the lines of the huge phone bill that you have got to pay, and the fact that you may be losing your job, and you only want it for practising on anyway. Drop hints about having just started a new hobby of furniture restoration and that you expect to be buying a lot of furniture from him in the future (as long as the price is right). Once he has offered you the final discount and he is crying, then you can offer him 10 pounds less for cash; this one always works. If all of these ploys work then the dealer should be paying you to take the item away.

However, if you want to shop there again I suggest that you settle for just the one discount. After all, next time he may have just what you are looking for, only on this occasion he is bound to see you coming and double the price in readiness for your assault (that's if he doesn't lock the door and pull down the blinds).

If you follow just some of these suggestions then you will certainly be paying the lowest price. If nothing else you will, without doubt, save the cost of this book. The important point is, in this type of business, whether junk or antique, it is acceptable and even expected for you to haggle. If you follow some of the tips given above, with a little practice, you can save yourself a fortune.

One final thought I would like you to consider is the value of older, second-hand furniture in comparison to the cost of a modern piece of similar

**Fig 2.10** A B O V E : **'So what would you say to an extra £10 discount for cash?'**

size and quality. It is not commonly recognized that most second-hand furniture is vastly under-priced. If you were to buy a good, solid second-hand oak or mahogany table from a junk shop, then have the same item made to the same quality by a present-day craftsperson, the difference in price would be phenomenal. If you choose your second-hand furniture well you will find a bargain every time, whether you receive a discount or not. In a very short space of time you will become aware that many of those hideous-looking piles of scrapwood piled up on the pavement outside junk shops are actually swans masquerading as ugly ducklings, just waiting to be discovered by you.

# CHAPTER 3

# SAFETY

PHOTO COURTESY OF ARCO LTD.

*With any subject that you have never had experience of before, it is important to be made aware of its inherent dangers and health hazards.*

## COMMON SENSE

Happily, many of the dangerous situations that you will encounter with furniture restoration are obvious and subject to common sense. For example, if you are finishing a piece of furniture with a highly inflammable finish, common sense should tell you not to smoke your pipe at the same time. I shall not bore you with the more obvious safety instructions. If you are not aware that a sharp knife can cut then, frankly, there is not much hope. However, some of the dangers are not so self-evident and I shall ensure that these are emphasized in the relevant chapter.

**Fig 3.1** A B O V E : **First aid kit.**

## ACCIDENTS

Accidents by their nature are unexpected: you do not expect to fall off a ladder or trip over a wire; if you did you wouldn't. You cannot predict your own accident. The best way to avoid accidents is to get into the habit of working safely, and to be aware of what you need to do if something goes wrong. Be prepared. Formulate and adhere to a safety checklist. If you are a sailor you wear a life-jacket. If you are a driver you wear a safety belt. If you are a skydiver you take a spare parachute. If you work in a crafts workshop you abide by a safety checklist.

Often large accidents occur due to a combination of smaller accidents happening at the same time.

This is an interesting area for investigation by people with an interest in the paranormal. It is not dropping something on your foot that causes the accident, it is the fact that when you jump out of the way to save your foot, you knock the blow torch over and ignite the meths that you spilt yesterday; consequently, the house burns down. It is not leaving the piece of wood on the floor that puts you into hospital, it is the fact that when your neighbour came round to borrow a cup of sugar, they side-stepped the piece of wood at the last minute and stepped instead on the cat's tail; con-

sequently, the cat leapt on to the heavy cabinet that you were just lifting on to the bench, upsetting the delicate balance and causing you to fall through the conservatory windows.

These sorts of accidents could be avoided if the chain of events that make up an accident was broken. In the above cases the chain could have been broken a number of times by adhering to a few common-sense rules. What follows is a safety checklist of the more general safety points. If you abide by them, they will guarantee – as far as can be possible – an accident-free workplace.

**Fig 3.2** B E L O W :

**Domestic fire extinguisher.**

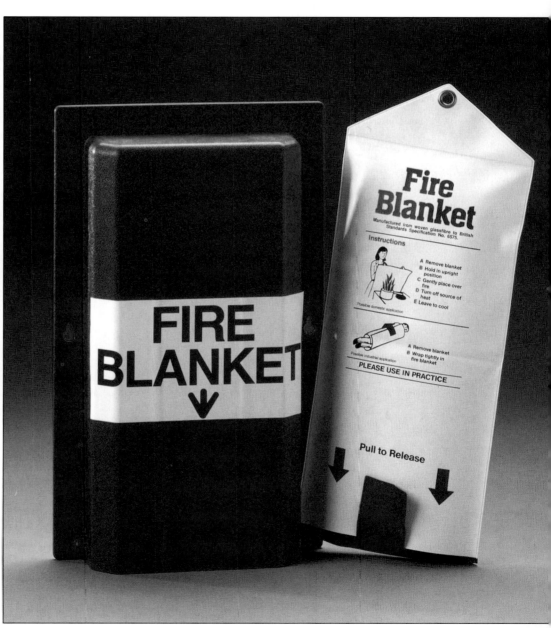

**Fig 3.3** A B O V E : **Fire blankets.**

## THE SAFETY CHECKLIST

Before you start work look around, think safety and mentally go through your checklist. Every time you come back from a break, repeat the process. If you are particularly safety conscious you might wish to write this checklist out and pin it up in your workspace.

- Don't eat, drink or smoke whilst working.

- Every 30 minutes or so, clear your working surface of tools and unwanted materials.

- Replace the lids and tops of all containers as soon as you have used them. Wipe up spills straight away.

- Keep all children, pets and interfering adults out of your workplace. Before starting any long and complicated processes, take the phone off the hook, hang a 'do not disturb' sign up, and take everything out of the oven or off the boil (accidents don't just happen in the workshop).

- Think about the working height of your project. It is worth spending some time raising furniture off the ground, particularly if you suffer from a bad back.

- Keep the floor clean and clear of electric cables, bits of debris and slippery surfaces.

- Be aware of fire. Many wood finishing procedures and chemicals are inflammable. Think safety, bowl of water, fire blanket, extinguisher (*see* Figs 3.2 and 3.3).

- Know where the first aid kit is and keep it well stocked (*see* Fig 3.1). I found out recently that there is nothing more irritating than searching for an eyebath when you are blinded in one eye by a painful, foreign object.

- If you make up any preparations, label them clearly and keep poisonous and dangerous chemicals in a locked cabinet.

- If you are worried, find a helping hand. If you are going to try something that you think you may have problems with or will be unsafe to attempt alone, invite a friend to help. If you prefer, have a friend in earshot who knows what you are up to and what the likely dangers are.

- Only use 'strong' chemicals in well-ventilated areas. Abide by the instructions on the container.

- If you have problems with your health then take this into consideration. The significant illnesses are lung complaints, skin problems (beware of allergic reactions to certain chemicals), back injuries and tennis elbow (repetitive strain injuries to arms and wrists).

- Wear suitable protective clothing: a mask to protect against dust for the mouth and nose, earmuffs or earplugs to defend against noise from power tools (if they are used), gloves for the hands, and visors or goggles to protect the eyes and face (*see* Figs 3.4, 3.5 and 3.6).

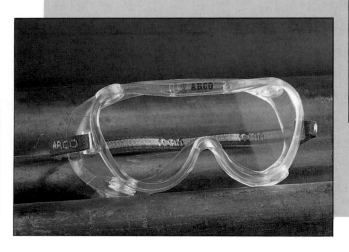

**Fig 3.5** L E F T : **Protective goggles.**

For those of you with a superstitious nature, it is worth noting that there are 13 items in this check-list. If you are unduly worried perhaps you could add another one or two. But don't remove any!

I have included these words on safety not to scare or worry you but to make you aware of the dangers. Remember, the biggest cause of accidents is ignorance.

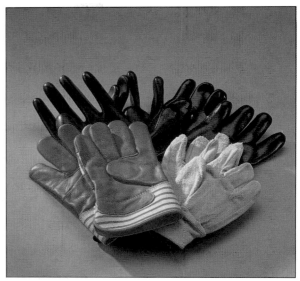

PHOTO COURTESY OF ARCO LTD.

**Fig 3.4** R I G H T : **Protective gloves.**

**Fig 3.6** B E L O W : **Dust/mist respirator. Protects against fine respirable dusts, fibres and aqueous mists.**

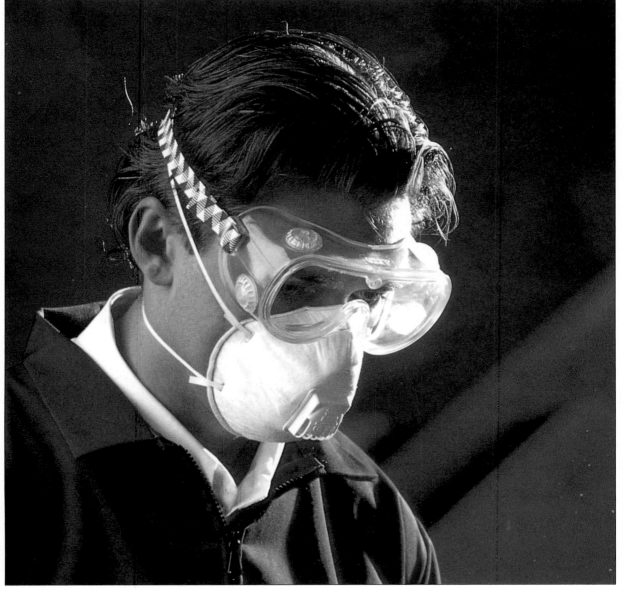

PHOTO COURTESY OF AROC LTD.

# CHAPTER 4

# WORKSPACE, TOOLS AND
## —— MATERIALS ——

PHOTO COURTESY OF STEVEN LEYLAND OF BUCKS COLLEGE.

*In this chapter we will look at some of the factors which should be taken into consideration when choosing a space to repair and restore your project. I will also discuss the likely tools and materials you will require.*

## WORKSPACE

After a suitable piece of furniture has been found, the next essential is a space in which to work. Where you work will depend on a number of factors, but you should consider some of the following points when choosing.

Your workspace should be large enough for you to place your project in the middle and leave enough room to walk all the way around it. For some projects you may need an old table or bench to raise the project off the ground.

**Fig 4.1** A B O V E : **Good light, no ventilation problems, plenty of space – on a good day, the best place to restore furniture has to be outdoors.**

It would be useful to have an area away from the project where you can place materials, tools and other equipment without them being knocked over.

If you are working in a garage, shed or workshop, try to limit the amount of dust that often abounds in these places. It may be worth running a vacuum cleaner over the workplace.

The other requirement of your workplace is shelter from air movement; wind, breezes and draughts will whip up a small dust cloud that will undoubtedly find its way on to and into your finishes as they dry.

If you find a suitable workplace, plan to have the use of it for at least a few days. Depending on the processes that you are going to get involved in, you may need to leave projects overnight undisturbed to dry. Take this into account in your planning.

Having said that, it is quite possible to do restoration work in a kitchen space, as long as you are careful not to get one set of ingredients mixed up with another, and are prepared to be flexible and put up with some of those terrible smells: garlic, boiled cabbage, kippers etc. (When experienced, working in a kitchen does have its advantages: you can strip, fix, stain and refinish a small table in a few hours, and whip up a four-course meal for six at the same time.)

## LIGHTING

Ideally, there should be some form of natural light. It is not commonly recognized that natural light, even on a cloudy day in the middle of winter, is many times stronger than artificial interior lighting. As such, it will illuminate and expose much more effectively. If you want to see the true colour of a piece of wood or a stain, view it in natural daylight. This also applies when inspecting a surface for blemishes, or when applying finishes.

There is a strange and spooky occurrence that happened a number of years ago in one of the first classes I taught, that illustrates perfectly the need for natural light.

It was a balmy evening in the middle of June. It had rained earlier, but the clouds had cleared swiftly to reveal a glorious sunset. In my studio I was speaking with a new student who went by the name of Damien. He had made an unusually good job of restoring the four damaged corners of an Edwardian mahogany games table, inherited from his recently deceased grandmother. When complete, the damage to the corners had been totally irradicated. Naturally, Damien was extremely pleased with the result.

However, when he returned the following week to work on another aspect of the restoration, he brought something peculiar to my attention: the colours used in patching the blemishes, which only last week had looked absolutely perfect, were now as obvious as a church steeple.

As hard as I tried, I could find no explanation for this odd occurrence. Nothing made sense. It had been very hot last week; perhaps this had had an effect on the stain. Maybe the colours had faded

in bright sunlight. Perhaps we had been exposed to too much methylated spirits, or maybe there were some other spirits at work?

It was decided that Damien should do the job again, only this time I instructed him to keep a detailed note of the colours and the techniques he used in the preparation and application of the stain. This was so we could re-enact the oddity if it happened again.

For the rest of the evening, I was involved with the enquiries and problems of the other students, so I did not manage to see Damien again until the end of the lesson. When I finally got to see what he had done I was flabbergasted. I called the class together to witness the incredible sight: there was no sign that there had ever been any damage to any of the corners. Damien had done an amazing job. The restoration was perfect.

It was not until I had finished my lengthy congratulations that Damien, looking somewhat puzzled, stopped me and explained. For some reason unknown to him, he had decided to busy himself with another project that evening. He had not worked on the table since last week! A bemused quiet fell over the room.

Eventually a perplexed voice broke the silence: 'How could this be?'

'Surely there is something uncanny going on.' I must confess to some heavy duty consternation at this stage. But eventually the penny dropped. The answer was simple: the lesson started at 7 o'clock in the evening and ran through to 9. At the beginning of the lesson the table had been viewed in natural sunlight and had looked 'wrong'. By the end of the class the artificial strip lights had been turned on and in these conditions the work looked perfect. It was in these conditions of artificial lighting that the restoration had been completed the previous week.

The moral of the story of course is be aware of the effect of different lighting. Always check your work in natural daylight. As a rule, if it looks passable in daylight, then it is going to look magnificent in the less searching illumination of artificial lighting.

While we are on the subject, there is one other way that our perception of colours can be affected, best illustrated by a little experiment. If you hold a white piece of card up against a large expanse of colour, such as some heavily coloured curtains or wallpaper, the card will 'take on' and will be affected by this reflected colour. Beware of your sense of colour being upset by this type of 'colour infiltration'.

If you are a night owl like me and are working in a garage or workshop, it is worth investing in some extra lighting. This is less tiring on the eyes than a single bulb or strip light, which will cast heavy shadows on your work. It will also provide you with a much safer working environment.

### THE IDEAL WORKSPACE

My favourite place for restoring is the garden. This has a number of practical benefits: the lighting is unsurpassed; on a still day there is no dust; ventilation is excellent and there is more than enough space to move around your project. If you decide to use an outdoor space (a patio or balcony are just

**Fig 4.2** B E L O W : **Oak sideboard under oak tree.**

PHOTO COURTESY OF JOHN BODDY'S FINE WOOD & TOOL STORE LTD.

as effective), then it is wise to wait for a favourable weather forecast, i.e. dry and still. Strong winds can be particularly hazardous (*see* Fig 4.2). Also, be prepared to have the project finished before sundown, or make plans to move the furniture undercover overnight to avoid condensation on the work.

Direct sunlight should be avoided as this can affect the wood adversely and can make some finishes difficult to apply. Low temperatures can also affect the drying and application qualities of some finishes. The effect of these conditions on each type of finish is addressed in the relevant chapter.

If you are working indoors you can enjoy all the comforts of home, although it is important that you protect the floor and the wallpaper etc. Also, allow enough ventilation, and beware of kids, pets and disapproving adults.

The best place to work will depend on the time of year, the size of your project, what techniques and finishes you intend to use and your individual circumstances. Be flexible; plan ahead, and nothing is impossible.

## TOOLS

A furniture restorer's tool box must be one of the smallest in the craft world. Even the most well-equipped furniture restorer will travel and be prepared for every eventuality with the equivalent of a vanity case. And this will include all the stains and finishes. The following materials and tools should be obtained only as and when they become necessary.

### SCRAPERS

You will need a selection of scrapers for removing old finishes. Some of these should be shop-bought and will cost a few pounds each (*see* Fig 4.3). Other scrapers can be home-made and can be improvised as and when you need them; old kitchen knives, lollipop sticks, old craft knife blades are a few possibilities.

**Fig 4.3** ABOVE: **A selection of scraping tools. Top row are scraping planes, except for second from left – a scraper wheel burnisher. Bottom row (l to r): three sizes of cabinet scraper, a goose neck scraper, a concave convex scraper and three types of scraper burnishers.**

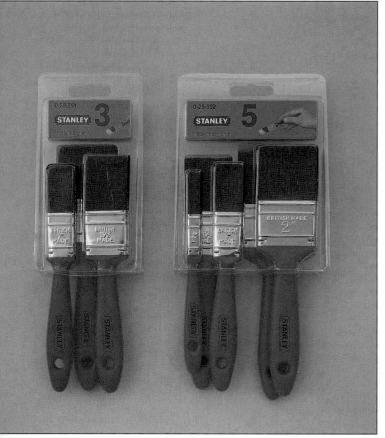

PHOTO COURTESY OF STANLEY TOOLS.

**Fig 4.4** A B O V E : **Various sizes of paint brush.**

**Fig 4.5** R I G H T : **A selection of artists' brushes.**

## BRUSHES

You will also need a selection of old and new paint brushes in various sizes (*see* Fig 4.4). The quality of brush that you buy will depend on what use you plan to put it to. Check the relevant chapters for advice on the type and size of brushes required for each job.

If you have done any home decorating you are likely to have old brushes that have been ruined by normal use and ineffective cleaning. Rather than throwing them out, use them for applying stripper.

You will also need smaller artists' brushes to paint in graining effects and textures when fixing and camouflaging with colour. These brushes can be bought from any artists' supply shop (*see* Fig 4.5).

## RAGS

You will need an endless supply of absorbent rags for applying stains, cleaning off, wiping your hands, applying finishes, cleaning up spillages and for crying into if things go wrong.

You may also need old newspapers to protect floors, upholstery and walls.

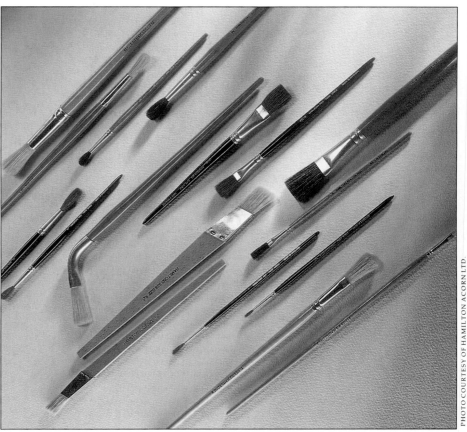

PHOTO COURTESY OF HAMILTON ACORN LTD.

## CLAMPS

When re-gluing you may require wood clamps to hold everything together while it dries, and to squeeze the joint as tightly as possible (*see* Figs 4.6 and 4.7). These can be expensive, so it is wise to check that you are going to need them before you rush out with your chequebook
(*see* page 65).

**Fig 4.6** A B O V E : **C clamp.**

If you decide that you need some clamps try borrowing them first from friends, relatives or neighbours. If that fails there are a number of possibilities to be considered; you could try hiring some clamps of the required size. If you decide to buy, you will find there are a number of different types on offer. Which ones you decide upon will depend on the size of your bank account and the nature of the job.

You may be able to manage with some home-made clamps. The easiest and cheapest one to make is the windlass or tourniquet clamp. At its simplest this is a piece of string or thin rope looped around the furniture; the slack is removed by twisting a piece of wood into the string to tighten. Try several of these on your dry run and see if that cures the problem before investing in 'proper' clamps. Figs 4.8 and 4.9 show the web clamp, made by Stanley Tools, which does a similar job to the tourniquet clamp.

**Fig 4.7** A B O V E : **A selection of clamps used by furniture restorers.**

**Fig 4.8** L E F T : **The web clamp.**

**Fig 4.9** R I G H T : **The web clamp in use.**

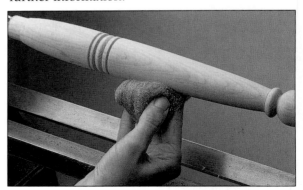

## ABRASIVES

**ABRASIVE PAPER** There is a bewildering array of abrasive papers available on the D.I.Y. shelf. Each one proclaims some quality enticing you to buy it. Fear not, we do not use that much of it to care.

All you will need to start you off is one or two sheets of fine-grade sandpaper and the same amount of 600 grit wet-and-dry. The fine-grade sandpaper is, funnily enough, a sandy colour. It is used to smooth down wood surfaces such as a rough table top before refinishing.

The 600 grit wet-and-dry is traditionally used by panel beaters in the repair of car bodywork. It is also called silicone carbide paper. If you cannot get it in the D.I.Y. store, you will find it in any car accessory shop. It is dark grey, almost black in colour and is used for rubbing down finishes between coats. It is a much finer grade of abrasive paper than ordinary sandpapers. If it becomes clogged it can be washed out in the sink with some soap and running water, and will therefore last much longer than ordinary sandpaper (*see* Fig 4.10).

**WIRE WOOL** You will need some wire wool (sometimes called steel wool) (*see* Fig 4.11). I suggest two or three different grades: fine, medium and coarse. Wire wool has a nasty habit of dispensing invisible steel splinters into the fingers during use. It is

horrible stuff but has many uses to the furniture restorer.

For this reason it is wise to have a pair of protective gloves when using wire wool. Gardening gloves are tough but a bit thick and clumsy. Washing up gloves are more sensitive but tend to tear and wear out quickly. Old driving gloves can be very useful.

**SUEDE BRUSH** You will need a suede brush for stripping complicated areas such as mouldings and carvings. These are available from shoe repairers and supermarkets (*see* Fig 6.7). See Chapter 6 for further information.

**Fig 4.10** T O P : **A selection of abrasives.**

**Fig 4.11** A B O V E : **Fine wire wool in use.**

## GLUES

There are a number of glues available to the wood-worker, and each has its positive and negative aspects. The absolute beginner needs knowledge of the following:

**POLYVINYL ACETATE** This is more often referred to as PVA. It is the most commonly available wood glue and there should be a number of different makes to choose from in your local D.I.Y. shop. It is relatively inexpensive, water washable and easy to use. Drips and spillages can be wiped up with a damp cloth. It is white in colour, although it dries clear, resembles thick cream in consistency and look, and has a pleasant fresh smell. It is available both in an indoor and an outdoor formulation and is completely safe in normal use (children's nurseries use a variety of it for their craft activities).

Manufacturers often insist on supplying it in totally ineffective cut-off nozzle-type containers. The nozzle is rendered pretty useless after its first use as it invariably gets bunged up with congealed glue. I use quite a lot of the stuff on a regular basis, so I decant mine into a pot and apply it with a spatula (*see* Fig 4.13). For weekend users, I suggest

**Fig 4.12** A B O V E : **A wide selection of adhesives. The absolute beginner will only need four of these (*see* text).**

**Fig 4.13** R I G H T : **PVA glue (shown here decanted into a jar) is marketed by a number of manufacturers and in a variety of formulations, but it always looks the same.**

you cut a largish top off the nozzle and then, after each use, wipe around with a damp cloth and re-seal with thick sticky tape.

This glue will cover 90 per cent of the absolute beginner's needs. It works best when joining closely fitting joints. Its drawback is that it is not very good at gluing joints where the wood is not very close fitting and, as you can imagine, loose-fitting joints are a common occurrence with old furniture.

The other problem is that sometimes it can be too effective. To give an example, imagine that you have a chair which has been dismantled and you are now ready to reassemble. All the joints fit nice and tightly, so you choose PVA glue for the job. The problem occurs when you have to pull open a joint which you have just glued so that you can fit in another section of the chair, or, if you make a mistake and want to take it apart and start again. Unfortunately, the tighter the joints are the better and more quickly the PVA glue works. In some circumstances the glue can adhere immediately, leaving you with a major problem. In short you are stuck!

**UREA-FORMALDEHYDE GLUE** What you need in a situation like this is a glue that does not work quite so quickly, allowing you time to make small adjustments so that you do not have to rush the whole operation. If the joints are very tight and you need some time to scratch your head and adjust, or the joints are very loose and you need a glue to fill the gaps, what you need is urea-formaldehyde glue.

In the UK the most common make of this type of glue is called Cascamite. This glue comes in the form of a white powder and has to be mixed with water to the manufacturer's specifications. These instructions are not the easiest to follow so I prefer the gravy-mix method. I mix a spoonful of the powder with a few drops of water and then stir. If it is too thick I add a little more water; if it is too thin then I add some more powder. I am sure someone will tell me that this method will adversely affect the adhesive properties or whatever, but it has always worked for me. On the other hand, my gravy is lumpy and tastes pretty awful too.

Cascamite mixes to a creamy texture and has no discernible smell. It dries clear to a glass-like hard-

ness by chemical reaction. The glue starts to go sticky 20 minutes after being applied, allowing plenty of time to make any adjustments or corrections to your assembly procedure.

There is a health and safety problem linked to this glue. Contact with the skin can cause dermatitis and, for obvious reasons, inhaling the fine powder will not improve the quality of your breathing.

It is not as readily available as the PVA, but most timber and builders' merchants will sell it. It is also obtainable through trade supply houses. It is not as economic as PVA because any glue not used on the job has to be discarded. Also, it is more expensive.

Its chief benefit is in filling the gaps (excuse the pun) that are left in the range of uses of PVA glue. Also, being weatherproof, it is widely used out of doors and for boat making.

**TRADITIONAL SCOTCH GLUE** The other type of glue used by professional furniture restorers, though rarely by absolute beginners, is traditional scotch glue (sometimes called hide or animal glue). This

**Fig 4.14** ABOVE: **A traditional glue pot for the preparation of scotch glue, with a cast-iron interior and an aluminium exterior.**

**Fig 4.15** R I G H T : **If the pieces of wood on either side of the top of a cabriole leg – known as the ears – come unstuck, they can be difficult to stick back into place without the aid of the old type of animal glue.**

has some benefits but it is notoriously difficult and involved to use, particularly when compared to PVA.

It is heat-sensitive and so has to be heated in a pot to the required temperature before applying (*see* Fig 4.14). In use it cools quickly and will contract slightly so pulling the pieces of wood or joints firmly together. This can all happen in seconds and there is often no need for clamps or a long drying time before moving on to the next process. In the hands of a skilled craftsperson heavenly things can be achieved. In the hands of an absolute beginner all hell can be let loose.

In some cases, however, no other glue can be used. Certain traditional construction methods are only possible with scotch glue, such as glue blocks on the back of mirrors (*see* pages 79–81). And sometimes, because of the shape of the items to be joined – for example, when sticking on the ears of a cabriole leg (*see* Fig 4.15) – this is the most appropriate glue to use. However, you should try every other possibility before opting for scotch glue, and if you decide to use it, contact a trade supply house

and they will supply it and offer advice on its use.

Apart from being heat-sensitive, traditional scotch glue is also moisture-sensitive and so will often fail in furniture that has been subject to damp (a common occurrence). Most pre-war furniture, and all antique furniture, will have used some form of this glue in its manufacture.

One benefit of this glue is that it is capable of being unstuck if the need arises. It is possible to dismantle anything where scotch glue has been used either by wrapping hot cloths around a joint or, in difficult cases, by drilling a small hole and injecting hot water into the joints.

**GLUE FILM** This comes in a roll and is backed with paper, and is used for applying and repairing veneers. It is heat-sensitive and can be tacked to the back of a veneer, then ironed on to the ground work. This makes working with veneers extremely simple. (If you are ambidextrous you can iron a couple of shirts at the same time.) It is inexpensive but can only be bought from specialist suppliers (*see* page 188).

# CHAPTER 5

# IDENTIFYING
# FINISHES

PHOTO COURTESY OF BUCKINGHAMSHIRE COLLEGE.

*When you become more experienced in restoring furniture, identification of finishes will become second nature and you will be able to tell some finishes just by looking at them. Often the style and age of furniture, or the way the finish has deteriorated, will give you an indication of what finish you are dealing with.*

For the absolute beginner there is a series of experiments you can try to reveal the identity of a finish: first, spill a small drop of methylated spirit on to an inconspicuous corner and scratch the moistened area gently with the fingernail of your index finger (*see* Fig 5.1). If it is a French polish finish, within a very short period of time (less than 15 seconds) the finish will soften and some gunge will be noticeable under your fingernail. If it takes longer to soften

(within two minutes), and the finish is quite thick and it looks as if it has been applied with a brush, it is probably a type of spirit varnish. Spirit varnish is a derivative of French polish that was used before the more modern varnishes were developed. Fur-

---

**Fig 5.1** A B O V E : **A chest of drawers (c.1875) made from Hungarian ash. But what finish does it have?**

niture produced before 1945 is 90 per cent likely to have a French polish finish.

If the finish doesn't soften, rub a similar area with a fingertip of cloth soaked in white spirit. If it goes dull and eventually rubs back to bare wood, you have a wax type of finish. If the surface is cleaned by this action and becomes a little sticky, it is likely to be an oil type of finish.

If none of the previous experiments have worked, you are dealing with a more modern (post 1945) finish. The next step is to try a drop of chemical stripper. If the finish softens, bubbles up, thickens, and looks as if it may have been applied by an amateur brush, then it is likely to be polyurethane finish.

Another clue to the finish is the style of the furniture itself. If it looks post-war and mass-produced, the finish is likely to be an early type of cellulose finish.

If all these experiments do not work and the finish looks as if it has been sprayed on, then try cellulose chemical stripper, available from car ac-

cessory shops. It should be remembered that there can often be a combination of finishes on any one piece of furniture: wax over French polish is very common, as is wax over an oil finish.

If the furniture looks dirty and waxy, give the surface you are experimenting on a thorough cleaning with white spirit before testing.

Painted furniture is usually obvious, but there are a number of different types of paint: the main two are oil paints and emulsion paints. If oil paint has been used, it will be softened by chemical stripper; if it is emulsion paint then it will need scraping off.

Sometimes emulsion paint is used and a French polish or polyurethane finish is applied over the top, followed by years of wax polish. These sorts of combinations can cause some head scratching and experimenting to unpick the muddle.

---

**Fig 5.2** B E L O W : **Fingernail test of meths on French polish.**

# CHAPTER 6

# STRIPPING

*Do you need to strip? In 95 per cent of the cases that I have come across, the answer is yes. By stripping off the old finish, you will remove decades of scratches, marks, water stains, and other evidence of a long and battered life. Often, all you will need to do is replace it with a new finish and the furniture is as good as new, if not better – ready for another two or three generations of use.*

## ALTERNATIVES TO STRIPPING

If the project is an antique, removing that all-important finish may be ruinous, stripping it not only of its finish but also of the value and character that made it so different from a new piece of furniture. If you have any doubts then do nought. Think and ponder and peruse; then ask other people for their thoughts. The question you are asking is, will stripping and refinishing this piece of furniture ruin it or improve it? Of course, if it is of little value there is nothing much to worry about (this is one of the benefits of having old and decrepit furniture).

If you decide that it may be worth keeping the original finish, then I suggest you turn to Chapter 8 for advice on what to do next. The furniture may have a waxed finish, in which case it may be wiser to try and rejuvenate this finish before you make the decision whether or not to strip. This area is dealt with in Chapter 14.

If you decide to strip, then try out some of the techniques and remedies contained in Chapter 8 before going any further. This gives you the opportunity to experiment and play around with remedies for removing blemishes without having to worry about the outcome. In this way you can build up a body of knowledge and confidence very quickly.

**Fig 6.1** A B O V E : **An ideal table for stripping.**

## CHEMICAL STRIPPER

In the meantime I shall presume that your furniture is of little value and that it can only be improved by stripping and refinishing. For the majority of projects I would recommend paint/varnish stripper (*see* Fig 6.2). Do not be misled by the name – it will strip most finishes. Use this unless you have a very good reason for using one of the alternatives.

Stripper is a caustic chemical compound which softens most types of wood finish, thus allowing the finish to be easily scraped off the wood. You may have the choice of either a thick variety, or a thinner version. Opt for the thicker gel. They all do the same job, but the thicker stuff has a tendency not to drip so much. Once the bulk of the finish is removed, any remaining stripper is washed off the wood and neutralized. This is done with water, white spirit or methylated spirit, depending on the type of stripper that you buy.

Do not buy water-washable stripper. It is usually cheaper and may initially seem to be a better buy, but unfortunately, water has a habit of doing unspeakable things to wood: raising the grain and lifting veneers, as well as having an adverse effect on subsequent finishes. Save yourself these problems by choosing a stripper that is washed off with white spirit or meths. Since you are in the store, you may as well buy the spirit at the same time, so read the small print on the back of the stripper container, and see what spirit they suggest.

### SAFETY

When you do the stripping, make sure there are no children or pets present. Outside on a clear day is a good place to do this job. If you are doing the job indoors, allow yourself adequate ventilation, as the stripper does have a strong chemical smell. Read the instructions on the back of the can, and Chapter 3 on safety before starting.

The bad thing about paint stripper is that it burns the skin. That sounds very dramatic, but don't worry, it won't dissolve your hand into an unrecognizable blob of smouldering flesh. However, you will feel an unpleasant burning sensation and it will often leave a temporary red mark on the skin. I liken the sensation to having a very localized sunburn. It disappears very quickly when washed. So,

either wear gloves or have a bowl of water present to wash off accidental splashes. You should also wear a pair of protective goggles to defend the eyes. However, if you use the following technique, you should not have any problems. A good rule of thumb is, if you can feed yourself without poking yourself in the eye with a fork, then you are capable of stripping without putting your safety in jeopardy.

### HOW TO USE CHEMICAL STRIPPER

Place the item to be stripped on a carpet of old newspaper to protect the floor. If possible, raise the furniture to a height that enables you to work without having to bend over too much. You could

---

**Fig 6.2** B E L O W : **A can of paint/varnish stripper.**

be spending some time stripping, so you should make your workplace as comfortable as possible.

Pour some of the paint stripper into a wide-brimmed jar. Use a suitable size of old paint brush (here's why you saved all those old paint brushes). A large piece of furniture requires a large brush (3in or 75mm); a small piece of furniture requires a small brush (1in or 25mm).

The method is to strip small sections at a time. The most common mistake made by absolute beginners is to cover the whole piece of furniture in a thick layer of slimy, dripping varnish remover then spend the next hour howling like a scalded cat because they have become smothered, like some toxic mud wrestler, in the ensuing mess. Do *not* cover all of the furniture in stripper. If, for example, you are stripping a chair, apply a heavy coating of stripper to one leg, then stand back and let it do its stuff. Leave for a few minutes, and then test to see if the finish has softened.

The tool you use to remove the finish depends on the area and shape of wood to be stripped. A paint scraper can be used in many cases, but for larger flat areas a wallpaper scraper would be preferable. Likewise, for smaller flat areas, use an old chisel or knife. If the article is carved, or the surface is not flat, then you will have to devise other scrapers to get into the little nooks and crannies. Lollipop sticks are a very good tool. They can be shaped with a craft knife to enter the required nook and are hard enough to scrape out the gunge (*see* Fig 6.3). Wire wool can be used on curved surfaces.

Gently scrape away the gunge that is a combination of the stripper and the chemically dissolved finish. If the finish comes away easily leaving bare wood, then you should continue scraping, depositing the gunge in an old rag kept specifically for that purpose (*see* Fig 6.4). If the finish is still firm under the stripper, leave for another few minutes until it is soft.

**Fig 6.3** L E F T : **Using a shaped stick to strip a moulding using Rustin's Strypit.**

PHOTO COURTESY OF RUSTIN'S LTD.

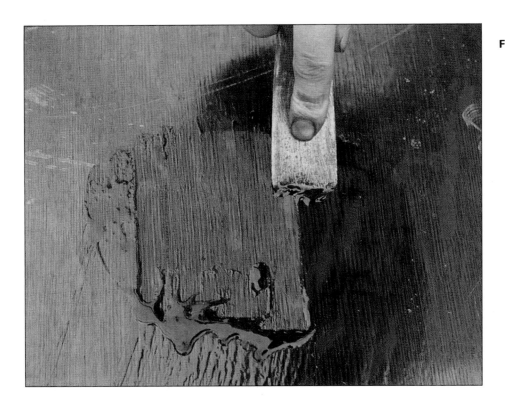

**Fig 6.4** L E F T : **Allow the stripper to soften the finish, then scrape the gunge into a cloth.**

## FINISHING OFF

If after clearing all the gunge off, there are still some remnants of finish left, then repeat the process until all the finish is removed and you are left with bare wood and some residual gunge. This is removed by dipping some medium-grade wire wool in some white spirit or meths, and rubbing gently over the wood with a cleaning action (*see* Fig 6.5). Leave to dry and you have finished. Now repeat the process on the rest of the article, but remember, small sections at a time. If you use white spirit to clean off and neutralize the stripper, you may find

**Fig 6.5** R I G H T : **When you have finished removing the gunge, rub the area with white spirit. This will remove any remaining gunge and stripper in preparation for refinishing.**

the surface of the wood is coated with a white powdery deposit. This is normal and should be ignored (*see* Fig 6.6).

I have already described some of the tools that can be used for scraping away the gunge. However, the best tip I can give you (and this is worth the price of the book) is to obtain a suede brush. These are normally used for cleaning suede shoes and other suede items and can be bought from a shoe repairer or from the shoe polish counter at a supermarket. Suede brushes are just the correct stiffness to scrub away the chemical gunge from carved and intricate areas. They are particularly effective when stripping very open-grained woods such as oak, ash, elm and mahogany. These are very common hardwoods, much used in all sorts of woodwork. When used in older furniture the wood has often been finished in a dark brown French polish which fills the open grain. The only way to strip these woods effectively is to remove the finish as des-

cribed previously, and then to give the surface of the wood one more thin coating of stripper and scrub the pores of the open-grained wood with the suede brush. This will clean the old finish out completely, revealing the natural beauty of the previously obscured wood (*see* Fig 6.7).

Once you have been through the stripping process a couple of times you will gain in confidence and will be able to strip a small table or uncomplicated chair in about one hour. If you have anything larger to strip then take it easy. Don't try and do it all in one go. Plan your work and spread it out over a number of sessions. A common tendency with absolute beginners is over-enthusiasm. Good stripping takes time and it is important that you do it properly. If you try to get it finished too soon you will inevitably end up disappointed and frustrated and perhaps be tempted to give up. Switch the radio on, relax, and you will soon be halfway there. If you start getting bored then stop, read a few more chapters of this book and start again tomorrow.

You will often find that it is just part of the furniture that needs stripping. Table tops, for example,

**Fig 6.6** A B O V E : **A harmless white powdery residue often remains when white spirit is used to clean off the stripper.**

receive a lot of wear compared to table legs and you may think it advisable to strip and refinish the top and leave the legs alone. This can be done, however the trouble lies in matching the colour of the refinished top to the colour of the legs. This should be no problem for a skilled furniture restorer with many years experience. The absolute beginner may be lucky and by coincidence match the two separate parts, but as a rule I always suggest that the beginner strips the piece completely. In the long run it will be a lot easier.

When refinishing furniture in need of reupholstery, first remove all of the old upholstery, then strip, fix and refinish the woodwork, before proceeding with the reupholstery. If the upholstery is okay, you can refinish the woodwork without removing it, as long as you are careful and protect the edges of the material with thick polythene and masking tape.

Emulsion paint on furniture is usually the result of a misinformed amateur furniture restorer. It will rarely respond to chemical strippers and it is best sanded or scraped off. Sometimes it will scrape off quite easily; at other times it is easier just to repaint it and be done with it. This second option is known as 'going with the flow' or 'being sensible' and occasionally, by more masochistic craftspeople, as 'giving up'. Give the furniture a trial scrape and see which option you prefer.

Cellulose lacquers are very hard, clear and often shiny finishes frequently applied to more modern (post-war) furniture. If your finish looks like this and does not respond to ordinary paint stripper, then try some cellulose paint stripper (available from car accessory shops). If this does not work it is probably even more recent. Try a hot air gun to soften the finish before scraping and lifting the finish away.

**Fig 6.7** B E L O W : **A suede brush is indispensible when stripping carved and complicated areas.**

# OTHER METHODS FOR STRIPPING WOOD

### SANDING

The process of removing a wood finish by sanding is easy to describe. If you are sanding by hand, obtain a selection of grades of abrasive paper (*see* page 34). Starting with the coarsest grade, start rubbing the finish off the wood. As the finish is slowly removed, move through the grades of sandpaper to finish with a fine grade of paper on bare wood.

The only time I would recommend this method, in preference to chemical stripping, is when chemical stripper will not work (such as with some modern finishes or emulsion paint), or when the finish comes off with ease when sanded with a medium-grade paper. This is often the case with old, deteriorated French-polished surfaces. The main drawback of this method is that, if you are not careful, it will often remove a small quantity of wood along with the finish. It is also extremely labour intensive, and produces a fair amount of dust, so wear a suitable dust mask (*see* page 27).

### POWER TOOLS

I do not recommend power tools and their attachments for stripping finishes from furniture. They are far too severe and can cause a lot of damage. If you do use a power tool, you will still have to finish off any mouldings, carvings or inaccessible areas with chemical stripper, as power tools are not capable of reaching these areas. Also, the abrasive papers used with the power tools tend to clog up quickly making them inefficient.

### SCRAPING

Like sanding, scraping is a labour-intensive method and will also remove a quantity of wood along with the finish. I must confess that it is not a method I have ever employed for anything largescale, but I do know that some restorers find it most satisfactory, perhaps due to the absence of chemical smells and skin burns and the fact that it is inexpensive.

The process employs any number of suitably sharp implements which are used to physically scrape off the old finish. These tools can include chisels, knives, purposely fashioned bits of metal, broken hacksaw blades and broken pieces of glass. In one case I heard of a coin being used, but perhaps more orthodox is the cabinet scraper.

The cabinet scraper is a tool specifically designed to scrape wood. It comes in a variety of sizes and shapes (*see* Fig 4.3 on page 31) and can be purchased inexpensively from tool merchants. It consists of a piece of tool steel, sharpened along one edge, and is employed to scrape away old finishes and the top layers of wood leaving a very fine surface. There is a certain amount of skill involved in their use, but the only way to see if cabinet scrapers or the other scraping tools are for you is to give it a go.

### BLOWTORCH

Another method of removing a finish is by blowtorch. This tool is designed specifically to remove paint and other finishes. Blowtorches can be bought from D.I.Y. stores and come complete with a can of inflammable gas. The one advantage of this type of removal system is that it removes thick layers of finish very quickly. It is most usefully employed when stripping thick accumulations of household paint from window frames, doors and staircases.

The method of removal is to hold the lit blowtorch in one hand, pointing at the finish to be removed; the heat causes the finish to soften and this is then scraped away by the paint scraper which is held in the other hand (ambidexterity is useful with this process). This process entails a certain amount of practice before acquiring the knack of not charring the wood underneath or turning one of your hands into pork scratchings.

Obviously there is a fire risk with this form of stripping so be very careful where you point the torch (in bright daylight the flame is almost invisible). Wear a thick (non-flammable) glove and keep other finishes and chemicals well away from the flame. The smoke from some finishes can be toxic, so open a window. Have a bowl of water to hand for skin burns or in case something catches fire.

I would not recommend this method for furniture unless it is of very simple design, or you intend to paint or ebonize the wood, thereby covering the inevitable charring.

**Fig 6.8** A B O V E : **Hot air gun.**

## HOT AIR GUN

A modern development of the blowtorch is the hot air gun (*see* Fig 6.8). This does not have a naked flame and it works on a similar principle to the hairdryer, but is much hotter. It is a lot easier to control the heat and less likely to cause charring and fire. It is therefore considered a great improvement on the ordinary blowtorch.

## SODA CRYSTALS

Many moons ago, in my innocent youth, I took the advice of an Uncle George and I tried using hot soda crystals to strip a piece of furniture. This used to be quite common advice before the advent of modern chemical strippers, and unfortunately the advice is still bandied around and accepted as valid. From my own hard-earned experience I offer you a word of advice: don't. It is tedious, time consuming and hazardous to your skin and anything else that gets splashed with the stuff; more importantly it has an appalling effect on the wood. It soaks the wood with water and will change the colour of most woods to a dull grey. Not recommended.

## DIPPING

This is another method often favoured by Uncle George. It involves immersing the article in a large vat of chemicals, leaving for a period of time and then retrieving it. The benefit of this system is that it involves no work whatsoever: the job is usually undertaken by small firms and sometimes by second-hand shops who advertise this service in the local papers.

The success of such processes depends largely upon the type of item to be dipped. I have yet to see a piece of furniture that has been dipped that could not have been stripped more effectively by hand using chemical stripper. Doors and larger architectural pieces are the sorts of item that usually receive this treatment. I do not recommend it to furniture restorers as it can cause serious damage. If you are interested in this form of stripping, contact a local specialist firm and ask them about the possible results. Ask to see some examples of furniture that they have stripped. Do not dip items of any value, or anything with a veneered surface (*see* Chapter 11 on veneers).

# CHAPTER 7

# ANTIQUIKSTRIP

*The eleventh commandment as spouted by anyone with a passing knowledge of antiques is: do not strip antique furniture. This is extremely good advice, particularly for the absolute beginner. If the furniture is of any value, leave it alone, at least until you have had a chance to build up some experience and confidence on less costly pieces.*

The aforementioned commandment is often accompanied by a little story (usually told with amusement) that runs something like this:

'I heard of a man . . . bought this beautiful Georgian commode at auction about three months ago. Paid 600 quid. Lovely it was. Took it to be restored by someone he knows very well. It cost him an arm and a leg. Wanting to make a fast buck (and who doesn't), last week he put it back into the same auction house. After much pushing, shoving and swatting of flies, it finally reached £150 before the tall guy dropped his mallet. The man was in tears. He had to sell his house to pay off the restorer, his wife left him and he has started drinking very heavily.'

The moral of the story of course is, if you are a potential furniture restorer, do not under pain of death, or worse, an appointment with the VAT inspector, attempt to strip a piece of antique furniture. You will only manage to render it totally worthless with your hapless blunderings.

When stripping a piece of furniture you will remove much of its 'patina' (*see* page 182), and for many enthusiasts of old and antique furniture the patina is the proof of its age and one of the reasons for buying it. A connoisseur can see the age of a

**Fig 7.1** A B O V E : **Antiquikstrip in action. By rubbing gently over the top of old French polish with some meths and wire wool, you can clean and partially strip the finish.**

piece of furniture through the depth and colour of its surface. Often, when stripping a piece of furniture, we remove many of the signs of its age, and if it is a collectable antique, stripping is therefore detrimental to its value.

Of course what is and is not antique will depend on your definition of the term. I like to define items made before 1920 as antique. There are many fine examples of furniture of this age around that are of little monetary value. In fact much 'antique' furniture is inexpensive if not virtually worthless, and valued for its function as opposed to its rarity or collectability.

However, just because it is not expensive does not mean that we should not appreciate its patina, character and charm, and treat it with sympathetic techniques which will preserve these attributes. Antiquikstrip is one such technique.

## HOW TO DO IT

This technique is for use on old French-polished furniture in need of stripping. If you wish to try it, I suggest that you also read Chapters 16 and 17, and achieve a reasonable level of confidence with the French polishing process.

The way that antiquikstrip works is to remove just some of the blemished French polish finish, leaving the wood (which contains elements of the patina) and the underlying polish undisturbed.

If you have large gouges or scratches to fix, fill these with thick French polish, as detailed on page 106, before using the antiquikstrip method.

Take some medium-grade wire wool and a bowl of meths. Dip the wire wool into the meths and squeeze away the excess so that it does not splash or form puddles on the work. Stroke small areas of the old finish, working with the grain. Work around the furniture systematically. The top layers of the old polish will soon soften and be removed by the abrasive action of the wire wool. Change the wire wool frequently so that it does not become too clogged (see Fig 7.1). Methylated spirit is highly inflammable, so do not smoke or use it near open flames.

The idea is to remove the part of the French polish that contains the scratches and deteriorated polish, and any other aberrations that are offensive

to the eye, leaving a surface free of blemishes. With a little experience this may be achieved very quickly, just by removing the very top layer. On other occasions you may need to remove the finish almost back to the wood; it is for you to decide when enough polish has been removed.

Once you have removed the top layers you should let the remaining polish dry out for a few hours, leaving the polish to go hard again. Then rub down with 600 grit wet-and-dry paper to flatten the surface, in preparation for the next stage.

The next stage is to French polish, as directed in Chapter 16, only now you have a head start. The foundation, or first day's work, is already in place. All you have to do is to continue the 'building up' process and spirit off or wire wool a satin finish depending on your preference. It's as easy and as complicated as that.

The agreeable thing about this technique is that, given the right conditions and a little experience, you can choose which of the scratches you leave and which you remove, or lessen the visual impact of. However, there are some problems that should be noted: the technique works best on relatively thick polish which has been damaged by scratching and other marks. Occasionally with this technique, the French polish is too deteriorated to be used as a foundation; often the polish is very thin and will come off completely when rubbed. Having said that, if the conditions are right, the wind is blowing in the right direction and you haven't upset anybody with supernatural powers, spectacular results can be obtained. With a little practice it can be done very quickly.

One last thing to consider: if you have a piece of French-polished furniture that is definitely in need of chemical stripping and you have got half an hour to spare, why not try out antiquikstrip on it first, to gain some experience.

## TOOLS AND MATERIALS REQUIRED FOR ANTIQUIKSTRIP

A piece of French-polished furniture, medium-grade wire wool, wet-and-dry abrasive paper, a bowl of methylated spirit and protective gloves.

# CHAPTER 8

# REPAIRING FINISHES

*Furniture restorers are often referred to as furniture doctors. In many respects the analogy is a good one. As with human doctors, the furniture doctor is never certain that any particular remedy will work. So we adopt a 'try it and see' approach and continue trying until the malady improves. In keeping with this analogy a restorer should always try the least invasive techniques first, before moving on to more aggressive methods. Stripping and refinishing should always be the last resort.*

If you have decided to strip a piece of furniture, stop! Experiment on the finish with some of the following recipes before you finally strip. This will give you an opportunity to experiment with various remedies without the fear of making a mistake. This is similar to experimenting on a corpse before trying it out on the living.

Starting with the simplest repairing remedies I shall work my way through the common problems that occur with old furniture. Many of the remedies will direct you to further information in other sections of the book, where you will find more complete or further information.

## WHITE MARKS

These are extremely common ailments, particularly on French polish finishes, but on others also. They are caused by moisture being absorbed into the finish. If the mark is ring-shaped, it is likely that a plant stand, vase or glass is responsible. If the mark is an amorphous cloudiness then it could have been caused by moisture in the air, a damp atmosphere, or even damp cloths or spillages being allowed to sit on the surface of furniture (*see* Fig 8.2).

First of all, establish what type of finish you are dealing with. Refer to Chapter 5 and try some of the experiments suggested. If it is a French polish finish there are a number of possible prescriptions.

## RUBBING COMPOUND

The first one that I suggest you try involves rubbing compound, which is obtainable from all car accessory shops. With a fingertip of damp cloth, gently rub the compound into the white mark. In 85 per cent of cases you will see the mark slowly disappear in front of your eyes. This is a great party trick; you can dine out on this one for many years if your friends are careless with their furniture.

You can use other abrasive cream preparations to get the same result: burnishing cream, metal polish, bath-scouring compounds and even toothpaste have all been used to good effect. The traditional Victorian prescription was to concoct a paste from cigar or cigarette ash and single cream or cooking oil. This makes a very fine abrasive paste.

One of the problems with this remedy is that if you have a very shiny surface and you remove the white mark with an abrasive that is too coarse, you will be left with a dull patch where the white mark used to be. Likewise, if you have a satin or matt finish and you use a fine abrasive, you will be left

**Fig 8.1** A B O V E : **'Thank you. Now kindly step behind the screen and remove your drawers.'**

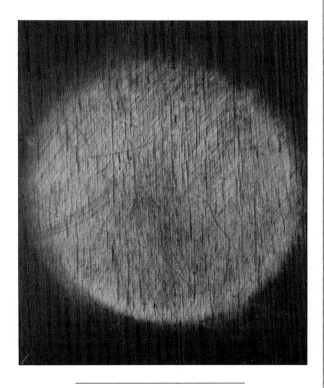

**Fig 8.2** A B O V E : **White marks like this are a common feature on much old furniture.**

**Fig 8.3** A B O V E : **Rub the abrasive cream into the white mark with a soft cloth.**

with a shiny patch where the white mark was. If you want perfection, you will have to find by trial and error the abrasive cream that will give the same shine as your French polish. The rule is, the coarser the compound the duller the finish.

The other problem with this remedy is that if you rub too hard or too fast, you can abrade away very thin or old and deteriorated coatings of French polish. There is no real answer to this one. I always think that if the polish is that far gone, then it needs to be renewed anyway. If this happens to you, try repolishing the area (*see* Chapter 16) or strip back to bare wood and start again.

### AMMONIA

If you suspect that the finish is thin, you may wish to try this remedy. However, a word of caution: this remedy uses ammonia, an extremely powerful and pungent chemical. In undiluted form it will give off very strong caustic vapours and the liquid will burn the skin. Use with care. If you have respiratory problems I suggest you get someone else to do it for you. Always use this chemical in well-ventilated areas, preferably out of doors, and away from children and animals.

Now that I have scared the living daylights out of you, I should point out that dilute ammonia is used in many household cleaning preparations, so balance my warnings against this information.

Obtain some ammonia from the chemist. Add some water to make a 50/50 mix. (This mixture is now a lot safer and more tolerable to work with, but do wear gloves.) Working slowly and purposefully, rub the solution into the white marks using a soft cloth. Look out for any adverse reactions, in particular a darkening in the colour of the wood. If this happens you will have to strip the surface back to bare wood, then stain it all the same colour and refinish, so *beware*! We don't want to chop off a leg just because we used the wrong size nail clippers.

If the finish starts to soften, the mixture is too strong and you need to add more water, but if all goes according to plan you should see the white mark slowly disappear before your eyes.

### REMEDIES FOR OTHER FINISHES

If you have tried both of these remedies and it still doesn't work, you have probably misdiagnosed the type of finish you have got. If it is a hard type of finish it is sure to be either polyurethane varnish or some form of cellulose lacquer. In this case all you have to do is rub a little harder with the abrasive compound, or use a coarser compound. If the mark persists, then it is time to go for the 'rough stuff'. Rub the compound in with fine wire wool. Do not worry if this creates a dull mark as you can always reshine the area with some finer grade compound when the white mark has gone.

In the case of Japanese laquer, moisture marks can be an orangey yellow colour, and can be removed using the ammonia method. Do not use any abrasive compound on the surface. The picture sections of Japanese laquer work are usually raised above the rest of the finish. This means they are closest to the surface and can be damaged or removed by too heavy a hand.

A white mark in a wax finish can be removed by lightly swabbing the area with a thin liquid wax mix and polishing (*see* Chapter 14). If it is an oiled finish then try rubbing in a thinned oil mix (*see* Chapter 15).

---

## BLACK MARKS

---

There are three types of black mark you may come across on your furniture.

### INK STAINS

The first is ink stains, commonly found on any furniture that is associated with writing. The ink is the old fountain pen or quill type and is a very close cousin to the spirit stains that furniture restorers use to stain wood (*see* Chapter 13). Often these ink stains only penetrate as far as the finish and can therefore by removed with the finish if and when you strip.

If the ink stain is superficial and the finish is thick, you can try to remove the stain by rubbing with the abrasive creams mentioned on the preceding pages. This is sometimes successful and always worth trying, but keep your fingers crossed.

If the ink stains penetrate through the finish to the wood, you will have to strip the finish and try the following remedy:

First, try scraping the surface of the wood where the black stain is with the tip of a sharp chisel or

## Removing a black mark from an oak piano lid using a sharp chisel

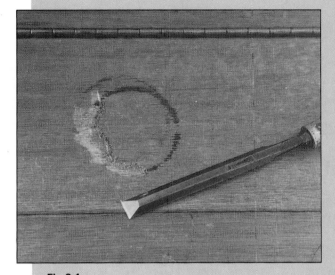

Fig 8.4

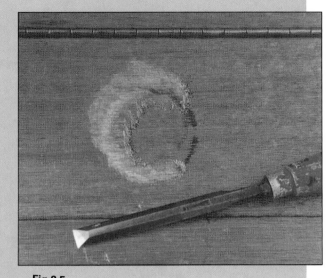

Fig 8.5

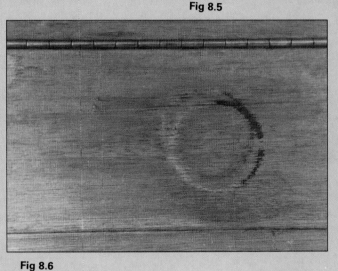

Fig 8.6

blade from a craft knife (*see* Figs 8.4, 8.5 and 8.6). Often the problem can be gently scratched away. If you do not have to scratch too deeply the colour of the wood will be left undisturbed, but this is largely dependent on luck rather than skill.

I should mention at this point a much simpler remedy, and that is changing your perception of the problem. It is, after all, expected for old writing furniture to have this form of blemish, and often it will not affect the price or value of the piece. For example, many furniture fakers will even add ink stains to writing furniture to make it look authentic (*see* Chapter 23).

### BURNS

All doctors will tell you that smoking is bad for your health, and you will receive the same advice from furniture doctors. Black marks are frequently caused by cigarettes and cigars left on the edge of table tops. This sort of mark is easily identified by its shape and position.

If it is caused by a burn, there is no alternative but to scrape the burnt fibres out of the surface of the wood with a sharp-edged implement. That should take care of the burn, but if the resulting depression that is left is an eyesore then please turn to Chapter 12 on fillers for a remedy.

## CHEMICAL STAINS

The final cause of black marks is the chemical stain. Tannic acid naturally occurs in certain woods such as oak, chestnut and mahogany, and when these woods come into contact with water and ferrous metal (iron) a chemical reaction takes place: tannic acid will attack the metal and a black stain will form. This stain can penetrate deep into the fibres of the wood. The result of this reaction is commonly seen out of doors in the black streaks that run down from screws and nails in some woodwork. You can see the same effect in the tops of pickle jars: the vinegar will react with the metal lid, causing a black stain. The method of removing this sort of stain from wood is exactly the same as that for removing ink stains.

It is interesting to note that craftspeople of by-gone times used this chemical reaction to create a black wood stain from vinegar and iron filings. (Please don't try this yourself as the mixture can be explosive.)

## SANDING

Another general method for removing black marks from wood is sanding. If you are not concerned about the antique value of your furniture, you can sand down the surface that contains the blemish. This will remove a fraction of a millimetre off the surface of the wood, baring fresh unpatinated wood.

If you only need to sand the table top, you may find that the top ends up lighter in colour than the rest of the table. In this case you will have to stain the wood to match (*see* Chapter 13).

When sanding, always sand with the grain, and finish off with the finest grade of paper you can get (*see* Fig 8.7). There are a number of power tools that will make the work of sanding large flat

**Fig 8.7** B E L O W : **When sanding by hand, always rub in the direction of the grain, never across it, and use a fine-grade paper.**

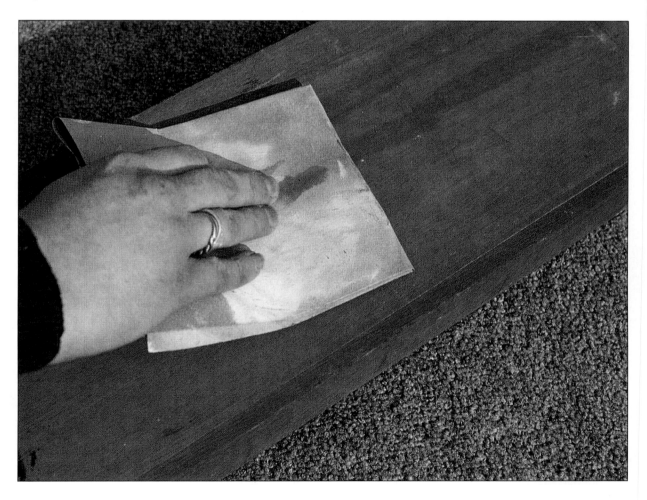

PHOTO COURTESY OF ROBERT BOSCH LTD.

**Fig 8.8** A B O V E : **A power sander.**

surfaces easier (*see* Fig 8.8), but you will still need to do some hand sanding on the places that are difficult to reach with a power tool.

Remember, even the slower hand-sanding method will produce a lot of dust. Wear a suitable dust mask and any other protection you deem necessary, such as hats and glasses.

I suggest you try some of the other remedies before opting for sanding. They are less labour-intensive and, if they work, will produce a better result. If they don't work at least you won't have lost anything and you may gain some useful experience. Remedies involving drastic action such as sanding should only be adopted when you have exhausted all other posibilities.

### BLEACHING

The other way to remove black marks from wood is to bleach them out. This is far more problematic than other removal methods. The behaviour of the bleach, the stain and the various chemicals in the wood make the job very unpredictable. As a rule I do not suggest absolute beginners use this method of stain removal.

There are two reasons why I include the process in the list of remedies. The first is in case you hear about it from Uncle George and you are curious. The second is to give you the opportunity to have

a go if you really want to. If you wish to try some bleaching, there are three possible methods you can follow:

First try ordinary household bleach. Don't use a brush to apply this stuff as it makes the bristles fall out, but draw it directly on to the stain using a lollipop stick shaped with a craft knife (*see* Fig 8.9), then wait for the bleach to have an effect. This may take some time (if it happens at all) and should be repeated every 30 minutes.

The second method uses a two-part wood bleach. This can be obtained from specialist suppliers and instructions are included with the package. Essentially you apply the first chemical to the blemish and this is then left for a short time to soak in. Then you apply the second chemical, and the resulting chemical reaction can have a bleaching effect.

**OXALIC ACID** This form of bleach is the Victorian craftsman's favourite. However it is a toxic poison, the chemicals used are strong and can burn the skin, so take all of the usual precautions: wear gloves and goggles, keep out of the reach of children and mark containers clearly. It can be obtained from specialist suppliers and is mixed into a weak solution and applied to the blemish. Abide by the supplier's instructions.

**Fig 8.9** L E F T : **Lollipop
stick used to draw bleach
on to a black mark.**

I do not recommend bleaching to the absolute beginner for a number of reasons:

- It is very unpredictable. In my experience of bleaching woods, I have seen wood turn snow white, yellow, orange, undergo no change whatsoever (very common), and once it even turned green.

- It can be dangerous (see above).

- It is difficult to keep the bleach in one place and it has a tendency to soak into the surrounding areas.

- If the bleached area goes too light, you then have to re-colour the bleached area with stains. This is not an easy job, particularly as the bleach can make the area more absorbent than surrounding areas.

- Bleaching will act like water and raise the grain. This then has to be sanded back.

- There are better and more predictable methods of removing stains.

In short, give bleaching a go if you wish, but if the gods are not with you, be prepared to sand. (If you decide to sand after bleaching be very careful of the dust as this can be toxic.)

## DENTS

Dents and depressions are another very common ailment afflicting both old and newer furniture. In Chapter 1 I described the microscopic composition of wood as being like a bunch of straws (*see* page 11). When the wood is dented these straws become compressed. All you have to do to reinflate the compressed fibres is to apply a cotton wool poultice.

Soak some cotton wool in tap water, mould the cotton wool into the size and shape of the dent and lay this on the surface of the wood (*see* Fig 8.10). Leave this to do its job and monitor progress every hour. For really nasty wounds seal the wet poultice with 2in (50mm) wide packing tape to stop the cotton wool drying out, and leave overnight (*see* Fig 8.11).

If you are impatient, or have a serious wound in need of intensive care, you can accelerate the process by touching the tip of a hot iron on to the wet cotton wool. This forces the moisture deep into the fibres of the wood and speeds up the process. This operation can be performed repeatedly until the dent is removed.

If this doesn't work it is likely that some fibres of wood have been removed at the time the wood received the knock, in which case there are no fibres to be reinflated and they will have to be replaced by some sort of filler. Refer to Chapter 12 for guidance on fillers, and the following paragraphs on scratches and gouges.

Some of the problems you may encounter with the dents prescription described above are as follows:

If you are trying this prescription on a project which is unstripped, it is important that the finish is broken to allow the water to penetrate into the wood. If the area is unbroken you can pierce the finish with a pin or a craft knife blade to allow the moisture access to the underlying wood fibres.

If the finish is French polish, invariably you will be left with a white mark where the water has been absorbed into the finish. Allow the area to dry out completely, which can take anything from a couple of days to a couple of weeks. To speed up the drying operation, play a warm hair dryer on the damp patch (probably the most boring operation that anyone has invented since cricket). Once completely dry, the white marks can be removed in the manner described on pages 51–2. If you try this operation on bare-stripped wood, you can over-inflate the fibres, leaving them proud of the surface. When you rub this down with fine sandpaper to level it you will remove some of the patina of the wood, leaving a lighter area which will be in need of patching in with stains.

This is making a lot of work for yourself. A better approach is to check the damaged area every hour to see how the operation is coming along. Prevention is always better than cure (as any good doctor will tell you).

## SCRATCHES AND GOUGES

These are the most common ailments found in furniture. As such, they are not dissimilar to the common cold in humans. Just as colds can vary in their severity, so can scratches, from the 'snuffle' of the fine scratches that you can find in any furniture, to the Grand Canyon – Spanish flu – of the schoolboy penknife.

The answer to these problems is invariably some form of filler (*see* Chapter 12). If your project has a French polish finish the scratches could be removed by employing the antiquikstrip process followed by repolishing (*see* Chapter 7).

## DETERIORATED FINISHES

If a finish is badly deteriorated, then it is probably best to strip it off and start again. Every now and then you find a finish that is not so bad it needs stripping, but is too bad to live with. The answer here might be an antiquikstrip (*see* Chapter 7).

**Fig 8.10** A B O V E : **Cotton wool poultice.**

**Fig 8.11** A B O V E : **Poultice with 2in (50mm) wide packing tape.**

## REVIVERS

A general remedy for finishes, be they waxy, dirty, deteriorated or scratched, is the reviver. These are the wonder drugs of the furniture doctor, much prized by antique dealers for their amazing rejuvenating effect on old and neglected furniture, involving very little expenditure in time, effort or money.

Safety note: Revivers are for furniture only. If taken by humans there will be a very different reaction. Label the container carefully and do not store next to the first aid kit!

### FRENCH POLISH REVIVER

There are a number of different formulas for revivers, depending on the finish, and the type and extent of damage. These very simple preparations are rubbed into the finish of the furniture and are very easy to use. The most common type of reviver is one used on French polish finishes. It is regarded as indispensable to the furniture doctor's workbench.

Mix equal quantities of white spirit, methylated spirit and boiled linseed oil. Shake them vigorously to a yellow creamy mixture (*see* Fig 8.12). If you allow the concoction to stand it will separate into its constituent parts. It should always be shaken before use.

Dip a cotton cloth into the reviver and rub it into small areas with a polishing action, then polish off firmly with a clean cloth. It is important not to leave any residue on the surface (*see* Figs 8.13 and 8.14).

Another way of using it is to decant the reviver into a garden spray bottle, spray it on to the surface and polish off immediately.

This reviver contains methylated spirit. As you will know if you have read Chapter 5, methylated spirit will soften and eventually remove French polish. Do *not* allow the reviver to sit on the surface of the furniture for more than a few seconds when not polishing.

The function of the meths in the reviver is to slightly soften the surface of the French polish, allowing the cotton cloth to polish and shine the surface. The function of the white spirit is to soften and remove any wax, dirt and fingermarks on the

**Fig 8.12** RIGHT: **When the reviver is left standing, it will separate into its constituent parts. Always shake well before use.**

**Fig 8.13** BELOW: **Before reviver has been used.**

**Fig 8.14** ABOVE: **After reviver has been used.**

surface of the wood. The linseed oil is there to darken and camouflage any scratches that are apparent, and to seal and tone down any areas where the finish has been removed.

The older, more damaged and dirty the furniture is, the more effective the reviver will be. It can also work as a wonderful cleaner for old leather and other bits and pieces.

### OTHER REVIVERS

Now that you understand what the functions of the various ingredients are you will be able to adjust the formula so you can make a reviver to fit the needs of your particular project. For example, if you have a project that is excessively waxy and dirty, you can increase the amount of white spirit in the formula. If your project suffers from numerous chips and scratches you can increase the amount of linseed oil, and if you have a finish that is in need of much polishing then you can increase the amount of meths. But do not overdo the meths or you may end up removing the finish instead of polishing it.

If you have identified the finish as polyurethane or some other modern finish, clean off the surface with white spirit plus a little car rubbing compound stirred in, then wipe some Danish oil on any areas that have bare wood exposed by scratches or deterioration.

If the finish is a wax or oil finish, mix equal quantities of white spirit and water, then stroke this reviver over the surface with a clean cloth. Follow with a fresh application of oil or wax.

## CHIPS IN THE FINISH

With very thick finishes there is a possibility of the finish being chipped, leaving a crater-like formation. This can be repaired by replacing the missing finish. First establish what type of finish you are dealing with; if you are not certain make an educated guess. If any colour has been added to the finish, you will have to try and match it by mixing in a comparable stain (*see* Chapter 13). If it is a polyurethane finish then it should be coloured with oil stains; if it is a French polish or cellulose finish it can be coloured with spirit stains.

Clean out the crater with a brush dipped in white spirit and allow to dry. Fill the crater with the correct finish by dropping the finish in on the end of a stick or artist's brush. Try to overfill the crater. This operation may take a number of applications. Allow to dry thoroughly (three days at least), then carefully level the surface with some wet-and-dry paper followed by some fine rubbing compound until the surface is absolutely smooth. If the chip is on a corner or edge you may have to tip the furniture over so that the new finish does not run out of the crater. If necessary, you can build a clay or plasticine wall around the crater to keep the finish in while it dries (*see* Fig 8.15).

N.B. Cellulose and other modern finishes can be repaired with clear nail polish.

---

**Fig 8.15** BELOW: **If you want to patch up a chipped area in a very thick finish (a problem most commonly found on modern lacquer finishes), build a clay or plasticine wall around the damaged area and pour some finish into it. When the finish has gone very hard (after perhaps seven days), remove the wall and rub down with fine-grade wet-and-dry before polishing with rubbing compound.**

## GARDEN FURNITURE

Garden furniture is often finished with linseed oil or some other preparation that in time becomes discoloured. On older furniture there may also be grime and algae growing. All of these substances can be removed by using strippers and a wire suede brush as described in Chapter 6. When stripped, refinish with a Danish oil (*see* page 129).

# CHAPTER 9

# REPAIRING STRUCTURAL
## —— DAMAGE ——

*Whereas the surface ailments of the previous chapter were superficial, the structural problems dealt with in this chapter are of a more serious nature and will often result in a totally disabled piece of furniture. Structural damage is the sort of problem that in the past would have consigned most furniture to the rubbish dump.*

To the furniture restorer this sort of damage is a double-edged sword. Firstly, these sorts of ailments are more difficult and time-consuming to put right, though certainly not beyond the capabilities of the absolute beginner. On the other hand, structurally damaged furniture is the cheapest furniture to buy, for the obvious reason that it needs more work doing to it (I find many prize specimens in skips and at rubbish dumps).

Fixing this furniture will involve some tools and equipment and, in severe cases, will require woodwork. Often dealers will not even bother showing this type of project in their shops, and will just throw it away. If you ask them nicely, I am sure you will be offered many structurally damaged pieces at a very good price.

Structurally damaged furniture is the most satisfying to complete; the more work you have put in to it, the more satisfaction you get out. However, as has been stated previously, beware of

---

**Fig 9.1** A B O V E : **A structurally damaged chair suitable for fixing.**

furniture that has major parts missing. Replacing these can prove expensive and falls outside the brief of this book.

If you prefer not to get involved in fixing structurally damaged furniture, just pick projects without severe damage and you can spend the rest of your life happily restoring without recourse to this chapter.

## WOBBLY CHAIRS

Wobbliness is the most common symptom of structural damage found in furniture. This section is concerned with this complaint in chairs, but the principles and processes can be applied to any wobbly or loose furniture.

Wobbliness is usually due to the failure of the glue joints that hold the furniture together. The strange thing is, wobbly chairs seem to last for centuries in this state, seemingly on the edge of total collapse. One of the reasons for the increased prevalence of this type of malady is that bugbear of all old furniture, central heating (*see* page 14). A chair that was in perfect condition before its introduction to a centrally heated environment, suddenly starts reeling and rolling like a drunk on a works' outing.

In the days before central heating, it was common for furniture to become wobbly during summer months. One of the old-time remedies for wobbly chairs was wrapping a damp cloth around the joint or joints overnight. This would restore the moisture to the wood and make the wood swell. Consequently, all would be well again until the next long dry spell.

### DISMANTLING A CHAIR

Presuming that you are not going to have your central heating removed to fix that wobbly chair, the remedy is as follows: the chair must be dismantled and all of the weak joints separated. If the joint is particularly strong then do not engage in a vendetta against it. But if you have taken the whole chair to pieces except one joint it seems a pity not to do the complete job and give yourself the satisfaction of knowing that every joint has been reglued.

Before dismantling, I advise you to describe and label the position of each component part (*see* Fig 9.2). These labels should describe exactly what side and in which direction the part was facing. If it is complicated then a small sketch or photo would be useful. You will be amazed at how difficult it can be to get even the simplest of pieces back together again. For example, one of my students recently

**Fig 9.2** R I G H T : **Label each component part before dismantling.**

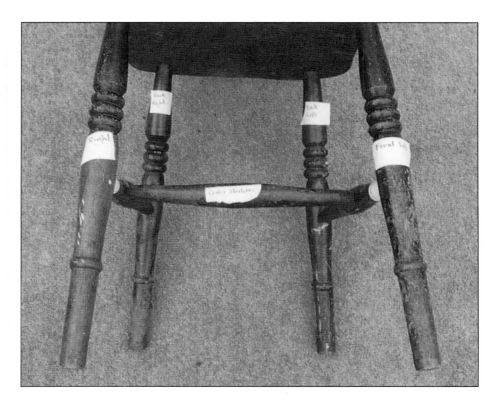

If you have any violent tension you wish to expel, this sort of activity can be very therapeutic, and it may help to think about someone you dislike intensely. For added impact you can snarl violently and bare your teeth, but try not to wilfully damage the wood.

If the joints are proving difficult to part, give them a thorough inspection to make sure you are pulling them in the right direction and there are no concealed dowels, screws or nails holding the joint together. Sometimes one part can only be removed after another piece has been removed.

If you still have problems, here are two or three tips you may find useful:

Perhaps the simplest way to apply force to the joints is the time-honoured method called using a mallet. Tape some protective cardboard or cloth pads to the areas where you intend the mallet to strike (see Fig 9.3). With the furniture being held by a trusting friend, or in a vice that has had the jaws lined with leather or cardboard, you can start gently tapping the joints apart.

Another method is to use a car scissor jack (see Fig 9.4). Place the jack in the most appropriate position, pack any gaps with blocks of wood or old books and then start winding the jack up.

If the joint survives this sort of treatment it will almost certainly survive another 100 years, so unless you are determined to reglue every joint, leave well alone.

arrived for a lesson with a three-dimensional jigsaw that had once been a small stool. The intention was to glue it back together again that evening. By the end of the two-hour session she still had not worked out the correct position of each of the members. Beware! If you want to re-stick, don't get stuck: use stickers.

Often joints will fall apart in your hands, and sometimes they will need brute force. If you lack the strength by yourself enlist the help of a friend.

**Fig 9.3** A B O V E : **Tapping joints apart with a mallet.**

**Fig 9.4** R I G H T : **Forcing joints apart using a car scissor jack.**

## CLEANING THE JOINTS

Once you have dismantled your project as far as necessary, the next step is to clean up all of the joints in preparation for regluing and reassembling.

Cleaning the joints involves scraping off the old glue from around the wood that comprises the joints. This is not as difficult as it sounds and should take between 30 and 60 minutes. I prefer to use an old chisel but anything with a sharp edge that will fit into the areas that need cleaning will do (*see* Fig 9.5). Protect the eyes for this job as the old glues can be very brittle and are liable to fly in all directions. Also, protect your hands from sharp chisels and knives.

Whatever the method of construction, there will be some sort of hole to clean. For this operation I use a ¼in (6mm) chisel. You do not have to clean all of the glue out, but the more you do the better the eventual glued joint will be.

## BROKEN JOINTS

If, when you have your project in pieces, you find that the wood comprising a joint or joints is broken you have a choice: the joint can be cut out and a new piece of wood 'let in', but this needs the skills and equipment of the cabinetmaker.

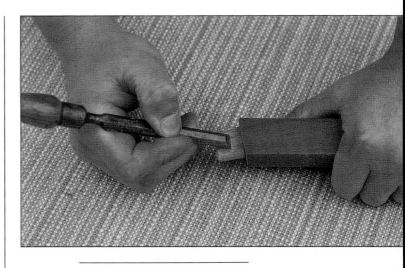

Fig 9.5 A B O V E : **Scraping the joints clean with a chisel.**

Fig 9.6 B E L O W : **A selection of dowel pegs.**

If the joint has some stable wood remaining you may be able to rebuild the joint using car body filler. If you elect to do this, clean the wood thoroughly with white spirit and a suede brush, then drill some ⅛in (3mm) holes into the remaining wooden part of the joint so that the filler can get a good grip and bond successfully with the remaining part of the joint. After this you can rebuild the

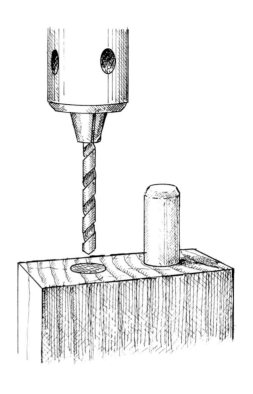

**Fig 9.7** A B O V E : **Dowelled joint and dowel pegs.**

**Fig 9.8** A B O V E : **To drill out broken dowels, first start with a small drill bit. Drill in the centre of the dowel. (You may find this easier if you cut the remaining dowel at the base.)**

**Fig 9.9**

**Fig 9.10**

A B O V E : **Two types of joint used in chair construction.**

joint with car body filler (*see* Chapter 12). When reassembling, use a urea-formaldehyde-type glue for this joint.

If the furniture is assembled using dowels you may find that some dowels get broken when you take the joint apart. Most D.I.Y. stores sell dowel (usually in inconvenient 8 foot (2.4m) lengths) and many sell ready-made dowel pegs (usually in inconvenient packs of 50) (*see* Fig 9.6). Decide the best type for your project by inspecting the joint (*see* Fig 9.7). Measure the depth of the dowel hole by inserting a pencil into the hole.

If a dowel gets broken off in a hole you will need to drill the remnants out before replacing with a new one. First cut the protruding dowel off at the base with a hacksaw so it is flush with rest of the joint then, holding the wood in a vice, drill a ⅛in (3mm) pilot hole in the dead centre of the inbedded dowel (*see* Fig 9.8); next, drill a slightly bigger hole. Continue increasing the size of the hole until it is the same size as the dowel. If the drill goes off course or you make the hole too big you can fill the hole with car body filler and redrill.

### REASSEMBLY

Unless you have reassembled a chair or other type of complicated project before, you cannot imagine the feeling of panic, frustration and loneliness that can go through you as all the things that can go wrong go wrong, and you end up slouched in a corner, a snivelling wreck, covered in glue surrounded by bits of chair and clamps.

If you want to avoid that situation then follow this advice: stay calm, take the phone off the hook, hang a 'do not disturb, craftsperson at work' sign on the front door, send the kids out of the country and give any pets to the neighbours. Invite your best friend: these are invaluable for tea, sympathy and an extra pair of hands. Do not invite someone who, as soon as anything goes slightly wrong, starts recounting your past failures and tells you that they knew it wouldn't work and that you never were any good with your hands were you? etc. etc.

Place the item to be glued on a table or bench. This is so that you don't have to spend the next half hour lurching around like Quasimodo looking for a contact lens. Then do a dry run. This is when you assemble the furniture without any glue so

that you can make sure all the pieces are there, have been properly labelled, you know where they go, and they all fit. Once you have reconstructed the furniture without glue, go through the process in your mind's eye a number of times, so you know exactly what you have to do. With complicated projects, it may be wise to glue and reassemble smaller sections first, then assemble the rest. I shall leave that decision to your common sense.

Have a damp cloth ready to clean up any excess glue drips from your hands, joints etc. Establish whether you need any clamping devices. If a joint or joints won't stay together by themselves you will need some form of clamp to hold the joints together while drying; arrange this now before gluing (*see* Fig 9.11). It's no good smothering everything in glue and then disappearing down to the hire shop.

Check whether you will need to use clamps when you are doing your dry run. If at this stage your construction can stand up by itself without falling apart, the joints are firm and don't open up, you can probably get by without clamps.

If the chair groans a little and reforms itself into an impression of a stick insect, or joints insist against all of your efforts to close, then you are going to need help from some sort of clamp to hold it all together while the glue dries (*see* Chapter 4 on tools and equipment). If you are using clamps, adjust them to the correct opening and have some cardboard or wood protectors taped into place. Before assembly you will need to have chosen the right glue for the job (*see* Chapter 4).

Working methodically through the dry-assembly furniture, disconnect one joint at a time. Coat both members of the joint with glue. Do not be mean with the glue; too much can be cleaned up; too little is a disaster. Err on the side of excess. After you have done this a couple of times you will learn how much is just enough. Bond the members of the joint lightly together, and move swiftly on to the next one. When you think that all of the joints have a coating of glue, double check them to make sure you haven't missed one. Now squeeze all of the joints together and check that the project is sitting square.

Sitting square is a phrase I use to describe a chair that is standing upright without leaning oddly

Fig 9.12 A B O V E : **Joint with glue oozing. This should be cleaned away with a damp cloth.**

Fig 9.11 L E F T : **Chair with clamps in place.**

in one direction. At the same time, check all four legs are touching level ground. To emulate a perfectly level floor I place a flat piece of thick plywood on the bench. If you are reassembling cabinet-type furniture and you do not have a set square, then check for squareness by holding a piece of large drawing paper up to the corners. (Set squares are tools used by cabinetmakers; one of their functions is to check that furniture constructions are 'sitting square'.)

Apply the clamps in two stages: first, hold the clamps in the correct position, and second, tighten them just enough to nip the wood and hold the clamps' own weight. Once all the clamps are in place, you can slowly tighten the clamps one turn at a time until they are fully tight. When you have fully tightened the clamps, check again for squareness, then clean up the glue with a damp cloth.

Cleaning up is an art in itself; keep changing the damp cloth so it does not redeposit glue on to the furniture. Use knives and bits of stiff card to get close into the joints where most of the glue exudes (*see* Fig 9.12).

Ten minutes after you have glued, check to ensure that no joints have opened up, but don't pull at the joints. Leave overnight to set. Clean off any glue that has oozed out during the night with a sharp knife or chisel, and you have finished.

If the chair does not sit four square on the floor, check that the floor is level; they rarely are. Do this by rotating the chair through 90° and seeing if the same wobble occurs; if it does, the floor is flat and the legs are at fault. If the wobble changes to another leg or disappears altogether, then the floor is wonky and the chair is okay. Double check by repeating the test, rotating in the other direction. Occasionally you will find that the floor is wonky and the chair is not square, in which case, stop drinking, it's bad for you.

It is worth noting that the three-legged stool was a favourite design with our ancestors because it was guaranteed to sit firm and square even on the most irregular flooring.

If the legs are still out of order then you will have to true up one of the legs. The easiest way to true up a chair is to buy a chair stud (available at most D.I.Y. shops) and apply it to the shortest leg. If you prefer, you can cut a piece of wood to the correct shape and size, then glue and nail it on to the leg. After the glue has dried you can stain and finish accordingly. Do not saw bits off the legs; this way leads to madness.

## REMOVING OLD SCREWS

This is always a problem. If the screws do not come out easily first time, ask yourself whether they really need to be removed. Old screws will frequently become corroded and very difficult to remove. If you decide that they have to be removed and they are going to be difficult, do not do anything else until you have the right tool for the job: a good-quality, correct-fitting screwdriver (*see* Fig 9.13). If you haven't got one, beg, steal or borrow one. Failing all that, go out and buy one – it will earn its keep a hundred times over, in all sorts of jobs.

Next, make sure the slot in the top of the screw is perfectly clean and not blocked up with filler, glue, finish, rust or wax etc. Scrape any debris out with an old chisel or knife so the screwdriver sits

**Fig 9.13** R I G H T : **A selection of good-quality screwdrivers.**

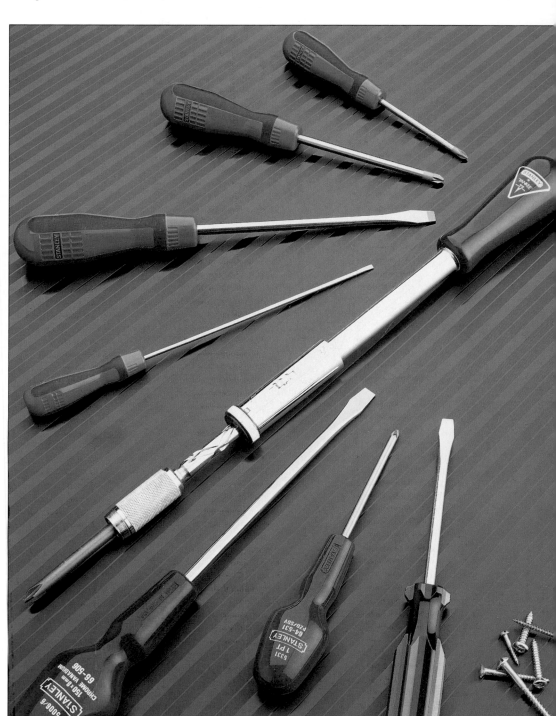

PHOTO COURTESY OF STANLEY TOOLS.

perfectly in the screw slot. Now, either get someone else to hold the furniture firmly, or clamp it to the top of a bench so that the screw head is pointing skywards.

Grip the screwdriver in both hands, and then, whilst bending your knees, turn your whole body at the waist. Do not try to twist your wrists or arms. They do not possess nearly so much strength as the rest of your body (see Fig 9.14). First try to tighten the screw (this is always clockwise). This sometimes breaks the corrosion around the screw. Then try to undo the screw by twisting it in the opposite direction (always anticlockwise).

Resist all attempts by the screwdriver to jump out of the screw's slot by pushing downwards with all of your weight. If you are doing the job properly

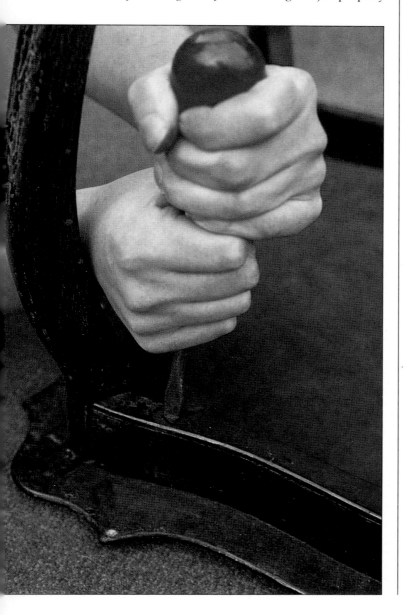

you will resemble a constipated sumo wrestler, but don't let that sway you – this is war and you are not going to lose.

Having tried that a number of times to no avail, try spitting on your hands and rubbing off the excess fluid down the front of your work clothes. This may not seem a very useful action at this stage, but it will give your hands a superior grip and look like you mean business to anybody who happens to be watching.

If all this still does not budge the screw, then you will have to start getting nasty. Place a thick blanket on the table top to protect any delicate surfaces, then with the screwdriver located in the slot of the screw, strike the top of the screwdriver three blows with a mallet or suitable lump of wood.

The first blow just taps the top of the screwdriver, the second hits a little harder, and the third does the trick. Do not overdo it, and make sure your screwdriver has a shatterproof handle; if you are not sure wrap the handle of the screwdriver in some towelling cloth or other suitable material. Do this two or three times, then repeat the sumo wrestler method.

If all else fails, you can (assuming you haven't changed your mind about getting the screw out) heat a length of metal rod with the same dimensions as the top of the screw head to a dull red heat and touch it on to the top of the screw head, leaving it there until the heat has had enough time to conduct itself through the screw. Make sure you put any flammable preparation out of the way before trying this one.

Once you have done this, swiftly adopt the sumo pose. You can repeat this process a number of times, being careful not to burn any surrounding timber or damage the tip of your screwdriver by inadvertently heating it up. If all of these techniques fail to shift the screw, then give up. It is more than likely that the screw will have broken. If this is the case you will have to call it a draw. When you remove the other screws you will find the remains of the screw in the wood. This you can remove with pliers or by cutting it back with a hacksaw.

**Fig 9.14** L E F T : **Use a correct-sized screwdriver and a firm grip to remove stubborn screws.**

## DRAWER RUNNERS

These are the bits of wood that drawers use to rest upon the corresponding bits of wood in the cabinet (*see* Fig 9.15). There are usually two parts to the drawer runner that need repair – the part inside the cabinet and the part that is attached to the drawer.

It is difficult to describe when drawer runners need replacing, but when the drawer starts getting stuck and will not sit level in its opening in the cabinet, take it out and inspect the insides of the cabinet and the bottom of the drawer sides for excessive wear.

There are a number of configurations of drawer runners, and these are tricky jobs for the absolute beginner, involving the use of woodworking equipment and skill. I suggest that if you have a project that is in need of this sort of work, and you are not experienced in woodworking, you find someone with the skill and the equipment to do it for you.

For every drawer in need of repair you will have two sides, and each side can involve the replacement of two sections: inside the cabinet and on the drawer. So a four-drawer cabinet that needs all of its drawer runners replacing requires 16 separate pieces of woodwork. Be warned, this job is not for the absolute beginner.

However, this problem of worn drawer runners is very common, so if you can learn the skill from a weekend cabinetmaker, or invest some time, money and trouble gaining the necessary skill and equipment, then it could be to your advantage in the future.

## REPAIRING BROKEN DRAWERS

Often drawers decide to collapse due to overwork and misuse. If this has happened to you then you will need to scrape off the old glue and reassemble. If any of the components have broken or split you will need to glue, clamp and allow these to dry before you glue the drawer back together again.

**Fig 9.15** A B O V E : **One example of a drawer runner configuration. The channel in the middle of the drawer side is matched by an insert in the body of the cabinet. These will often wear and, in extreme cases, need replacing.**

## NATURAL BREAKS IN THE WOOD

Natural breaks in the wood, where the wood has split along the grain, are caused by wood drying out and shrinking (*see* Chapter 1). It will usually split along the grain of the wood starting from a section of end grain (*see* Fig 9.16). The easiest option is to fill the crack and then colour accordingly (*see* Chapter 12).

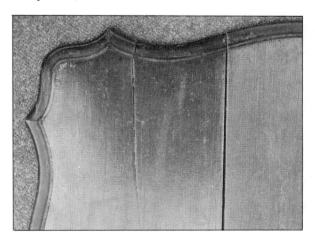

**Fig 9.16** A B O V E R I G H T : **Showing both an unnatural (right) and a natural break in a table top. The split on the right was caused by the wood shrinking and consequently breaking the joint between the two boards that make up the table top. The split on the left is a natural break caused by a defect in the timber.**

## SPLITS IN TABLE TOPS

As well as natural splits in wood, there are un-natural splits. During the manufacture of table tops, two or more pieces of wood are often joined together to form a larger or more stable piece of wood. Over the years, the constant fluctuations in moisture from summer to winter can move apart, twist and warp these joints (*see* Fig 9.16).

The problem is often exacerbated when people use small tables out of doors during hot summers and these then become caught in sudden summer storms. This has the dual effect of first drying the wood out and then saturating it.

Many table tops have been riven down the middle by the force of these elements. If they are completely split into two, three or even four, then your life can be made much easier and the job much quicker. This is because the best way to fix these table tops is to allow the wood to dry, then plane true again the edges of the boards that make up the table top, and glue them back together in the same manner as they were first made. The problem here is that you will need some woodworking equipment and quite a lot of skill to manage to do this job with any alacrity. I therefore suggest that you contact your weekend cabinet-maker and employ his or her talents in planing the edges of the boards perfectly true, before regluing and replacing.

If the split is only halfway up the join or less, take the top off and see if the joint can be artificially broken, so that you can fix it using the above method. If the split is not too serious, fill it with a wood filler, then colour (*see* Chapter 12).

## WARPED TABLE TOPS

Warped table tops often come in tandem with the above problem. The warping and twisting of table tops and cabinet tops is a disaster and cannot easily be repaired (*see* Fig 9.17). The force exerted by a twisting piece of wood is phenomenal and far beyond the capabilities of the absolute beginner, or even more experienced craftspeople to control.

The best remedy for this problem is to remove the table top and replace it with a new top. The new top can be made quite easily from thick plywood, or you could get a copy made of the original top, then replace it and refinish accordingly.

## VENEERS

Lifted and damaged veneers is an extremely common problem and I direct you to Chapter 11 for advice on this subject.

**Fig 9.17** L E F T : **This beech table top became bowed after being left outside in the rain.**

**Fig 9.18** A B O V E : **Use a block to increase leverage and protect the wood.**

## REMOVING OLD NAILS AND PINS

Nails and pins are the thorn in the furniture re-storer's side (if you'll forgive the pun). They should not be in the furniture at all and are usually a sign that a bodger (*see* page 75) has been at work. They are often seen in wobbly chairs. This would not be so bad if it were not for the fact that the nails rarely have any beneficial effect. More often than not they just make the job more difficult for future restorers when the furniture needs to be repaired.

If you can get the nails out using a pair of pliers or the claw of a claw hammer, then do so. However, it is rarely as simple as that. Often you will have to use brute force to wrench the two pieces of wood apart, removing any nails and pins after the joint is separated, and then deal with the consequences of the split and broken timber by the judicious use of filler.

Often you need a little extra leverage to remove deep-bedded nails, in which case place a block under the claw hammer or pliers. This will have the dual benefit of protecting the wood underneath the tool, and increasing the leverage power (*see* Fig 9.18). Obviously the least damage you do the better. With this in mind you are free to try any tool that you can think of, but remember, those nails and screws have to come out.

## REPAIRING COMPLETE BREAKS IN FURNITURE

Often you will come across a stretcher or a slat in a chair or other piece of the furniture that is broken in two. To dismantle the furniture, remove the broken pieces, fix and replace would be unfeasible. It would be far better if you could fix the slat while still in place.

If this is to be successful it is important that the two pieces of wood are thoroughly clean. Do a dry run ensuring there are no foreign bodies or way-ward splinters of wood stopping their union. To find the best way to hold the two pieces together whilst the glue dries you will have to use trial and error. In the past I have used bulldog clips, rubber strips cut from inner tubes, masking tape, splints made from lollipop sticks, small clamps, small screws, hose clips, and rubber bands. There are no rules; if it works it is good. Whatever you use, find it while you are doing the dry run, not after you have spread the glue (*see* Fig 9.19).

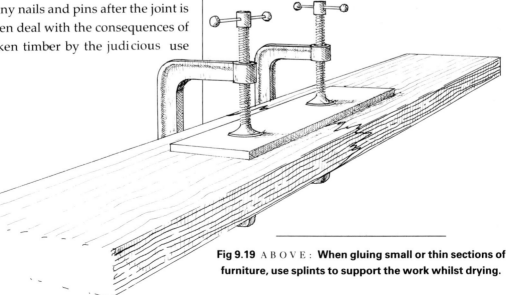

**Fig 9.19** A B O V E : **When gluing small or thin sections of furniture, use splints to support the work whilst drying.**

PHOTO COURTESY OF RENTOKIL LTD.

## WOODWORM

The activities of the common furniture beetle, otherwise known as woodworm, are world-renowned. The mere mention of its name can send grown men into a thumb-sucking stupor, and not without some reason: woodworm can, in a relatively short space of time, devour your furniture from the inside out leaving a wormhole-riddled shell. One day you can be hunting for a fresh pair of socks in your antique chest of drawers, and the side of the cabinet will suddenly disintegrate into a pile of wood dust.

This is rare, but not rare enough; you can understand why, over the centuries its activities have

PHOTO COURTESY OF RENTOKIL LTD.

**Fig 9.21** A B O V E : **Exit holes of the common furniture beetle.**

**Fig 9.20** A B O V E : **The common furniture beetle, or woodworm.**

gained such notoriety, and why, finding even one of the tell-tale flight holes will scare little old ladies and collectors of expensive furniture out of their underwear.

The truth is, although woodworm can do irreparable damage, as long as the furniture owner is aware, knows what to look for and nips it in the bud, they will have no problem. So do not panic. More often than not woodworm damage is superficial and is typified by a smattering of tiny flight holes. These are of no real concern to the restorer. In fact I always enjoy seeing it in furniture as it assigns a certain amount of character to a piece.

The treatment of light infestation is simple. Buy some woodworm-killing fluid from a D.I.Y. or hardware store and squirt it liberally into the flight holes (*see* Fig 9.22). This will eradicate any insect still at home and will stop any woodworm fly returning to lay their eggs. Problem solved. The liquid is a poison so treat with common sense, don't smoke it or make any sandwiches with the stuff or stir it into your tea.

Woodworm are a little sneaky in their eating habits; they prefer the rougher wood that is found around the back and underneath of furniture. Always pull the furniture away from the wall and inspect it thoroughly in these places, looking out for any fine-powdered sawdust which is indicative of rampant worms at work.

If you find the problem too late and parts of the structure have been undermined, there are two approaches possible:

First, you can drill some ¼in (6mm) diameter holes through the deteriorated wood into solid wood underneath. Then fill the drill holes with some fibreglass resin and allow it to soak into the deteriorated timber. Fibreglass resin can be bought at car accessory shops and, when mixed according to the instructions on the pack, will solidify and stabilize the wood. Any holes that are left can be filled with filler. Once the structure is complete you can colour as necessary (*see* Chapters 12 and 13).

The other approach is to cut out the deteriorated wood and replace with some new wood of the same size, shape and type. This is usually beyond the absolute beginner, so use the skills of a weekend cabinetmaker.

**Fig 9.22** L E F T : **Squirt woodworm-killing fluid liberally into flight holes.**

**Fig 9.23** B E L O W : **Rampant worms at work.**

## Chipboard corner built up with car filler

Fig 9.24

Fig 9.25

## CHIPBOARD

Using the same fibreglass resin you can also repair chipboard. Chipboard is made by mixing small fibres or chips of wood in a glue and then compressing. It has hundreds of uses in modern furniture design. However, when it breaks it is very difficult to repair, unless you have this book.

The most difficult part of the operation is the preparation. Place the two broken sections together and clean out any chips that are obstructing the close union of the two sections. Next, using plasticine or clay, make a wall around the break. On the underside, seal the break with 2in (50mm) packaging tape so that no resin can seep out, and support the two sections by placing blobs of plasticine beneath the two halves on the corners, keeping the two sides on the same level.

Pour the fibreglass resin into the break and allow it to set. The chipboard will absorb the resin and then set, making a perfect bond. Finish by filling any holes and colouring (*see* Chapters 12 and 13). If the chipboard has just had a piece removed or a corner damaged, it can be repaired by building up with car body filler (*see* Figs 9.24 and 9.25).

## BODGERS

Before finishing, I must mention the biggest problem facing the furniture restorer: no, it's not central heating, nor is it musical chairs at the slimming club. The biggest problem encountered by the furniture restorer by a long chalk is previous amateur restorers, or rather, previous amateur restorers who have not seen a copy of this book.

These well-meaning uninitiates are commonly referred to in the furniture restoration trade as 'bodgers'. As has already been stated in Chapter 3 on safety, ignorance is the biggest danger, and this also applies to bodgers. What the average bodger gets up to is bad enough; when they really make an effort the results can be staggering.

If you are a more experienced restorer and you want to save yourself wincing at the following litany of disasters, I suggest you skip the next bit.

Nails in loose joints; furniture stripped with blowtorch or caustic soda; table tops covered with flooring linoleum; chipboard used to 'upholster' chairs; legs shortened to accommodate uneven floors; fine mahogany antiques painted yellow, pink and blue; contact adhesive used to fix wobbly tables; ceramic tiles used to decorate bookshelves; table tops stripped with power-sanding discs; bedside cabinets veneered with wallpaper; wobbly chairs fixed with metal straps; breaks fixed with the wrong glue (in one case jam and sticky tape); veneer bubbles filled with chewing gum.

If you have chosen a project that has been worked on by a bodger, you have my sympathies. The answer to this ailment is to remove as much evidence of bodging as posible from your project. There are two main weapons of torture in the bodgers' armoury: metalwork and glue. Both of these will have to be dealt with mercilessly. Remove any metalwork that may be evident: screws, nails, fixing straps, brackets, staples. Then dismantle the furniture and scrape away any glues. Once all bodging has been removed, you can fill and repair any holes or other damage.

This all sounds very simple and you may be wondering what all the fuss is about. The difficulty lies in these two charmingly innocuous phrases: 'remove all metalwork' and 'scrape away any glues'. Within these two phrases can lie weeks of frustrating, nerve-shattering, sweaty-browed, eye-popping, teeth-gritting work. Unfortunately I can offer you no help; only sympathy and the certain knowledge that bodgers do not go to heaven.

# CHAPTER 10

# FIXING ODDS AND
## —— ENDS ——

*This chapter is concerned with those odds and ends that will not fit neatly into the previous two chapters. Here we have a selection of the common problems that are difficult to pigeon-hole, but none the less frequently crop up in my classes.*

## KNOBS AND FINIALS

Knobs and finials are often missing or are in need of changing on furniture (finials are small decorative knobs) (*see* Fig 10.1). Large D.I.Y. stores will vary in their range of knobs, and other furniture accoutrements available to the restorer.

For more individual requirements there are a number of specialist firms who deal with this sort of product. It is worth obtaining their catalogues and getting to know them. The right finishing touch can 'make' a piece of furniture.

Broken furniture which has major structural damage will often be thrown out by a dealer as unworthy of the space it takes up. However, before disposal the dealer will often remove useful smaller parts such as locks, knobs, finials etc. with the intention of either repairing a future piece or selling on to someone like yourself or another dealer. If you ask very nicely and offer a reward, you may find what you are looking for.

Decorative finials are frequently lost or broken. If you cannot find another one that matches in the suppliers' catalogues and you do not want to go to the expense of having a new one made, you can cast one yourself.

Lightly wax and make an impression of a matching finial in plasticine (*see* Fig 10.2), then mix some car body filler and spoon it into the mould, pushing it gently into the crevices of the mould (*see* Fig 10.3). When set, you now have half a finial. Cast the other half in the same way, but before it has set, gently push the two halves together, matching the complete finial (*see* Fig 10.4). Clean up rough edges, fill any air holes, stain, finish and replace.

**Fig 10.1** A B O V E : **A selection of knobs.**

PHOTO COURTESY OF JOHN BODDY'S FINE WOOD & TOOL STORE LTD.

## In the absence of a suitable replacement, you can cast your own finial out of car body filler

**Fig 10.2** A B O V E : **First take a mould of half of an existing finial.**

**Fig 10.3** A B O V E R I G H T : **Push some body filler into the impression.**

**Fig 10.4** R I G H T : **Repeat this to make a second half, but before the second side is dry, push the two halves together to make a complete finial. When finished, fill any air bubbles, tidy up any rough edges and stain with spirit stain, and French polish to the correct colour.**

## LEATHER TOPS

Old leather tops are always in need of replacement. Surprisingly, this operation is not at all difficult. The problem lies in ordering the correct size of leather. Contact a supplier (*see* page 188) to find out their terms of business; most will require the exact measurement in millimetres of the width and length of the leather. If the leather is not square, you will need to make a paper template of the recess that the leather is to be fitted into. You also need to choose the colour and type of decoration. The supplier can advise you on many aspects of this particular facet of restoration, so be prepared with a few choice questions.

The recess that the leather is to be fitted into must be perfectly flat and clean. Be particularly fussy around the edge where the recess is. To check for flatness, lay some thin paper where the leather is to be placed, and rub your hand over the top to see if any foreign bodies mark or raise the paper.

Brush some thick wallpaper paste on to the area to be leathered, then check there are no lumps or dry spots. Now lay the leather on to the surface and smooth from the centre outwards, removing any creases and air bubbles. Beware of stretching the leather at this stage. Line up any decorative tooling so that it is parallel with the edges. Using the back of a dinner knife, gently push the edges of the leather into the recess. Then with a craft knife fitted with a brand-new blade, cut around the line that has been made with the dinner knife.

If you have a broad-bladed wallpaper stripping knife you can use this to guide your craft knife and to hold the leather in place whilst cutting. Lean the craft knife outwards from the centre of the leather slightly so that it is undercut at the edges as described in Fig 10.5. This will help to disguise the lighter-coloured edge of the leather. When all sides are cut, push the leather against the edges of the recess and clean up with a damp rag.

If you happen to scuff or otherwise damage your new leather during installation, it can be repaired using spirit stains (*see* Chapter 13). Occasionally, old leathers can be improved rather than replaced by using the correct-coloured spirit stain with a little French polish added. This can be rubbed on gently with a cotton cloth, followed by a thin wax. How effective this will be depends on the condition of the leather.

Household tip: spirit stains can also be employed to restore scuffed shoes and other leather items.

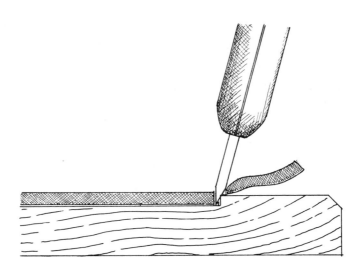

**Fig 10.5** A B O V E : **The leather should be cut at a slight angle to give a neat finish to the job.**

Fig 10.6 L E F T : **When refinishing the frame of a mirror, shield the glass with tape and paper.**

## GLASS AND MIRRORS

Glass and mirrors are frequent visitors to the restoration workshops and they always make me nervous (particularly when I catch a glimpse of my reflection in one). Handle with extreme care, not only because glass is a very dangerous material, but also because mirrors and glazing can be time-consuming and expensive to replace.

If the frame is not in need of structural repair, it is always best to leave the mirror in place while refinishing, and just be careful that you don't earn yourself seven years bad luck. Cover your workbench with a thick blanket and protect the glass with some masking tape to save the edges of the glass becoming coated when refinishing (*see* Fig 10.6). Mirrors can last for millenia when hanging on a wall, but as soon as someone takes it from its usual surroundings the chances of it having an unhappy ending escalate enormously.

If you have to replace a piece of glass or mirror then take measurements along to a glass merchant and ask them to cut you the required piece. Although Uncle George may entice you, don't bother trying to cut it yourself. Glass is dangerous to work with; it needs special tools and space. Let the glass merchant take the responsibility and the risks. He is well worth the money he charges.

To clean dirty glass, polish with newspaper print dampened with methylated spirit. Any spots of paint can be carefully removed with the edge of a sharp blade or a little metal polish. Glass used in cabinet doors is thin – if it is old it is notoriously easy to break; be very careful and do not apply any pressure when cleaning.

Old mirrors are often fixed into their frames with glue blocks (*see* Fig 10.7). If you decide to remove the mirror before refinishing the frame, these glue blocks can be awkward to deal with, as the glue used is the old type of animal glue (*see* Chapter 4).

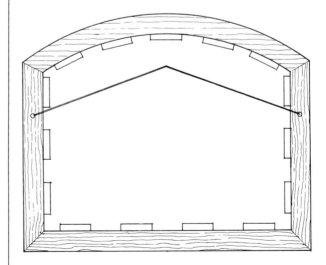

Fig 10.7 A B O V E : **The glue block used to be a common way of constructing furniture. They are often seen on the reverse of old mirrors.**

## GLUE BLOCKS

When the mirror was being assembled many moons ago, the wooden glue blocks were a very practical and quick process. The blocks were given a quick wipe with some animal glue, then hand-held into place until the glue cooled; often this took no more than a few seconds per block. This technique, which can also be seen underneath and around the back of many pieces of old cabinet furniture, was very efficient in its day and widely used (*see* Fig 10.8). Today animal glue is rarely used outside the professional restoration workshop, and definitely not recommended for use by absolute beginners (*see* Chapter 4).

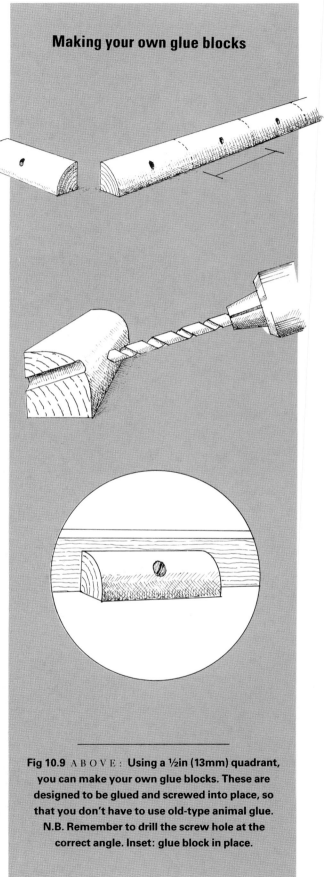

## Making your own glue blocks

**Fig 10.9** A B O V E : **Using a ½in (13mm) quadrant, you can make your own glue blocks. These are designed to be glued and screwed into place, so that you don't have to use old-type animal glue. N.B. Remember to drill the screw hole at the correct angle. Inset: glue block in place.**

**Fig 10.8** A B O V E : **Glue blocks are commonly found on the inside of cabinet furniture.**

Therefore the absolute beginner has to find a way around the problem of fixing the glue block with modern glues. Removal is easy. If you want to remove them without any force or damage, then lay some cotton wool or cloth soaked in hot water over the individual blocks and wait for the glue to soften. If the project has been in a damp situation or is very old, then a sharp tap with a light hammer on one end of the block usually releases them. When doing this to old mirrors, protect the back with cardboard, or if this is difficult use a chisel to lever them off.

Replacement is the problem. If you don't want to use the old-type glue (and I don't recommend it) there are a number of other ways of proceeding. The method you choose depends on your particular circumstances.

You will have to find a way of holding each glue block in place while the modern slower-drying glue dries. Before replacing, you can drill a hole into each glue block and screw them into place. Sometimes you may find it easier to make new glue blocks; drill holes at 1in (25mm) intervals into some suitable size quadrant moulding (available at all D.I.Y. stores). Then cut 1in (25mm) sections from the moulding leaving the hole that you have drilled in the middle of the block. Glue and screw these into place (*see* Fig 10.9).

The size hole that you drill will depend on the width (gauge) of the screw that you use. Buy these two items together and ask for advice in the shop on the best size drill bit for your chosen screws (*see* Fig 10.10).

PHOTO COURTESY OF JOHN BODDY'S FINE WOOD & TOOL STORE LTD.

**Fig 10.11** A B O V E : **Arrow glue gun (with lever action).**

If the glue blocks you need are quite large, strong and not to be seen, there are some plastic pre-formed, predrilled fixing blocks available on the market. These do not require glue, just screws. Most D.I.Y. stores will have a selection for you to choose from.

Otherwise you can use a heat-sensitive glue gun (*see* Fig 10.11). This piece of equipment is widely used in other craft activities. If you can beg, borrow, steal or buy one, do so. Make sure you use a glue stick that is designed for sticking wood, and that all the old animal glue is cleaned off the wood.

I do not recommend using nails to tack the glue blocks into place – many mirror and cabinet frames are very fragile and will not take the hammering.

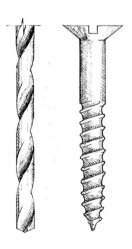

**Fig 10.10** L E F T : **You will normally need two drill bits to accommodate a wood screw – one for the threaded part of the screw and one for the shank. Hold the drill against the screw to judge the best sizes. If in doubt, when buying screws ask the shopkeeper to recommend the right drill sizes.**

## UPHOLSTERY

If your furniture requires new upholstery, recaning or rushwork, you need to completely strip it of the old upholstery material, do the restoration of the woodwork, then reupholster. There are many excellent specialist upholstery, caning and rush-work books on the market to help you accomplish this aspect of the craft. Among these are *Seat Weaving* by Ricky Holdstock (GMC Publications, 1993), and *Upholstery: A Complete Course* by David James (GMC Publications, 1990).

If your furniture is not in need of reupholstery and there is a problem with a broken, wobbly or loose joint underneath the material, then you will have to untack and peel back the upholstery around the joints, try to effect a repair and then reupholster.

Common sense will tell you that the less damage you do to the upholstery at this stage the better. However, be prepared to completely redo the upholstery if your efforts are not successful – this is another area where luck rather than skill is important.

If your furniture's upholstery is in good condition but the woodwork needs refinishing, cover all of the material with thick polythene held in place with 1½in (38mm) thick masking tape (*see* Fig 10.12). The masking tape should come right to the edge of the material and then be tucked underneath. Once the material is protected you can refinish to your heart's content.

## LOCKS

The same specialist firms that supply knobs, finials and hinges will also supply keys and locks (*see* Fig 10.13). It is rare to find a lock with its original key on a cabinet, wardrobe or writing box. Keys are so easily lost that finding a 50-year-old lock with its original key is as common as snow in July.

The price of a box with its original key can be as much as double that of a box without one. This is why many dealers keep a large bunch of homeless keys in their backrooms. Many boxes and other furniture were given very primitive locks, often duplicated in other furniture. It is worth asking

**Fig 10.12** L E F T : **Protect intact upholstery with paper or thick polythene when refinishing.**

your friendly neighbourhood junk dealer if he has a bunch that you can try. If this does not work you can send the lock off to a cabinetmaker's locksmith. Many of these will cut a key for your particular lock. If you haven't got a lock then the same suppliers will sell you one by mail order.

Often, locks have been broken or lids prised open, damaging the remaining setting for the lock. Fill around the lock recess using car bodywork filler and screw the lock back into place. But beware of clogging the workings of the lock with filler. Once the filler has dried you can colour as described in Chapter 13.

## LOOSE SCREWS

One loose screw can, like the proverbial nail in a horseshoe, be the undoing of many a piece of furniture. The remedy for this is simple: remove the screw, push a matchstick or matchsticks dipped in glue into the hole, cut off any protruding matchstick with a sharp knife, and replace the screw. If the area around a hinge has split and the screw won't hold, then fill with car body filler or urea-formaldehyde glue. It may be necessary to clamp the wood together as well.

**Fig 10.13** T O P : **A selection of locks and keys.**

**Fig 10.14** A B O V E : **An example of plated metal worn away.**

## METALS

To clean metalwork, use rubbing compound or metal polish. For badly corroded, rusty or tarnished metal, use a suede brush or fine wire wool.

Sometimes metals used in furniture can be plated. This means that one metal is coated with a very thin coating of another metal. Over the years the outer coating can get worn away showing the base metal underneath (*see* Fig 10.14). This can look unpleasant. Remedies include replacing the metal-work, or rubbing off the remaining plating with rubbing compound to reveal the lesser but homogenous base metal (this often turns out well if the metalwork is of simple design); or if the metal work is purely decorative and of a complicated design, you can try painting it with gold or silver paint. Again, the method you choose depends on your circumstances and the condition of your project.

**Fig 10.15** A B O V E : **A selection of solid brass cabinet fittings in antique and bright finish.**

# CHAPTER 11

# VENEERS

PHOTO COURTESY OF BUCKINGHAMSHIRE COLLEGE.

*This chapter is for those of you who are unfamiliar with veneers, how they are used in the production of furniture, and the best ways of restoring them.*

Veneers are very thin sheets of wood. They can be as thick as the cover of a hardback book or as thin as a newspaper. They have been used in the decoration of every class of furniture for thousands of years. In discussing such a wide-ranging subject as veneers, it would be easier if we split the subject into two sections: their decorative use, and their practical use.

**Fig 11.1** A B O V E : **Horizontal veneer cutting of sycamore, angled for grain effects.**

**Fig 11.2** R I G H T : **Veneering in progress on a pine base.**

PHOTO COURTESY OF BUCKINGHAMSHIRE COLLEGE.

# Examples of marquetry pictures

**Fig 11.3**

**Fig 11.4**

**Fig 11.5**

## DECORATIVE VENEERS

When used purely as decoration, veneers can be employed in a number of ways. In the specialist craft of marquetry, different-coloured veneers are cut, assembled and glued to build up pictures. These marquetry 'veneer pictures' can be produced as individual free-hanging works of art (*see* Figs 11.3, 11.4 and 11.5) or incorporated into the furniture surface as decoration (*see* Figs 11.6 and 11.7).

**Fig 11.6** A B O V E : **Cabinet, oak veneered with marquetry.**

**Fig 11.7** R I G H T : **English walnut table c.1685 featuring marquetry around the drawer handles.**

PHOTO COURTESY OF PETER LEGG.

PHOTO COURTESY OF PETER LEGG.

**Fig 11.8** T O P : **An example of Turkish banding.**

**Fig 11.9** A B O V E : **An example of cross banding on an old bureau door.**

Sometimes veneer borders are created on table tops and legs to add visual interest to furniture. This is achieved by inlaying a line of contrasting-coloured veneer. This border can be quite small – ⅛in (3mm) – and is called stringing. Sometimes it can be more complex and be up to 2–3in (50–75mm) thick; this is called banding (*see* Fig 11.8). If the veneer borders are laid with the grain facing inwards against the natural grain direction of the rest of the wood, then it is called cross banding (*see* Fig 11.9).

## PRACTICAL VENEERS

Many of the world's timbers are unsuitable for use in the construction of solid wood furniture. This can be for a number of reasons: sometimes the beautiful, wild and swirling grain of the wood is too unstructured to contain the necessary strength needed for solid furniture (the 'straws' are lying in such a random fashion that strength and stability is minimal). Sometimes the wood can be too expensive or rare to make it feasible for use in the construction of solid wood furniture.

Designers and cabinetmakers get around this problem by making furniture in a stable and cheap foundation wood, then covering this with a more attractive veneer. This sounds like a case for the fraud squad, but even to a semi-experienced eye veneers are easy to detect, and veneering is done largely for aesthetic effect.

In 1863 an American patented the system of using veneers glued one on top of another to produce very strong and large sections of board called plywood (*see* Fig 11.10). This material was soon taken up by cabinetmakers and designers as it was capable of many things that solid wood was not: it was available in large sections; it had the ability not to move, expand, contract and split in the manner that solid woods so frequently do; the visible outer veneers could be composed of whatever type of veneer the designer chose, so opening a whole new panorama of design possibilities. All of these aspects made it a lot cheaper and more convenient to produce furniture using this material. It was therefore much loved by the designer of mass-produced furniture and has been incorporated in furniture designs ever since.

Designers usually combine the use of solid wood and veneered plywood; in areas like legs, lippings and the carcass of the furniture, they will employ solid wood. For large flat areas such as table tops, central panels, backboards and side panels they

**Fig 11.10** B E L O W : **This stack of plywood highlights the manner in which the sheets are constructed using thin veneers.**

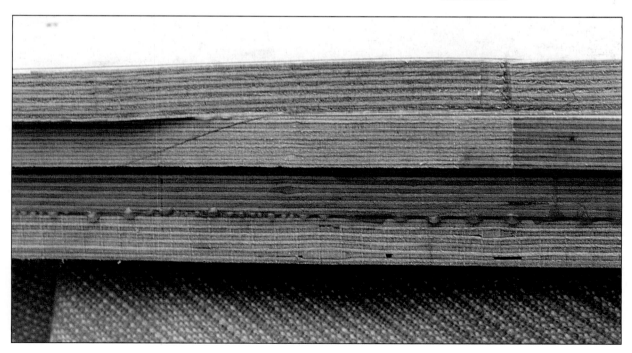

**Fig 11.11** T O P : **A mid-twentieth-century plywood sideboard, veneered in walnut.**

**Fig 11.12** A B O V E : **Chipboard with a very thin veneer.**

will use veneered plywood with a veneer that matches the solid wood. It is in these areas that veneered plywood is ideal; it will not split, it does not move and it is much stronger than solid wood of the same thickness. Much early twentieth-century furniture is made using plywood in this way and is usually of very robust and resilient construction (*see* Fig 11.11). More modern furniture can incorporate veneers glued to chipboard, blockboard and all sorts of other man-made board. These veneers can be extremely thin in some furniture (*see* Fig 11.12).

## SPOTTING VENEERS

From the furniture restorer's point of view, it is useful to be aware of when and where man-made boards and veneers have been used, so that we use the best possible techniques to restore them. Because of their thinness, it is important that veneers are not sanded or scraped with any degree of vigour, or introduced to too much water, which could soften glues, create bubbles or make the base wood swell up.

Most households contain some sort of veneered wood. If you have not been aware of this material before, take a look at your furniture and try to identify what is solid and what is veneered. Spotting decorative veneers is relatively simple. It's rare to find a picture of a rose in full bloom picked out in various grains in the middle of a natural log of wood, and it is safe to say that anything like this is veneered (marquetry).

Assessing where practical veneers are used is more difficult to describe. One of the easiest ways is to look at the edges of table tops or other areas suspected of being veneered plywood. The sides of veneered plywood will not have any end grain and the edges may be concealed with an edging veneer. This is just a thin strip of the top veneer applied to the edge of the board. Sometimes veneered boards can be 'lipped' with solid wood. Often edges are camouflaged with brown paint (this comes off when it is stripped).

Side and back panels of cabinet furniture are often made of veneered plywood (*see* Fig 11.13). Although they may be no more than ¼in (6mm) thick, they will be extremely strong and long-lasting.

If you investigate the inside or underside of a section of furniture, the wood may be of a different type or grain structure than the outer, more visible parts, and this is indicative of veneered plywood.

---

**Fig 11.13** B E L O W : **Detail of a sideboard showing side and back panels of plywood veneered in walnut.**

## DAMAGED VENEERS

But perhaps the best time to recognize veneered furniture is when the veneer becomes damaged. There are some ailments that only appear on veneered furniture and, unfortunately, old veneered furniture is often damaged. This is because, in some respects, veneers can be more fragile than solid wood. For instance, it is more likely to be damaged by the effects of wet, heat and wear and tear. Although a veneered piece of furniture can be very strong in its structure, if it is harshly treated the veneers are easily damaged, resulting in a very strong but tatty looking piece of furniture.

The two most common forms of damage are, first, veneers becoming unstuck at the edges, then snagged on something (usually a polishing cloth), and then lost. Or second, when the veneer becomes raised or 'bubbled'.

### LOST VENEERS

If the project involves some bandings or marquetry then often small sections of veneer can become dislodged and lost (*see* Fig 11.14). Fixing of these ailments can be easy. First we shall deal with the fixing of missing veneers. Perhaps the easiest way of fixing these ailments is to fill the gap or crater that is left with a suitable filler, then to colour the filler with the correct colour. This is reasonably easy to do; reference should be made to Chapters 12 and 13 to find the most suitable type of filler and colour for your particular job (*see* Fig 11.15).

However, if you are a perfectionist or you are replacing a large section of veneer, you may want to fill the gap with another piece of veneer. If this is your chosen route, first try and find the correct type of veneer for your job. To do this you will need a supplier of veneers (*see* page 188) and then purchase the necessary veneers. The best advice I can give you with regard to this is to talk to the suppliers and tell them what you want and listen to their suggestions. They will have supplied thousands of craftspeople just like you, many of them absolute beginners, and they will be well-versed in your needs.

Once you have obtained your new piece of veneer you will have to cut it to the required shape. If it is an irregular shape such as a portion from a section of marquetry, scrape any old glue and other debris from the bottom of the crater with a suitable knife or thin chisel, then clean it out with an old

**Fig 11.14** L E F T : **This sort of damage is very common in veneered furniture.**

toothbrush and white spirit. Place a thin piece of paper over the crater and rub some pencil graphite over your index finger. Rub the crater through the paper, concentrating on the edges of the depression. Soon an exact likeness of the recess will become apparent. Use this as a guide to cut out a replacement piece from your new veneer, taking care to choose the best grain configuration. Use a craft knife with a new blade to cut the replacement veneer. If the veneer is particularly coarse-grained you may find it helpful to iron some of the veneer glue film on to the back. This will tend to stop the veneer splitting and make the veneer easier to cut (*see* page 37).

Next, glue the replacement veneer into place by rubbing the tip of a medium-hot iron over the section. Try not to warm up surrounding veneers, as you may soften the glue and remove the veneer, making more work for yourself.

The same process can be applied to broken areas of sheet veneer. Cut a clean edge around a break and fill it with new veneer in the same fashion (*see* Fig 11.16).

Once you have succeeded in replacing the veneer, then you can refinish by brushing a matching finish on to the repair with an artist's brush.

Fig 11.15 A B O V E : **The damage to this veneered box is due to the solid wood that it is made from warping and breaking the veneer.**

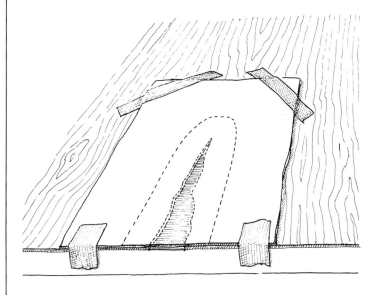

Fig 11.16 A B O V E : **To replace a piece of edge-damaged veneer, stick a new, matching piece of veneer over the damaged area, and then cut through both the new and the old veneer with a sharp knife. The new piece will then fit the old area exactly.**

## BUBBLES

Bubbles seem to be more prevalent on pre-war furniture (*see* Fig 11.17). This could be because of the glue and manufacturing processes they used then, or it could be that it is older and therefore more likely to spring a problem.

Bubbles can occur for three reasons:

- Heat or wet sometimes penetrates the veneer and dissolves the old animal glue that was used to apply the veneers. Consequently, the veneer will swell up and lift, causing a bubble.

- The craftsperson is sometimes to blame; during manufacture the craftsperson might inadvertently miss a small section of gluing. Once this area is subjected to damp, the veneer expands and lifts.

**Fig 11.17** A B O V E : **Bubbled veneer.**

- The craftsperson sometimes puts glue on but allows the glue to cool and dry before laying the veneer on top.

All of these are possible reasons for bubbles occurring. The problem is, you do not know which one has caused your particular bubble, so you are going to have to go through the remedies that I am about to describe one at a time, until one of them works.

The remedies are based on the understanding that the glue used in the past for laying veneers was animal glue (*see* pages 36–7). This is a heat-sensitive glue and can be redissolved by the application of heat.

The main tool for this job is an ordinary domestic iron. Put it on a medium setting and lay a piece of paper over the bubble to aid the slip of the iron and stop the wood from burning. If the bubble is severe and feels brittle, rub a little water over the bubble to soften it during heating, and to stop it drying out, causing shrinking and splitting.

Now, place the tip of the iron on the paper and move it around, pushing the bubble flat. Keep this up for two or three minutes until you think that the heat has penetrated the veneer and redissolved the glue that you hope is there. It is difficult to judge how long it will take for the heat to melt the glue; much depends on the heat of the iron and the thickness of the veneer. Once the veneer has flattened, if you take the iron off you may find that the veneer will slowly lift up again.

The molten glue has to cool down before it starts to stick. To stop the veneer rising and to aid the glue setting, place a flat block of wood or a second cold iron over the repair and press down hard until the repair has cooled. After a few minutes check to see if it has worked.

Sometimes the veneer will stick temporarily under the forces of the heat and pressure. Check this by tapping with your fingernail – a hollow sound will indicate that the glue hasn't set. If it has not, then give it another couple of goes with the iron to make sure.

If it hasn't worked, then the cause of the bubble is a lack of glue during manufacture. The answer now is to slice the base of the bubble with a sharp craft knife and then to insert a thin layer of PVA wood glue. I use an artist's palette knife for this job, although a thick feeler gauge or a thin knife will work just as well. Once the glue is spread, squeeze the veneer down to remove excess glue, then clamp the bubble down as shown in Fig 11.18. To clamp in this manner you will need two pairs of hands and some preparation, so do a dry run beforehand.

If the bubble has broken open, it must be assumed that over the years a small but significant quantity of dust, dirt and wax will have collected in the resulting pocket. This will make it impossible for any glue, if any existed in the first place, to

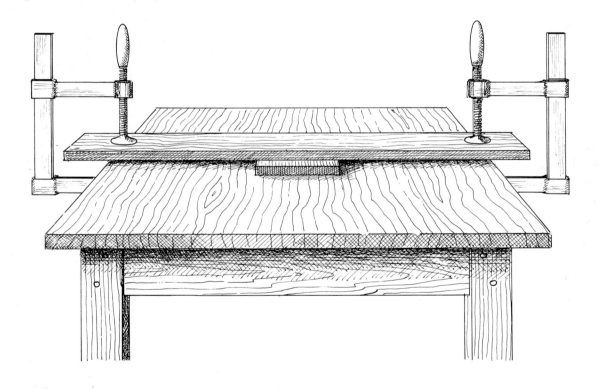

**Fig 11.18** A B O V E : **Clamping a bubble in the middle of a table top can be problematic. If clamps are unavailable, you can use any heavy weights – even buckets of water.**

stick the veneer back. If a previous restorer (bodger?) has tried to fix it then there may also be a quantity of glue from the inevitable failed attempt. Altogether this makes for a major disaster area. If this is the case, you will have to remove the veneer from over the bubble and clean out the dirt, glue, wax and any other antique compounds that have lodged themselves over the years. This is akin to a doctor breaking a leg to reset it again. To the absolute beginner it is like performing the operation without anaesthetic, but be brave – sometimes you have to be cruel to be kind. Indeed in the past I have found that the more of the bubble you remove first go, the better job you will make of it.

So take a deep breath and an old kitchen knife and force the veneer open, with your fingers crossed, then lift the veneer off the top. Keep your hand cupped over the bubble because small brittle pieces of veneer can sometimes fly across the room like a cork from a bottle. I can assure you from bitter experience, there is no fun to be had crawling around the floor of a sawdust-and-shavings coated workshop searching for half an inch of broken veneer.

I have found that it is better to break the veneer away rather than cut it away with a sharp knife. This is because when you eventually have to stick the pieces of veneer back, they will make a more invisible and natural join. Once the veneer has been removed, you can scrape away any old deposits with a small knife or thin chisel, then wash the area thoroughly with a toothbrush full of white spirit to remove any wax or dirt. Do the same to the back of the veneer and then allow to dry. Be meticulous in your preparation, as every minute spent on this will be repaid in a perfect job. Once cleaned and dried, iron the veneer into place as before.

It has to be said that this job can be fiddly and so should be approached with a mixture of caution, overconfidence (because you have such a good book to guide you) and hope.

If all else fails and you find that the job you have done looks disgusting, you can always replace your repaired veneer with some filler, as described earlier, and use an artist's brush and some spirit stains to 'paint' a veneer effect. On some woods this can be very easy and effective.

However, if you have a rather plain and light-coloured wood it can be difficult to make it look just right. Once again, luck will play its part. If even this fails, there are still the life-saver finishes: ebonizing (*see* Chapter 21) and painting (*see* Chapter 22). Or else you could just cover the table with a cloth and a vase and be done with it (*see* Fig 11.19).

This is all starting to sound very defeatist so I shall desist. There is no reason why you cannot do this job perfectly first time, but it is nice to know that if anything does go wrong you have a contingency plan.

Occasionally, veneered furniture will appear which has at some time been left out of doors and has a lot of small bubbles over the surface, indicating rain damage. Try the iron but you will also need a prayer mat and the acquiescence of a higher being if you are to be successful.

**Fig 11.19** A B O V E : **If all else fails . . .**

# CHAPTER 12

# FILLERS

*Filler is a broad term to cover the large number of compounds that can be applied to cracks, dents, scratches and other crevices found in furniture. Ideally, the good application of the correct filler is the first step towards eradicating and making invisible damaged areas of your furniture.*

If the right filler is chosen and the repair is done with a mixture of artistry, skill and luck, the damaged area can often be invisibly repaired. If the wrong filler is used and the repair is done with a mixture of bodgery, ignorance and mishap, you can imagine that the 'fixed' area will look far worse than any damage it could possibly have been designed to repair, and the best thing that can happen to it is for the filler to fall out.

From this you will realize that fillers play an important role in the restorer's arsenal. I intend in this chapter to examine the main fillers used by furniture restorers and to describe their use. There are three different classes of filler that the absolute beginner needs to be aware of: grain fillers, scratch fillers and wood fillers.

## GRAIN FILLERS

These compounds are used by craftspeople on open- or coarse-grained woods when the desired final finish is to be glossy and smooth. Grain filler compounds are rubbed into the bare wood and fill the texture of the wood. When dry they are lightly sanded and leave the surface smooth and ready for a finish. If they are not used, the texture of the grain will show through the eventual finish and spoil the glossy smoothness.

There are three methods of filling the grain that I am going to describe to you. The first is the simplest and to my mind the best, particularly for the absolute beginner.

**Fig 12.1** A B O V E : **Various fillers.**

## FIRST METHOD

Take whatever finish you are applying to the wood, brush it on to the open-grained wood, allow it to dry and then rub back hard with 600 grit wet-and-dry paper, moistened with a little white spirit. Repeat until the wood is as smooth as marble and the grain is filled with the finish. It is as simple as that. In effect, I am saying don't bother with filler, just give the wood two or three extra coats of finish. Admittedly it will take a little longer than other filling methods, but you are guaranteed a good colour match between the filler and the finish, and you do not have to buy any equipment or compounds that you do not already possess.

If you are trying to achieve a glossy finish with French polish and you are an absolute beginner then I suggest you apply these filling coats with a rubber. This way you can practise your polishing technique. Later, when you are more confident and you want to speed up the operation, you can apply the French polish with a brush (*see* Chapter 17).

## SECOND METHOD

The second method, which was a favourite with Victorian French polishers is to use plaster of Paris.

This is applied in a particular way: get two bowls; in one, place some plaster of Paris, and in the second, place a mix of half water and half meths. Dip a ball of cotton cloth into the wet stuff and then dab it into the powder. Rub this into the grain of the wood wiping off any wet slurry across the grain (*see* Fig 12.3). Try not to make the surface too wet as you will raise the grain. After about one hour this compound should have dried enough for you to sand it with a fine sandpaper followed by wet-and-dry paper.

A problem has arisen: your beautiful wood now looks as if it has been used as a chalkboard for the last three centuries (*see* Fig 12.4). Fear not; take some boiled linseed oil and thin this with enough white spirit to give the oil the consistency of milk. Gently rub this into the wood and plaster with a clean rag. The filler will become invisible before your very eyes (*see* Fig 12.5). Clean off any excess oil and allow to dry for 36 hours. You can now apply the finish of your choice.

Often when stripping old furniture you will find a white deposit in the grain (*see* Fig 12.6); this is the plaster of Paris in which the oil has dried out. Just apply some more linseed oil and the whiteness will disappear for another 100 years.

**Fig 12.2** R I G H T : **A can of grain filler.**

PHOTO COURTESY OF RUSTIN'S LTD.

## Stages in the plaster of Paris method of grain filling

**Fig 12.3** R I G H T : **Wet the cloth in the meths/ water mix, then dab it into the plaster of Paris. Rub this into the pores of the wood.**

**Fig 12.4** L E F T : **The chalkboard effect.**

**Fig 12.5** R I G H T : **On the left-hand side, the grain of the wood has been filled with plaster of Paris and then rubbed down with fine sandpaper. The right-hand side shows the effect of thinned linseed oil.**

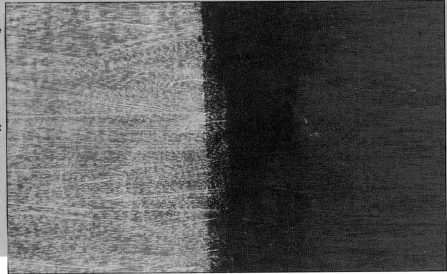

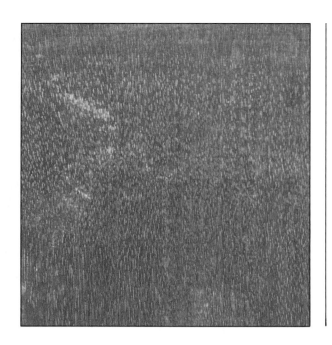

## THIRD METHOD

The third grain-filling method is to buy a pot of grain filler from the D.I.Y. store and comply with the instructions on the tin. Rub the compound into the grain, allow to dry, then sand off. These compounds are closely related to clay and will be available in a range of colours. Try to get a colour that matches your wood (*see* Fig 12.7). If this is not possible or the filler looks conspicuous in the grain (*see* Fig 12.8), then the best thing to do is to stain the filled wood before applying a finish.

**Fig 12.6** L E F T : **White deposit in the grain, often found when stripping old furniture. If you are not going to refill the grain, then this can be removed by rubbing with linseed oil in the same way.**

## Using grain filler

**12.7** R I G H T : **Ideally you should buy the correct colour filler for the job.**

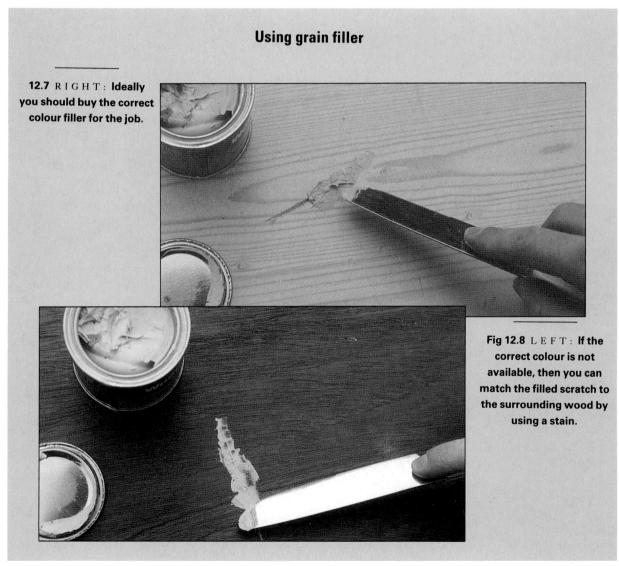

**Fig 12.8** L E F T : **If the correct colour is not available, then you can match the filled scratch to the surrounding wood by using a stain.**

## SCRATCH FILLERS

There are two types of scratch filler: filler for scratches in the finish, and filler for scratches in the wood.

By definition, scratches in the finish don't go deep enough to disturb the wood underneath. The catch-all remedy for this type of problem is some form of wax. A suitable wax polish (*see* Chapter 14) will fill these. This is normally applied as part of a regular cleaning and polishing operation, as part of the the household chores.

The restorer can extend this operation by treating larger or deeper scratches with harder waxes, or by pushing some ordinary-coloured wax (*see* Chapter 14) into scratches and allowing it to dry for 48 hours before buffing with a clean cloth.

### WAX STICKS

For severe cases, or for scratches that are visually offensive, there are available in large D.I.Y. stores and through other suppliers, coloured wax sticks. These are variously sold as scratch removers, scratch covers, or hole fillers, and they have a well-earned place in the furniture repairer's tool box (*see* Fig 12.9).

However, I have a number of reservations about this type of filler. Firstly, the cost of the sticks is often far in excess of the cost of the raw materials

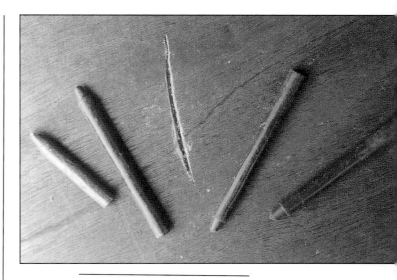

**Fig 12.10** ABOVE: **This scratch needs at least two colours to fill and camouflage it correctly. These are children's crayons, and can be mixed with each other in order to match the colours in the wood.**

(wax and pigment) – but then I am a world-renowned cheapskate.

Secondly, and most importantly, although the manufacturers of these sticks offer a wide range of colours, the number of colours in any one scratch can be in the order of two, three or even four (*see* Fig 12.10). When wax scratch sticks are employed they will fill a scratch with only a single colour of wax. Occasionally this can be quite sufficient, but at other times it is woefully inadequate. This is because the visually jarring scratch is replaced by an equally visually jarring streak of coloured wax.

**Fig 12.9** LEFT: **Scratch removers.**

PHOTO COURTESY OF LIBERON WAXES LTD.

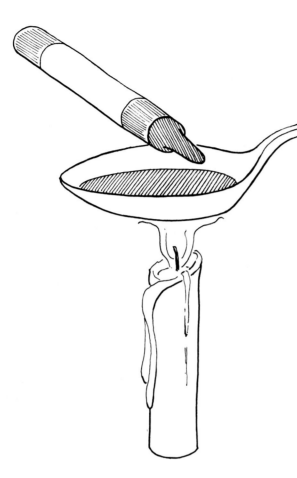

**Fig 12.12** L E F T : **How to make your own wax sticks: the spoon and candle method.**

**MAKING YOUR OWN WAX STICKS** If you want to invisibly mend scratches with wax sticks, then it will be worthwhile investing a little time and energy learning how to mix and make your own scratch sticks. After reading the instructions for this, some of you may consider the investment of a few pounds in some shop-bought sticks to be preferable to the following rigmarole. Others may welcome the opportunity to reach for perfection and get your hands dirtier than they already are.

First obtain some children's wax crayons; the thick ones are best. Now you will need an old tablespoon and a source of heat. I use the gas cooker but a blowtorch (*see* Fig 12.11) or candle (*see* Fig 12.12) is adequate.

Before mixing the colours it is worthwhile taking a peek at the short section on colour and the colour wheel on page 120 which may explain some of the vagaries of colour mixing in wood finishing (*see* pages 111–13). In short, most furniture restorers deal with colours that are some form of brown: light brown, dark brown, medium brown, reddy brown, browny brown, greeny brown, orangey brown; the list is endless. Browns are best achieved by mixing two complimentary colours: red and green, mauve and yellow, orange and blue. I try to identify the crayon colour that is closest to the wood colour that I want to fill. This is often an orange, so I shall use this as an example.

Holding the old tablespoon in a heat proof cloth (you only make the mistake of not protecting your hand once), heat the spoon over the flame. The spoon will warm up very quickly. Now remove it from the heat and touch the bottom of the hot spoon with the orange crayon. This will melt and become liquid. Once you have a sufficient amount of wax in the bottom of the spoon, do the same with the blue wax crayon. Swill the first few drops of blue wax around (you may have to return it to the heat for a while). As you swill it around, the colours will mix and you will see the orange wax going a shade closer to brown; the more blue you add the more brown it will become.

It is up to you to experiment and to find the right colour for your particular piece of wood. Look intently at the colour of the wood and see if you can observe traces of yellow or green or red or any other colour. If you can, add a little of that colour to your brew and evaluate its effect. Practice makes perfect. And don't forget, always check your colour match in daylight; do not rely on artificial lighting.

Usually the two or three colours needed to fill a scratch will be shades of the one colour. So when I have mixed the lightest colour needed and applied it to the scratch, I then add a little more blue, giving me a slightly darker shade of the colour. I add another touch of blue and this will give a yet darker tone. Once you are experienced in this, it can be surprisingly quick.

You can make wax stick moulds from cooking foil wrapped around a thick crayon and supported in sugar or sand when pouring. Otherwise, you can pour the molten wax straight into the scratch (*see* Fig 12.13). The latter method is preferable on larger blemishes as it has a better grip.

**Fig 12.11** L E F T : **Melt and combine colours until you reach the colour of your wood. Don't burn your fingers!**

**Fig 12.13** R I G H T : **Pour the melted wax into the scratch while it is hot.**

## Using wax to repair a scratch

**Fig 12.14** A B O V E : **The scratch is filled with wax.**

**Fig 12.15** A B O V E : **Scrape away excess with a blade, then rub away and smooth down the wax with white spirit and a cloth.**

**Fig 12.16** L E F T : **When smooth, use a sharp knife or pin to pick out the areas where you want a darker colour.**

**Fig 12.17** A B O V E : **Next, fill the scratches with the darker wax, and scrape and rub down with white spirit as before.**

**Fig 12.18** R I G H T : **Remove excess wax.**

If you find it is not exactly right the first time, you can scrape the wax from the scratch and have another go. With a little bit of playing around you will be able to make invisible mends in all types of scratches. In Figs 12.14 to 12.18 I have highlighted the technique of pouring one colour of wax into a scratch, then removing the area that needs to be a darker colour and replacing it with that darker-toned colour to achieve an invisible mend.

When you are satisfied that you have the correct colour match you can remove any excess wax around the repair by rubbing gently over the top of the repair with a cloth lightly dampened in white spirit and water.

### FRENCH POLISH

Scratches in French-polished furniture are common. One way to fill them is to clean up the bottom of the scratch with white spirit and a toothbrush and drop in some thickened French polish. This thick French polish is made by pouring some polish into a dish and allowing the polish to dry out. As the alcohol (meths) in the concotion evaporates, the polish will thicken. Pick some of this gooey stuff up on a matchstick and touch it into the hole or scratch (*see* Fig 12.19). Try to overfill the scratch,

then allow it to harden. You may need to repeat this filling a number of times. When completely dry, rub the protruding filler with a little wet-and-dry, then polish the area with some rubbing compound or other abrasive cream. The same job can be done with other types of hard finishes such as polyurethane or cellulose finishes. On deep scratches this can be a long-winded process, but be patient, it works.

The same process can be used during the application of French polish finish. Often you are not aware of a pit or hole in the otherwise perfectly smooth surface, until you have got a bit of a shine from the French polish. Then the problem stands out like a beacon in the dark. You can fill any aberration that is slow in coming to your attention with this method. After drying and rubbing down you can continue polishing.

Please note, if you are filling deep pits or scratches, it may be worth you searching out some transparent French polish so that the thickness of the French polish does not darken the filled area too much.

**Fig 12.19** ABOVE: **If you eventually intend to French polish the project, then scratches can be filled using thick French polish.**

## WOOD FILLERS

There are two types of wood filler I am going to recommend for the absolute beginner. The first is commonly called stopping, and the second is car body filler.

### STOPPING

There are a number of different variations of this filler. Some are water-based and some have a white spirit or cellulose base. The important thing to remember is that it should be very smooth and in no way granular. Its texture should be the same as clay. As long as it has a smooth texture it will be very malleable and easy to push into smaller scratches and dents.

This type of filler is supplied ready to use in small tins. Often the packaging of these items leaves a lot to be desired; the tins tend to allow the filler to dry out and go unworkably hard. If the filler hardens you can usually resoften the contents by the addition of the compatible solvent. Usually, the filler will be available in a number of 'woody' colours. The idea is to allow you to choose the colour that best matches the colour of your timber. This is not so simple in practice, and as a general rule I would suggest that you err on the lighter side. If your filler is not dark enough you can always darken it, adjusting its colour by using a little stain and artistry after it has dried (see pages 118–19 for full instructions on how to do this).

Using this method you will also be able to make totally invisible repairs.

So, once you have chosen your particular brand of filler and you are satisfied that the colour is to your liking, it is just a simple job of smearing the filler into the scratch or blemish, either using your fingers or a knife or similar instrument. Remember: 'the colour when wet is the colour you will get'. The filler will dry a different tone to that when it is wet. Use the wet colour as the guide when matching wood and filler.

It is best to overfill the scratch; when dry you can smooth it down to the required level using fine wet-and-dry abrasive.

The drawback of this type of filler is that it has almost no strength whatsoever and is consequently useless for corners, edges and large areas of damage. To repair this type of damage you will require . . .

### CAR BODY FILLER

This is the other type of filler that the absolute beginner should become acquainted with. It is available from any car accessory shop and will probably be frowned upon by antique restorers and other old fuddy duddies, but to the absolute beginner furniture restorer, it is like a cool drink on a hot day.

Once you have become accustomed to it you will be able to perform minor miracles. With this material it is possible to fill, mould and recreate

**Fig 12.20** LEFT:
**A can of stopping.**

## Repairing a table using car body filler

**Fig 12.21** R I G H T : **The foot of this table has been gnawed mercilessly by a teething puppy. Because of the amount of filler needed and the likelihood of its being knocked in its future life, car body filler is a good choice for the repair. To give the filler extra grip I have inserted two 1in (25mm) nails into the wound.**

**Fig 12.22** F A R R I G H T : **First, roughly fill and mould the filler to shape.**

**Fig 12.23** R I G H T : **The second application fills any of the finer details.**

**Fig 12.24** F A R R I G H T : **Finally, sand the filler using fine-grade abrasive paper and a mask, until it is as smooth as marble, and ready for staining (*see* page 119).**

whole sections of carving (*see* page 76). With a little imagination and enough time you could build your own Louis XIV commode with this material.

Once mixed with the hardener it will go rock hard between five and 30 minutes, depending on how much hardener you use. While it is still curing it is possible to carve it with a sharp knife. It will stick to the wood like a shipwrecked sailor and is therefore perfect for damaged corners and chipped edges. When it has gone very hard you can use wet-and-dry paper to make it as smooth as marble.

Then, and this is the real bonus, it will be hard enough for you to copy the texture of the surrounding wood grain into it using a knife or a needle.

For complicated jobs the filler can be built up, carved back and the process repeated. Recently one of my students replaced a section of carved swag that was part of the apron of an ornate side table and made a perfect job of it using this material. On other occasions we have made replica roundels and finials, by taking a cast of the existing orna-

Well it is. The trouble is that it costs about three times as much, and to my mind it is not of the same quality. It tends to be too granular.

One drawback of this type of filler that some readers might object to is the smell. It gives off quite a pungent chemical odour that will permeate through the whole building. If over-exposed to it, some people may be left feeling nauseous, and it can make the eyes smart. If you suffer from breathing problems, ensure good ventilation. Also, the dust produced when rubbing down can be an irritant to the skin, eyes and nose, so take suitable precautions.

## PLASTIC WOOD

Plastic wood is to wood fillers as vinegar is to wine. To the furniture restorer it is useless. It has been designed to be used by carpenters and decorators on the building site and is intended to be painted or used in areas where it will not be seen. It is far too coarse in texture to be of any benefit to the serious restorer.

## SAWDUST AND GLUE

There is one more filler that has to be mentioned – that is if Uncle George has not mentioned it to you already. This is sawdust and glue, which is widely rumoured to be the best, most wonderful wood filler available this side of Pluto. The idea is that you mix some wood dust (from the wood you are working upon) with some glue, stir them together, and you will have the perfect filler. Frequently, my students will try this before I have a chance to get to them. They will mix any old sawdust with some PVA glue and make a gruel-like concoction that comes two rungs below plastic wood in the ladder of wood-filling excellence.

I suspect that there is somewhere an excellent recipe for sawdust and glue filler that I have never heard of. Or maybe the recipe that I have just stated is considered by building site carpenters to be 'excellent' due to its low cost and easy availability, and has – along with most of Uncle George's advice – become confused with the sort of excellence required by the furniture restorer.

ments out of plasticine and then casting them in this type of filler (*see* page 76).

I have to confess that this is my favourite filler. If the circumstances allow, I use this one. Enough of the advertisement.

Unfortunately, car body filler only comes in one colour – light grey – so it is essential that, once it is dried, it is stained (*see* pages 118–19 for information on how to do this).

With so many benefits you may wonder why the same filler is not marketed for woodworkers.

# CHAPTER 13

# STAINS

*Perhaps the easiest and quickest way to change the appearance of a piece of furniture is to use a stain. From the brightest of shocking pinks to the subtlety of golden oak, the range of colours that wood can be stained is as wide as colour itself.*

There are four basic groups of stains traditionally used for changing the colour of wood: water stains, chemical stains, oil stains, and spirit stains (sometimes called aniline dyes). I recommend that the absolute beginner becomes conversant with oil stains and spirit stains. Water stains and chemical stains are described below so that you are aware of them and understand why they are not recommended.

## WATER STAINS

Water stains are very similar in application to spirit stains and are available from the same suppliers. As the solvent for these stains is water, they can be the cause of some adverse reactions in finishes and with some woods. Also, they raise the grain of the wood causing unnecessary work. I prefer not to suggest them to absolute beginners until they are experienced with oil and spirit stains.

## CHEMICAL STAINS

Uncle George's favourite lesson is chemical stains. I have lost count of the weird and wonderful preparations that Uncle Georges have suggested to my students to use. To be fair, some of them are very good traditional methods of colouring wood and many are still favoured today by craftspeople, particularly if you are trying to recreate antique methods.

The problem is that many of them are highly toxic poisons. I do not use them in my classes and I do not recommend them to the absolute beginner. You really do not need added worries such as whether that bout of flu that you can't shrug off is really a bout of flu or the results of ingesting some

**Fig 13.1** A B O V E : **A selection of wood stains.**

archaic preparation that you used three weeks ago or whether the fact that the dog's hair is falling out is due to fleas or because of the stain you unwittingly spilt in his water bowl this morning.

## OIL STAINS

This family of stains is the most commonly used by the D.I.Y. person. A range of oil stains can be found in any hardware or D.I.Y. store. The shopkeeper may not recognize these stains by the name oil stains, though don't let that deter you; it is the furniture restorer's name for them.

Oil stains have been specifically mixed by the manufacturers with the amateur D.I.Y. user in mind. They are usually supplied in rectangular tins, with each shop typically displaying about a dozen different colours.

The manufacturer will often give them a fancy name, ostensibly for your guidance. Try to think of the stains in terms of their colour and not these artificially conceived names. They will all sound very exotic and expensive but this is just marketing; it is not intended to inform, just to embroider something which is really very down to earth: i.e. colour. So, English Light Oak is an orangey yellow; Brazilian Mahogany and Rosewood will be shades of red; Black Ash, Ebony and Tudor Black Oak are all, you've guessed it, black; and so on.

A common misconception about wood stains is that the application of an 'Antique Walnut' stain to a piece of wood will make that piece of wood look like a piece of antique walnut. This is not the case.

**Fig 13.2** A B O V E : **To judge the true colour of a stain, observe the colour inside the cap of the tin.**

### HOW TO GET THE REQUIRED COLOUR

To find out how to get the colour you want for your project by using oil stains, follow this advice: take a stain from the shelf and give it a thorough shaking – much of the pigment contained in oil stains will settle at the bottom of the tin if left standing for any length of time. Unscrew the top of the tin and examine its underside. This will usually contain a silver or clear plastic insert which will be coated with a thin layer of the stain (*see* Fig 13.2). This is the true colour of the stain. It is this colour in combination with the colour of your wood that you will get. This is where you need to have a little imagination and a bit of an eye for colour. The best way to gain an eye for this sort of colour mixing is to experiment on spare pieces of wood.

Usually you will find a small sticker attached to the tin which is intended to represent the colour

**Fig 13.3** B E L O W : **A typical colour chart of stains.**

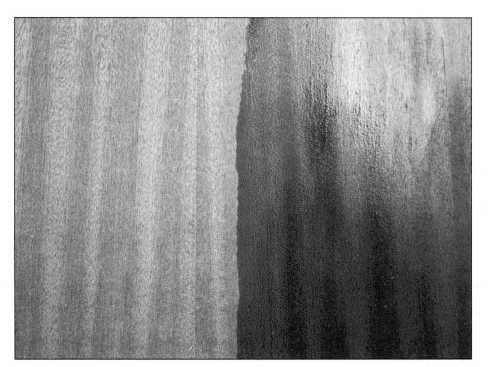

**Fig 13.4** L E F T : **To view the colour of the wood once finished with a clear finish, just wipe over the wood with white spirit.**

in the tin; use this as a rough guide only. Sometimes, alongside a shelf full of colours will be a colour chart showing the effect on wood of particular stains (*see* Fig 13.3). Take note of the colour of the wood used for the chart. It will usually be a light wood such as pine or birch. This is okay if you are staining a light-coloured wood, but on darker woods such as mahogany or elm, the resulting colour will be very different from the colour on the chart and on the sticker.

It is worth pointing out that the range of colours sold in this type of stain is usually quite limited. As a rule they keep to a brown, 'woody' range of colours. There are no bright yellows, greens or blues. However, they are usually light fast, meaning they will not fade in strong sunlight – a very important attribute for stains.

Oil stains are intermixable. If you decide to mix a particular colour for your project, ensure you mix more than enough. There is no experience worse than staining half your very important project a beautiful hand-mixed colour, only to waste five litres of stain and two months of Sundays desperately attempting to remix that same colour.

A word of warning: in the world of wood finishing there are very few processes which are not easily reversed, and one of them is staining. It is possible to remove *some* of the stain if you decide

later that you have made a mistake, but to remove all means you will have to sand away the top 0.5mm of wood containing the stain. This is unfeasible and unnecessary.

A far better method is to make sure you get the right colour first time. If you want to be absolutely certain, here's what to do . . .

Experiment on a scrap piece of wood. It is important that the experiment should be conducted upon a similar colour wood to that of your project. Make the scrap as large as possible and stand this next to your unstained project. Make a cup of tea, sit down in a comfortable chair and meditate upon the colour scheme. If necessary, make a number of different colour tests. Don't proceed until you are certain that you have the right colour. If the project that you have in mind is intended for a particular interior, then it may be worth taking some colour tests to that location for perusal.

One more thing: 'the colour when wet is the colour you get'. When you first apply the stain it will be much darker than when it dries out, but it is the colour you will see once you have applied a finish. It will be worth giving your tests a coat or two of wax or varnish, maintaining the wet look, to make it easier to see the true finished colour. Incidentally, unstained wood will also turn a few shades darker when a finish is applied to it. Before opting to stain, wet your wood with some white spirit or meths to see what colour the natural wood would be if it was given a clear finish (*see* Fig 13.4).

There is one major disadvantage to staining with oil stains that you should be made aware of. The best way for you to appreciate this is to undertake a little experiment. Take a piece of scrap wood, scratch it across the grain of the wood, then hit it a couple of times with a hammer to bruise the wood (*see* Fig 13.5). If it makes you feel any better you can pull a funny face and swear at it as well, but this isn't compulsory. Now, with a cloth or a brush,

apply some dark stains to the surface of the wood and wipe off the excess.

The problem becomes immediately apparent – any scratch, bruise, dent, rough surface or chip, will become aggressively highlighted by the stain 'gathering' at the point of injury (*see* Fig 13.6). These injuries can be quite numerous on older or neglected pieces of furniture. Unfortunately, these slight blemishes, which are invisible before staining and can even add to the character of a piece of furniture, often become eyesores with the injudicious application of an oil stain.

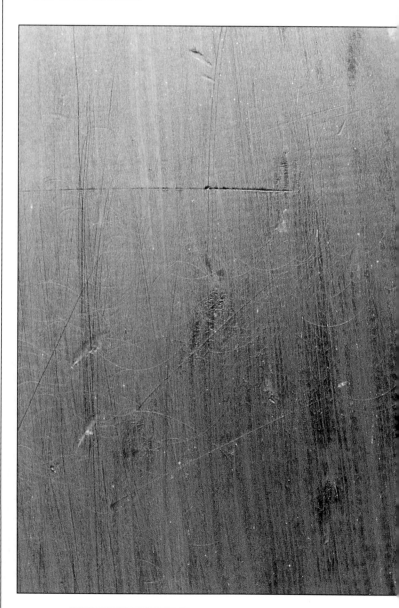

**Fig 13.5** A B O V E : **Damaged wood before the application of oil stain.**

**Fig 13.6** A B O V E : **The same wood, after the application of oil stain.**

## PREPARATION

Before applying oil stain, check over your project and try to get rid of as many defects as possible. Look for areas of roughness which can be scraped or sanded down. Investigate areas where glue may still be. Typically this occurs around joints, but drips or smears can appear elsewhere. Dried glues can be almost invisible to the eye, so look carefully. Repair and fill the deeper scratches and dents. And lastly, beware of any remaining old finish which has been overlooked when stripping.

This all sounds very fussy and time consuming, but in reality it is not. Most of this sort of checking is done automatically when stripping, and is quickly dealt with if found. The idea is to try and eliminate as many disturbances to the surface of the wood as possible so that the stain can be applied as smoothly and homogenously as possible.

If you want to be a perfectionist, you may wish to apply what I call a 'discloser' stain. This process involves rubbing a thin coat of stain over the wood in a superficial manner in order to highlight or disclose where the surface injuries may lurk, allowing you to put them right before applying the main stain. This is often useful when you can see there is an injury or even a natural defect such as a knot or wayward grain, but you are not too sure how it is going to look after a stain is applied.

There is only one last thing I should impart to you before we begin staining. Again it is best described by a practical demonstration. Take a block of wood that has been sanded on all sides. Apply an even coat of dark stain to all sides using a paint brush, and observe the results. You will find that the sides of the wood that display the end grain have become much darker than the rest of the wood. This is due to the fact that the end grain of the wood is far more absorbent than the rest of the

Fig 13.7 A B O V E : **On an even application of stain, end grain stains darker than the rest of the wood.**

timber, and therefore absorbs more of the pigments contained in the stain (*see* Fig 13.7).

All pieces of furniture will contain end grain. The successful application of oil stain depends on identifying which parts of the furniture are end grain and ensuring you do not saturate these parts with stain.

This would stop the effect often seen in modern reproduction furniture of a totally unnatural, almost black end grain when stained with a mahogany or other dark stain. This effect is caused by the production-line technique of dipping or spraying the entire piece without consideration for the varying rates of absorbency that compose any piece of furniture. It may be worth visiting the furniture department of a large store to see this effect so you can understand what we are trying to avoid.

## APPLICATION

Here is what you have waited so patiently for – how to stain a piece of furniture with oil stain. All the preparation has been done, you have read the chapter twice, and you are wearing a pair of protective gloves so you don't spend the rest of the week washing your hands. We are off!

Shake the can of stain vigorously for at least a couple of minutes. Take your cotton cloth and, covering the opening of the can with the cloth and forefinger, spill a small and controlled quantity of stain on to the cloth. Rub the cloth on to the wood. Work methodically around the project, staining one section such as a leg or a side before moving on to the next section. Continue until all the furniture is uniformly covered.

Convention says that the inside of drawers and underneath of furniture are not stained. The exception to this rule is Shaker furniture; for Shaker craftspeople the insides of the drawers etc. were considered to be as important as the more visible parts of the furniture. If you wish to subscribe to the Shaker tradition and stain the insides of the drawers, then feel free. Just remember, they will also need a couple of coats of finish over the stain, otherwise it may leach out and stain the eventual contents.

As stated earlier, end grain is more absorbent than the rest of the wood. Therefore it has to be treated a little bit differently. The easiest way is to stain the ordinary grain first, wait until the cloth has become almost dry and is ready for a top up from the tin, and then rub it into the end grain. Because there is hardly any stain on the cloth it will be impossible for you to overdo it. If you were to stain the end grain with a freshly charged cloth, the chances are the end grain will soak up the stain like a dry sponge and go much darker than the rest of the wood.

If you do happen to make a mistake, then write out a hundred times: 'I must not apply lots of stain to end grain', and then see if you can improve the area by rubbing with a cloth soaked in white spirit. This also works if you find a 'gathering' around an area that is damaged or contains some wayward grain. The reason that white spirit is used for this

**Fig 13.8** R I G H T : **I have marked the end grain on this chair with yellow paint. The location of end grain will vary depending on the type of furniture.**

job is because white spirit is used to thin oil stains. It will therefore dilute the colour and make it weaker.

The fact that white spirit is the thinners for oil stains means that any product that can be thinned with white spirit can also be tinted and coloured with oil stains. So, finishes such as varnishes, waxes and oils can and are coloured by adding oil stains. This ability to mix stains with other finishes to change the colour of the finish is an important one, and will be covered more fully in the chapters dealing with those finishes.

### THE GOOD POINTS

- Oil stains are widely available and popular wood stains.

- They are sold ready-mixed and the colours are intermixable.

- They are light fast (will not fade in strong sunlight).

- They are safe to use (though usual safety precautions should be taken).

- Oil stains go a long way and can be added to other finishes.

### THE BAD POINTS

- The colour range is limited to woody-brown colours.

- Care needs to be taken with end grain and damaged wood, otherwise this will become over-dark.

- It is often found that oil stains are not easily absorbed, particularly on some dense hardwoods such as beech and ash which occasionally take on a hard, burnished surface when they have been stripped; oil stains will sometimes find it difficult to penetrate into the wood under these conditions. In these circumstances you will need a stain that is a little bit stronger and more penetrative, which is one of the attributes of spirit stain . . .

## SPIRIT STAINS

These are not as easily available as oil stains. You will have to buy them from a specialist supplier of wood finishing products (*see* page 188). The spirit stain (sometimes called aniline dye) can be bought in powder form or ready-mixed. To make the powders soluble all you have to do is add methylated spirit to them.

If you have a choice, buy them in powder form. This will allow you to mix dozens of strengths of colour and make them much more versatile in their use. For instance, a spirit brown powder can be mixed in strengths varying from a thin 'tea wash' coat to an opaque 'black coffee' brown just by altering the amount of meths used (*see* Fig 13.9).

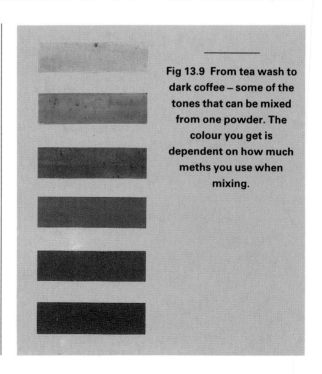

**Fig 13.9 From tea wash to dark coffee – some of the tones that can be mixed from one powder. The colour you get is dependent on how much meths you use when mixing.**

**Fig 13.10** R I G H T : **A toy stained with spirit stain.**

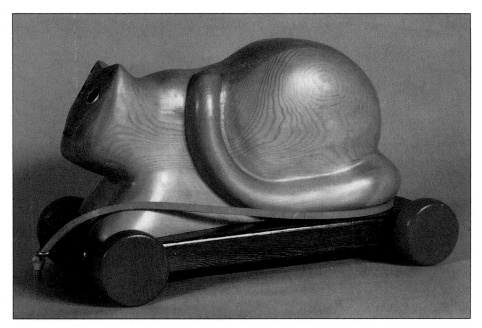

The range of spirit colour is much broader than oil stain colour, and will include all the colours of the spectrum. Along with mahogany, walnut and other woody mixes you can get the less subdued flaming pinks, sunset oranges and blood reds. If you want a different colour for each of your dining chairs, or your wardrobe stained all the colours of the rainbow, this is the stain for you. If you intend to use these stains on toys or children's furniture, ensure they comply with current safety regulations (*see* Fig 13.10).

Application is best achieved by brushing the stain on. Be careful not to flick the brush as this stain will travel light years. Protect any vulnerable items and wear old clothes.

Because the stain is based on methylated spirit it is very quick-drying, particularly in a warm environment. This can be a drawback because if the stain dries too quickly during application, the first coat is going to be overlapped by the second coat. Certain areas will receive two coats and unsightly dark marks will appear.

This problem can be alleviated in a number of ways. First, do not apply these stains in very hot and dry surroundings. Second, always try to keep a 'wet edge' to the stain when it is being applied. This is not so difficult when staining something small, but with larger items it requires a particular technique. The answer is to stain small sections at a time. Completely finish staining before moving on to the next section. If a table is your chosen project, stain one leg completely, then stain the stretcher, followed by another leg, then a rail and so on until finished. Using this method, as long as the sections are small enough, and you work quickly, there will be no problem of unsightly marks appearing.

Furniture with large expanses of wood, like table tops and cupboards, you may find troublesome, and for these there is another trick which you may find useful. Before brushing your stain on, brush on a coat of methylated spirit; this will wet the wood and keep it from drying out too quickly. But beware. It is not commonly known that methylated spirit contains water, and it may raise the grain of the wood if applied too liberally; do not overdo it. You may wish to enlist the help of another pair of hands to make the job a little easier, one person to brush on a thin coat of meths whilst the other follows behind with the stain.

A word of warning: some of the spirit stains can be toxic and also highly inflammable (due to the meths). Observe the usual precautions (*see* Chapter 3 on safety), wear gloves, goggles, don't smoke, drink or suck your thumb.

And finally it should be mentioned that because spirit stains are based on methylated spirit, and because meths is the base for French polish, the two can be mixed. This allows for all sorts of interesting possibilities.

## STAINS AND ARTISTRY

Apart from the wholesale staining of bare wood, spirit stains are also invaluable to the restorer for colouring areas that have been filled (*see* pages 107–9). If you have used a filler that matches the colour of the wood to repair a small blemish, this will often be enough to deceive the eye. If the blemish is larger, you will need to enhance the colour and the texture of the filler to mimic the surrounding wood.

The virgin filler is your canvas and you are Michaelangelo. Your brief is to make that filler look exactly like the surrounding wood so that nobody

### Using spirit stain to camouflage a repair

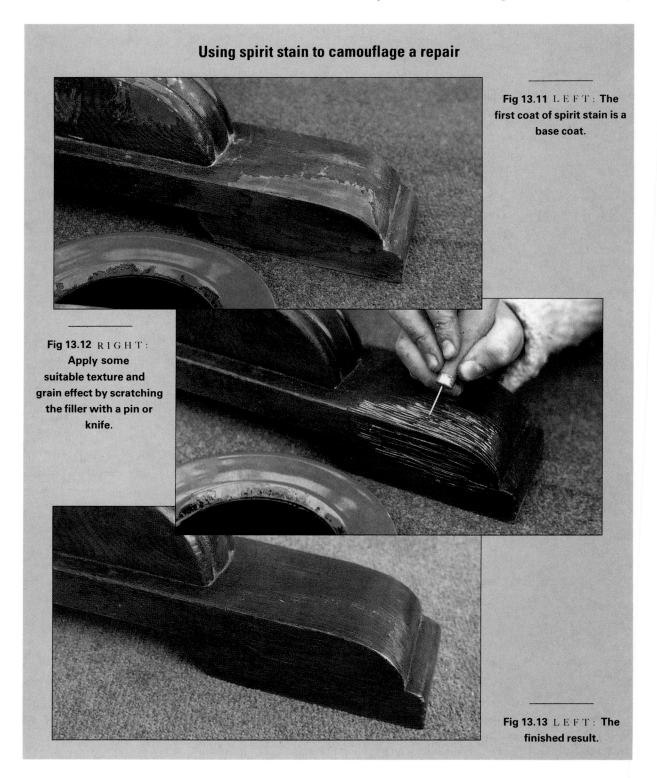

**Fig 13.11** L E F T : **The first coat of spirit stain is a base coat.**

**Fig 13.12** R I G H T : **Apply some suitable texture and grain effect by scratching the filler with a pin or knife.**

**Fig 13.13** L E F T : **The finished result.**

can tell the difference. In reality it only needs to act as camouflage so that the viewer's eye passes over the filled area and doesn't feel the need to stop and investigate. Your tools are spirit stains, meths, some French polish, two or three artist's brushes, a pin and some excellent technical direction . . .

First seal the filler with two thin coats of French polish. This will stop the spirit stain soaking into the absorbent filler, so making the brushing of fine lines much more precise. It will also act as a barrier between your colours and the filler. This means that you can make as many mistakes as you want, but the wood and the filler will be protected from the stain by the French polish. If you make a mistake you can easily clean off your 'artistry' with meths and wire wool and you will not have caused any discoloration of the surrounding wood. On the other hand, if you do a perfect job, you can seal your handiwork in with French polish and it will last for centuries. The system is foolproof.

Next, with a needle or pin, copy the texture of the surrounding wood by scratching into the filler with a needle or craft knife (see Fig 13.12). Then give another thin coat of French polish.

Now mix a base colour spirit stain. This should be the same colour and tone as the lightest colour in the surrounding wood. Brush this on to the surface and evaluate its effects on the wood. Should it be darker? redder? browner? lighter? Add some more colour, or alternatively, remove some colour with fine wire wool (see Fig 13.13). For pinpoint accuracy, wrap the wire wool around a cotton bud or matchstick.

If you want to take the easy way out you could stain the furniture and the filler at the same time, and in one swift move match the filler to the timber (though you will still have to put in the textures and darker colours).

Don't be afraid to experiment. When mixing colours, test them first on a piece of white paper. Next, examine the surrounding colours and try to mix the next darker colour. Apply this over the top of the base colour with an artist's brush. Often this is just a darker tone of the base colour, so add some more powdered stain to your existing colour. Apply the stain in grain-shaped strokes; this will help enhance the texture.

Soften any brush strokes and mistakes with the wire wool again. Now try to mix the darkest colours and paint these flecks in with deft strokes of the brush. If you make any mistakes or want to rub anything out you can use the wire wool as an eraser and remove the problem. When you finish, give it a couple of coats to seal it all in. In this way, by building up and cutting back, by experimenting and playing around with the colours, you can develop a perfect repair. It takes time and a few tears, but persist.

Sometimes you will need just two minutes and one colour; other times you can spend days and a whole spectrum of colours to achieve a perfect match. But every time you do it you will gain valuable experience of how the colours work and the best way to achieve the right effects.

The rule is, take it slowly and start with the lighter colours before working to the darker ones. The more coats you apply of a thin spirit stain the darker it will become. In years gone by, craftspeople used to 'manufacture' whole pieces of rare timber by using exactly these materials and techniques.

This technique can be used on all French-polished work, on the bare wood before polishing, or when disguising filler that has been used to repair scratches in French polish. But the most effective way is to apply the stains in between each layer of French polish, sandwiching the colour between successive layers of polish.

You can use this technique for small areas of wood that are due to have other finishes applied over the top, but it is always preferable for larger filled sections to use colours and finishes that are more compatible with the final finish.

For polyurethane varnish finishes you can use artists' oil paints to the same effect and seal your handiwork in with a couple of coats of polyurethane varnish. Alternatively, if the grain of the surrounding wood is not too complicated and you do not need to use much artistry, you can use oil stains mixed with a little varnish.

Spirit stains can be mixed with cellulose finishes in the same way as they are used with French polish, but experiment for compatibility before you spend too much time 'creating'.

## COLOUR AND HOW TO MIX IT

If you are not familiar with the way that colours can be mixed then here is a quick foundation lesson. There are three primary colours: yellow, red and blue. These are pure colours and cannot be created by mixing other colours together. There are three secondary colours: orange, purple and green. These colours are obtained by mixing the primary colours. To make orange, mix yellow and red; to make purple, mix red and blue; to make green, mix yellow and blue.

The notable omission from this scheme of things is the colour brown, a most important colour to the furniture restorer. Browns are achieved by mixing a primary colour with the opposite secondary colour in the wheel. These pairs of colour are called complimentary colours. By mixing complimentary colours – yellow and purple, or orange and blue, or red and green – you will produce a brown.

Knowledge of the colour wheel is indispensible to the furniture restorer. It would tell him, for example, that a red mahogany colour is often turned browner by the addition of green. With this knowledge and a little practice you should soon be able to mix the colours you need for your projects.

If you want to mix colours for use with white spirit soluble finishes, you can use artists' oil paints. Many suppliers sell spirit stains ready made up into 'woody' colours. These can be useful. I recommend a basic kit of mahogany, spirit brown, yellow, black and red. By varying the dilution and mixing them you will supply 95 per cent of your needs.

Here are some old-time French polishers' recipes for colours mixed with spirit stain, using black yellow and red:

| | |
|---|---|
| Dark Oak | 6 parts black, 1½ parts yellow, 1 part red |
| Middle Oak | 4 parts black, 3 parts yellow, 2 parts red |
| Brown Walnut | 3 parts black, 2 parts yellow, 2 parts red |
| Grey Walnut | 10 parts black, 1 part yellow then thin down |
| Green Walnut | 4 parts black, 1 part yellow |
| Mahogany | 14 parts red, 3 parts black, 2 parts yellow |
| Rosewood | 2 parts red, 1 part black |

These can then be thinned with meths to the required tone.

You may be surprised to learn that the three recommended colours are not the primary colours, nor are they complimentary colours. Closer inspection will reveal that the black and the yellow, when mixed, will make a dull green. The green and red are complimentary colours and will therefore produce browns.

This illustrates another important fact: nothing is straightforward when dealing with colour.

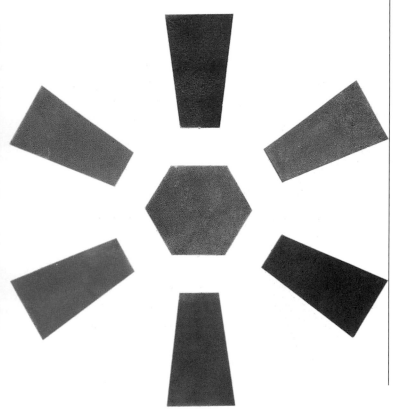

**Fig 13.14** ABOVE: **The colour wheel.**

# CHAPTER 14

# WAXES

PHOTO COURTESY OF LIBERON WAXES LTD.

*Your project has been stripped of finish. You have stained it to the colour of your choosing. You have filled any holes and fixed any wobbly bits, and you decide to give your furniture a traditional wax finish.*

## WHAT IS A WAX FINISH?

Waxing is one of the simplest and oldest processes for finishing woodwork. As such, it is an ideal finish for the absolute beginner. Because of its long history, many variations on the theme have been developed over the centuries. I shall explain the more common methods later.

One of the features of a wax finish is that it will need to be maintained by a periodic topping up of wax, as the finish becomes removed by wear and tear, is absorbed into the timber, or decayed by heat or water. The amount and frequency of re-polishing will depend upon the amount of use a particular piece of furniture receives. As the age and number of applications of polish increases, so will the depth and colour (patina) of the finish.

**Fig 14.1** A B O V E : **Applying wax polish.**

The full character of the wax finish is best illustrated by looking at old waxed chairs (*see* Figs 14.3 and 14.4). The areas that are being constantly polished by human usage, such as the backs and seats of chairs, will achieve a very high shine. The areas that do not receive a free polish every time someone sits down, the stretchers and the legs for example, or in between the splats of the back, will become dull, and deposits of dust and dirt will become embedded in the wax, creating a dark, variegated patina. This is an unmistakable feature of antique furniture, and highly prized by collectors as an indication of age (*see* Figs 14.4 and 14.5).

If the piece of furniture is many centuries old then it is likely to be pitch black in colour due to the accumulation of generations of this patina. (A fuller discussion of patina is undertaken in Chapter 23). It is worth noting that this darkening effect is often due to the primitive chimney arrangements of our forefathers which allowed much soot to accumulate within the house. For example, the difference between a Tudor Black Oak finish and a

**Fig 14.2** B E L O W : **English oak court cupboard (early 17th century).**

**Fig 14.3** T O P : **Old chair showing patina.**

**Fig 14.4** A B O V E : **Note the dark patina around the base of the slats on this old chair.**

Jacobean Dark Oak finish can be ascribed to the different chimney arrangements in those periods. In early Tudor times there was commonly a hole in the roof to let out the smoke from a bonfire in the middle of the room, hence a heavy deposit of black soot on the wax furniture. Later on they developed the fireplace and chimney at the side of the room, hence a lighter coating of soot was deposited on Jacobean furniture, giving it a dark brown patina (*see* Fig 14.6).

This highlights one of the chief drawbacks of wax: it is a slightly sticky substance which will attract a certain amount of dirt with each application. For this reason it is sometimes suggested that it should not be used on frequently handled

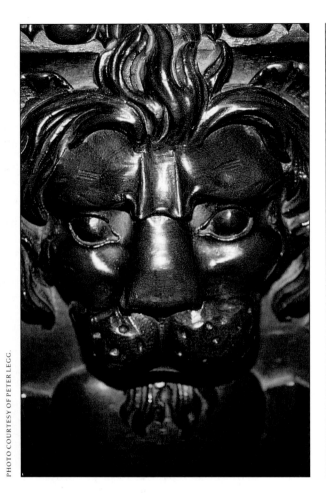

pieces. Also, when 'topping up', it smells of turpentine and is slightly sticky, and is therefore not advised for food cupboards or beds.

It can be damaged by heat and water, or if left for long periods in direct sunlight. Therefore, it should not be used in the kitchen, bathroom, outside, or anywhere where it is likely to receive heavy usage, unless it is also to receive the necessary upkeep.

It is, however, a very beautiful finish and very simple to apply, needing little skill even for the absolute beginner, and very little equipment. Other types of finishes will deteriorate over time and become scratched and patchy, eventually needing stripping and refinishing. A wax finish can quickly and easily be rejuvenated by a fresh application of a wax polish. This is a major advantage.

**Fig 14.6** B E L O W : **A typical late sixteenth-century living room. By this stage the fireplace had been positioned at the side of the room.**

**Fig 14.5** L E F T : **Deposits of dust and dirt have collected over time in the mouldings of this piece of furniture.**

## OBTAINING THE WAX

If you are friendly with a local beekeeper you may have the oportunity to concoct your own brew of furniture wax. This is quite a simple process which relies on the fact that beeswax is easily dissolved by turpentine and the judicious application of heat. If you decide to try this please beware, turpentine is highly flammable and heat is hot! There is a recipe for such shenanigans on page 127 for you to try if you so desire. However, for the absolute beginner I strongly suggest buying a pot off the ironmonger's shelf – it is just as effective. It may not be quite so satisfying, but it's certainly quicker and safer. The question is, which one should you buy? Today there are a number of different proprietary makes of furniture wax available. These split into two main groups: aerosol spray and non-aerosol spray.

The spray can version contains a cleaning agent designed to clean a range of surfaces from formica to the television. It is not suitable as a method of applying a wax finish to bare wood. It is also not suitable for cleaning or polishing furniture which has a long-established wax finish. This is because some of the chemicals contained in the spray could cause the old wax to dissolve and be removed.

The proprietary waxes that we are interested in will come in a tin or in a glass or ceramic pot and will have a butter-like consistency. These waxes are very basic preparations containing in the simplest of cases only beeswax and turpentine. Often there will be added ingredients intended to improve the mix in some way, but as long as the mix has got a large proportion of beeswax it will do the job (*see* Fig 14.7).

Often you will have a choice of coloured waxes, or a so-called 'antique wax'. However, in my experience it is rare for an absolute beginner to need a coloured wax. A stain is far better employed to colour the bare wood in a separate process, rather

**Fig 14.7** B E L O W : **A tin of wax polish.**

than using a wax with a stain added to do the two jobs in one go.

One time when you may require a coloured wax is when you are trying to make a piece of furniture look older than it really is (antiquing or distressing). For such an occasion, I have included an antique wax formula on page 127.

Another use is when fixing or patching in a damaged area (*see* Chapter 12). However, if you need any of these formulations, my advice is to buy a clear wax. From this you can mix all the other types of wax preparation including cream waxes, liquid waxes and all the different coloured waxes (*see* page 127).

## APPLICATION

There are two methods of applying a new wax finish to stripped furniture.

### FIRST METHOD

For the first method you require a clear, uncoloured wax and at least half a dozen soft clean cotton cloths free from buttons, threads of cotton or zips. If you have sensitive skin, wear a pair of protective gloves.

Take one of the cloths and, dipping into your wax mixture, apply a generous coating of wax to your piece of furniture. Rub the wax firmly into the wood. Imagine that you are grinding the wax into the wood. Do not remove any of the surplus wax, but just keep rubbing it around and around pushing it into the pores of the wood. Then leave the article for a period of two hours with a build up of wax on the surface of the wood. This will allow the wax to be absorbed into the fibres of the wood and the turpentine to evaporate, leaving the solid part of the mix – the beeswax – behind.

A word of caution: turpentine is flammable and strong turpentine fumes can be given off. Keep a window or door open and do not allow naked flames including lighted cigarettes near the workplace.

After a two-hour period, take the same cloth and start all over again. The hardened wax that is on the furniture should be rubbed over with fresh wax. This fresh wax will soften the dried-out wax and help it to shift around again.

Once you have rubbed the wax around for as long as you can, take a second cloth and start polishing the excess wax from the furniture. Eventually you will need to change to a third fresh cloth. Use this to polish the wood as hard as you can removing all traces of the loose wax.

There is a test to see if you have removed all of the loose wax: pull your (clean, unwaxed) index finger over the surface of the wood as if you were drawing a number one on the surface of the wood; if it leaves a noticeable smear on the surface, then there is still some loose polish to be removed.

You may have to apply the wax and repeat the polishing process a number of times before a satisfactory finish starts to appear, depending on the type of wood being waxed. Remember, you will have to maintain this finish with a topping up as and when it is necessary.

So there it is. The thing to remember with this particular finish is that the elbow grease is as important as the wax. And if you are a person with a sense of history, remember: when the beads of sweat start forming on your forehead and your arms start to ache, this process has been sworn at and enjoyed by craftspeople of every civilization since the start of history.

If you have a piece of furniture that has some intricate carving or mouldings, you may find it difficult to get the wax into the recesses, and harder still to clean them out when ready to polish. This is where the thinned down 'liquid wax' comes into its own (*see* page 127 for a recipe). If you wish, liquid wax can be brushed into complicated areas with a 3in (75mm) decorator's paint brush, then polished using a shoe-cleaning brush. If you have a lot of thick wax located in hard-to-clean-out areas, then you can wrap the cloth round the tips of lollipop sticks which you can cut to the required shape with a sharp knife.

## SECOND METHOD

The next method of application is a little easier, simply because the wax shine builds up quicker. It is also more practical in that, once applied, it does not need as much maintenance as the previous method. It will also resist grime being transported into the wood via the wax, so why is this method not used exclusively? Because some people say it does not provide the same depth and quality of finish as the previous process. Either way, both have their place and value.

First seal the wood. Traditionally this is done by applying two coats of thinned down French polish (*see* Chapter 16). At this point it is enough to know that there are three main varieties of French polish available through D.I.Y. shops. These are most easily distinguished by their colour. They are white

**Fig 14.9** A B O V E : **A bottle of liquid wax.**

polish, which is creamy white in colour and should be used on light-coloured woods; button polish, which is orange, and is traditionally used on golden-toned woods; and French polish, which is dark brown in colour, and recommended for use on dark woods.

They can all be thinned down by mixing with methylated spirit. The French polish and the button polish will alter the tone of the wood that you apply them to. However, for our purposes, we shall be applying two thin coats to the wood and the colour change will be noticeable, though light. Usually this change of colour is seen as welcome as it adds a warm tone to the wood. If you are concerned about the colour that your furniture will turn, do an experiment on a scrap piece of wood first.

Pour a quantity of French polish (colour of your choosing) into a container and add the same amount of methylated spirit. This is your sealer. Using a clean soft paint brush, coat your piece of furniture with this mixture as evenly and thinly as you can. Allow it to dry for 30 minutes in a warm and dry atmosphere, then repeat the process. Leave for two hours before rubbing down with a medium-to-fine grade of wire wool. Dust off any loose fibres that have been left behind from the wire wool and you are ready for waxing.

Now all you have to do is to follow the instructions for waxing that I gave in the previous method (*see* page 125), the difference being that the shine will build up a lot quicker and a lot easier with this method.

As with all things connected with furniture restoration there are a number of different ways of doing the same or similar thing. There are wood sealers that you can buy ready-made from the D.I.Y. stores. Alternatively, you can seal the wood with thinned-down polyurethane varnish or Danish oil or teak oil. This will create an even tougher foundation for the wax to be built upon, but I feel sure that many old-time craftspeople would consider the practice inferior to the methods that I have outlined above.

However, don't let that deter you from experimenting. After all, I'd bet a place on the Civil List that once upon a time French polishing was considered a long-winded foreign import of no value to serious craftspeople.

# HOW TO MIX YOUR OWN WAX POLISH

If you want to mix your own wax polish, melt some pure beeswax into a double boiler (one saucepan inside another saucepan is adequate), then add an equal quantity of pure turpentine (*see* Fig 14.8). Remove from the heat before you pour the turpentine in case of accidental spillage, allow enough ventilation and guard against fire. Continue heating and stirring, then pour into a suitable receptacle ready for use when cool. Don't smoke, and make sure your fire insurance policy is fully paid up!

**Fig 14.8** A B O V E : **The double boiler method for mixing your own wax polish.**

Often you will see a cream wax or liquid wax in the D.I.Y. store (*see* Fig 14.9). As their names suggest these waxes are a little thinner in their consistency. They can be very useful for polishing ornate areas of carving, moulding or fretwork where the thinner consistency makes it easier to get them into the nooks and crannies. However, rather than buy another bottle of stuff off the shelf, it is far more convenient and cheaper, to thin an ordinary wax with a little turpentine or white spirit.

Do this by spooning a little wax into a lidded jar, then add a small quantity of white spirit and shake vigorously. If you would prefer a cream wax (useful for cleaning waxed surfaces) then add a little warm water to the thinned wax and a couple of drops of washing-up liquid and shake once again.

By playing the 'mad scientist' with clear wax you can achieve your very own range of wax finishes. If you want to colour any of these waxes you can add some thin artists' oil colour or some oil stains (*see* Chapter 13). If, for example, you add a splash of mahogany oil stain to your clear wax and stir you will create a mahogany wax.

You can remove a wax finish sympathetically, to preserve the patina in much the same way as the antiquikstrip method is used to remove French polish (*see* Chapter 7), by cleaning it off with wire wool soaked in turps or white spirit.

If you want to clean a waxed finish then wipe over with a cloth slightly dampened with white spirit. The white spirit will soften the wax and the cloth will polish it and lift off any surface dirt. Alternatively, use the previously described cream wax.

Antique waxes can be bought off the shelf, but they are no match for this particular brew: take some clear natural wax. Mix in a splash of dark brown or black oil stain to taste (splash is roughly 3.6ml). Now add some fine dust from the vacuum cleaner bag, one teaspoon at a time, stirring all the time until fully dissolved. Then add a scraping of soot or fine charcoal or graphite from a pencil (or all of them) depending on taste.

First stain bare wood a dark colour. Then rub your home-made antique wax into the furniture leaving the wax to build up in the inaccessible areas which are traditionally the darker parts of old furniture. Leave overnight before buffing to a dull dark finish in the corners, nooks and crannies and removing from the areas in which a dark build up is not required. Repeat and adjust the mixture until satisfied.

N.B. Fraud carries a maximum sentence of 25 years upon conviction!

# CHAPTER 15

# OIL FINISHES

*There are a number of different kinds of oil preparation that can be used by the furniture restorer: Danish oil, oil from another country, raw linseed oil, boiled linseed oil, tung oil, teak oil, lemon oil polish and edible oils.*

All of these oils have the following in common: they all have a similar 'oily' constitution, they are applied in the same way, and they can all be thinned with white spirit. The difference between them lies in the number of applications needed to constitute a finish, the drying time of individual coats and their resilience to wear and tear once applied.

## SAFETY

Before proceeding any further, there is a problem concerning safety which you should be made aware of: the rags that are used during the application of oil finishes have to be treated with special consideration as they are liable to spontaneously combust. This means, when you have finished oiling, you must dispose of the rags correctly as there is a risk of fire. The oil-soaked rags will produce their own chemical reaction, that in the right conditions will cause them to burst into flames.

If you want to use the rags again, or are leaving them overnight in a workshop, drape them over a bench, or better still, hang them up outside on a washing line. Once dry they are perfectly safe. Do not, as one of my more absent-minded students has done, stuff them into a shopping trolley underneath a pile of upholstery wadding, methylated spirits, pieces of antique chair and other combustibles, and then catch the last bus home. In this case there was no harm done but on another occasion it may be different.

So next time you are on the bus late at night, and the little old lady that you are sharing a seat with suddenly bursts into flames, you may comfortably assume that she is on her way home from a furniture restoration class. With this knowledge, you can calm the fears of the rest of the passengers and thereby avert a panic.

## APPLICATION

The method of application is very simple, and this goes for whichever type of oil that you use. First, rub the oil into the wood. When it is dry, rub in some more. When the wood will not accept any more oil the finish is complete. It could not be simpler, the method of application for perhaps a dozen different formulas encapsulated in just three sentences.

The difference between the oils lies in the number of applications needed before full saturation is achieved. With a traditional linseed oil finish it could be as many as 30 applications, with weeks between drying; with a Danish oil, two may be sufficient.

I shall now be more specific and describe the properties and methods of application for different oils.

## THE DIFFERENT TYPES OF OIL

### DANISH OIL

I would recommend Danish oil as a first stop for the absolute beginner. It is the quickest and easiest of all the oil finishes, and will give you a taste of what this family of finishes looks like, and the methods involved. It is sometimes marketed as Scandinavian oil or Antique oil.

**APPLICATION** The oil is brushed on to the wood and allowed to 'soak in' for two or three minutes. It is then rubbed with a clean lint-free cotton cloth until the excess has been absorbed or pushed into the fibres of the wood. If the oil becomes too sticky, you can dampen the cloth with a little white spirit. Typically, end grain will need three coats to every one coat on the ordinary grain.

If you have stained the wood, thin the first coat of oil with some white spirit, apply a coat with a clean decorator's paint brush, and wipe off any excess or drips with a cloth. Do not rub this coat or else you will remove stain from the surface of the wood and create lighter patches.

The first coat will take about four hours to dry hard, after which you can 'denib' the surface with some wet-and-dry abrasive paper. Then apply a second coat in exactly the same way. This process can be repeated many times, but as a rule two or three coats are sufficient. Any more than that and the oil can build up on the surface of the wood and start to look glossy. To remove any unintentional gloss, rub the affected area with wire wool soaked in white spirit and finish off with a soft cloth.

Danish oil is ideal for use out of doors and on furniture needing protection from damp and heat

**Fig 15.2** R I G H T : **A can of Danish oil.**

and weather, such as kitchen, bathroom, conservatory and garden furniture. It is also recommended for external facing doors and garden gates, but perhaps its true beauty lies in its ease of application.

If you have spent the last six weeks scraping, scrubbing and wiping off the thick-coated finish of a large and cumbersome carved wardrobe, and are just about to take a chainsaw to the thing at the thought of having to spend another six weeks finishing it with the convoluted ceremonies that can accompany French polishing or polyurethane varnish, then you will fall down on your knees and bless the container that Danish oil comes in, when you realize that the process of finishing the largest of bare-wood areas amounts to little more than knocking the tin over with your elbow and wiping up the mess. This has got to be the easiest finish ever invented – made in heaven for furniture restorers everywhere.

If you apply it to garden furniture then I suggest a periodic 'topping up' every 18 to 36 months depending on weather conditions and whether you leave furniture out of doors in winter. Topping up consists of rubbing down with fine sandpaper and wiping or brushing another coat on. If this finish becomes damaged it is very easily repaired by the application of one more coat. If you prefer a glossy look on indoor furniture then Danish oil is a superb sealer before creating a high-gloss wax finish (*see* Chapter 14).

### OIL FROM ANOTHER COUNTRY

If you cannot find a supplier of Danish oil, or like me you are a cheapskate and want to concoct something similar yourself, try my recipe entitled 'oil from another country'. This can be applied in exactly the same way as Danish oil, to similar effect, and is a useful way of using up leftover polyurethane varnish.

It is composed of one part boiled linseed oil, one part polyurethane varnish (outdoor varnish if for use out of doors) and one part white spirit. Pour the ingredients into a pot and stir.

### LINSEED OIL FINISHES

Some craftspeople swear by it and others swear at it. Suffice to say that the full traditional linseed oil finish is a contentious subject. Personally, I'm not getting involved, but then I'm a coward. I shall tell you what it constitutes and then you can decide if you want to have a go.

'Use linseed oil.' This is one of Uncle George's most favoured pieces of advice. It is often described with the most poetic of language and a surfeit of superlatives extolling its wonderful attributes, but as with many other things in our lives, this has far more to do with image than reality.

The traditional linseed oil and similar vegetable oil finishes have a very long history that goes back to the time of cave-dwelling and perhaps even further. These types of oils have been used consistently all through man's involvement with wood. This fact alone is enough to cause a loving attachment in some craftspersons' eyes.

The reason for its longstanding use is clear. Until very recently it was the only finish that was capable of protecting wooden items used out of doors, or protecting items subject to much abuse. To this day it is still the traditional finish for protecting cricket bats and gunstocks, and is still a common finish for garden furniture and dining tables.

---

**Fig 15.3** B E L O W : **The tissue test. When there is little or no oil left on the tissue after wiping, then you are ready for the next coat.**

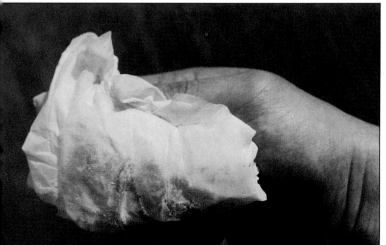

When applied to interior furniture it has the advantage of being heat-, scratch-, water- and alcohol-resistant, and is easily and quickly repaired in cases of hard wear or neglect. However, these attributes should be tempered with the knowledge that this finish is not very durable, and is therefore in need of regular maintenance.

In medieval times and later, it was the finish for any cooking or dining furniture. After a typical medieval banquet the surfaces would be sluiced down with hot water, then scrubbed clean and re-oiled to maintain its protective qualities, ready for the next round of festivities.

One of its other attributes is the fact that there is little or no skill needed in its application – just dogged persistence is required to keep rubbing the oil into the fibres of the wood. Once the oiled finish is soaked into the wood it will typically take on a low-key, soft-lustre finish.

**APPLICATION** The process for application is exactly the same as for any oil. Each coat requires thorough rubbing with a piece of blanket wrapped around a block of wood to push the oil into the fibres of the wood. Have a word with your doctor before using this finish as it can be hard work.

The biggest problem with linseed oil is that you will have to apply many coats and it will take a lot longer to dry between coats than other oil preparations. To test to see if it is dry enough to apply another coat, wipe a paper tissue over the surface to see if there is any oil still wet on the surface (*see* Fig 15.3). Perhaps if I give you an old-time guide to the application of a linseed oil finish, the problem will become clearer:

Apply one coat every hour for a day.
Then once a day for a week.
Then once a week for a month.
Then once a month for a year.
Then once every six months for the rest of its life.

This recipe would depend on the type of wood used and the ambient and environmental conditions of the item and should be taken with a pinch of salt, but it gives a good indication of the length of time and work involved in looking after a linseed oil finish.

**Fig 15.4** LEFT: **A can of Chinese tung oil.**

During application and drying, the oil will emit an all-pervading smell. This is not too unpleasant at first, but since it can take days, sometimes weeks, for each coat of linseed oil to fully dry, it may soon become obnoxious.

As you can imagine, over the centuries methods have been devised to speed up, or make the process more user-friendly. For example, you can warm the oil, or thin it with turpentine, so that it penetrates the fibres of the wood more easily, or you can use boiled linseed oil, bought from your local D.I.Y. store. Boiled linseed oil has been boiled and 'doctored' to produce a quicker-drying oil. Therefore to some it is preferable as a finish. Although boiling produces a thicker oil, it still needs as many coats and its durability is not improved. It is usually thinned down by the craftsperson with turpentine and heat (in a double boiler) to make absorption into the fibres of the wood easier.

Much of this information is of historical interest only. Except for the most dedicated craftspeople who are interested in recreating the finishes of the past, linseed oil finishes are largely redundant due to the time it takes to apply and the fact that there are far quicker and more resilient types of oil finish.

However, many of my students, with typical beginners' enthusiasm, have tried this finish and have produced extremely good results. And it has to be said, if you are at all romantic, using exactly the same finish as our most far-flung ancestors, does hold a certain appeal. When properly done it can look extremely beautiful. If you have the time and the inclination, please give it a go.

### CHINESE TUNG OIL

Pure Chinese tung oil (*see* Fig 15.4) can be expensive and is difficult to come by in the UK, but I have heard very good reports about it from the USA. In the UK it is relatively unknown. Many of the other proprietary oil mixes include a measure of tung oil in their constitutions.

### TEAK OIL

This substance is a proprietary mix designed to apply a finish to teak wood. Teak is a very hard and durable wood, much used in marine environments because it contains its own naturally occurring oils. Because of these oils, teak can cause difficulties when applying other types of finish. Therefore the traditional finish for teak is teak oil (*see* Fig 15.5).

However, it is not commonly known that teak oil works very well on other timbers. It is relatively quick-drying and will leave a slightly shinier finish than accompanies Danish oils.

### LEMON OIL POLISH

This is a thin, aromatic oil that is of no use as a finish. It is commonly sold as a scratch cover to disguise scratches in furniture in much the same way that the linseed oil component of revivers is used (*see* pages 58–9). As such I prefer to forego the very pleasant lemon smell and use thin linseed oil.

### SUNFLOWER OIL (AND OTHER EDIBLE OILS)

There is one more family of oils that is worth mentioning, if only because they are an interesting variation on this theme: edible oils. A number of these oils, such as sunflower oil, olive oil and corn oil, are used for cooking. These are most commonly used on woodwork found in the kitchen, most notably salad bowls and chopping boards etc. These oils have very little durability. The oil is rubbed in after washing up to maintain their look and protection.

**Fig 15.5** RIGHT: **A bottle of teak oil.**

# CHAPTER 16

# FRENCH POLISHING FOR THE
## ——— ABSOLUTE BEGINNER ———

PHOTO COURTESY OF RUSTIN'S LTD.

*The popular perception of French polishing is that it is an impossibly skilled craft taking many years of obsessive practice to master, and the beginner should not even bother trying because it is far too involved for mere mortals, and any attempt is bound to end in absolute failure – besides which, if you are not over 86 years old with grey hair, a pince-nez and a white apron, you have no right to meddle in such matters.*

This is an idea that has been fostered and encouraged over the years by the craftspeople and furniture restorers who earn their living from this particular skill. In short, all those with a vested interest in maintaining this image. Suffice to say, if I earned my living from French polishing, there is no way I would be writing this chapter about the subject and telling the world how easy it is.

The truth is, with careful instruction and a little practice, there is no reason why an absolute beginner should not get very good results, first time. It is one of this century's greatest conspiracies that I am about to expose . . . French polishing is easy peasy!

## WHAT IS IT?

French polish is a naturally occurring substance. It is produced in Asia where it is harvested from a particular type of aphid-like insect (*Laccifer lacca*). This insect attaches itself to certain trees and, as part of its lifecycle, exudes and eventually entombs itself in a thick, toffee-like substance.

This substance, along with the rest of the beetle and any bits of tree, are harvested and collected into muslin bags. These are then heated, and the toffee-like substance is squeezed from the bag and drips on to a slab of cold marble to form glass-hard 'buttons' (hence 'button polish' – the name of the least adulterated version of French polish). Further treatment yields different forms of 'toffee'.

This toffee-like substance has the interesting property of becoming liquid when mixed with methylated spirit. In this form it is known as French polish. When the liquid French polish is spread thinly over wood the meths evaporates, leaving a thin layer of the hard toffee-like substance behind.

## HISTORY

Since ancient times this liquid, sometimes called shellac, has been used for all manner of things, most notably as an ingredient in many wood varnishes. Legend has it that around 1820 an ingenious and anonymous French cabinetmaker developed the method of application which is now called French polishing. From that time on, until the 1940s, the bulk of all furniture, both mass-produced and smaller scale, was finished with some form of French polish finish. It may therefore strike you as rather peculiar, when I tell you that this widespread universal finish is the least practical of finishes to apply to your furniture.

## PROS AND CONS

It is easily damaged by scratching; it will decompose and be marked by heat; water or damp will turn the polish white; alcohol will dissolve it; and young children and uppity teenagers should be kept at least three streets away.

It is interesting to note that many of the household accoutrements of the Victorian age were designed to protect the fragile French polish on their furniture. Items such as tablecloths, lace doilies, coasters and table mats, were all designed to protect French polish from destructive forces. But even with these obvious drawbacks, in those days almost everything wooden was French polished, including doors, picture rails, skirting boards, right down to the wooden legs of seafaring gentlemen.

Application can be a long-winded process. To achieve the famed piano finish can take many hours of painstaking work. Consequently, it is very rarely applied in commercial work today. It is not practical to use on furniture that will receive a lot of hard wear such as coffee tables, desks and bar tops.

Because of its weakness in the face of water, it cannot be used in the bathroom, kitchen or out of doors. So why on earth do we bother using something so impractical?

Well, for many craftspeople there is no other finish to compare with the beauty and colour of a well-applied French polish finish. Among some craftspeople it has achieved an almost idolatrous status. Also, when dealing with antique furniture, you may need to retain its correct period finish. In this case it would be aesthetically wrong to apply anything but a traditional French polish finish.

And finally, it is comforting to think that in a hi-tech world, when millions of pounds are spent on research into ever more sophisticated finishing products, the skilled use of a couple of bits of old rag and some cotton wool, still provides a finish that is every bit as good, if not better, than that obtained by the most expensive modern spraying equipment.

In short, although it contains many negative aspects, it is still the way for the small-scale craftsperson to achieve the very finest of finishes.

## HOW TO APPLY

The method of applying French polish that I am about to explain is not the only one. With something as old as French polishing there are bound to be variations, and I like to refer to these different methods of application as recipes. Just as there are many different bread recipes, there are many different French polish recipes.

The recipe I am about to describe to you has evolved over many years of teaching absolute beginners how to French polish. It is not the quickest way to apply French polish, nor is it the simplest. However, it teaches you the basic principles of French polishing and produces a classic high-gloss French polish, sometimes called a 'mirror finish' or 'piano finish'.

I show you the high-gloss finish because it is the most difficult form of French polishing. Many other French polish recipes are derived from this one. If you master this recipe, the others will be easy and you will be able to build up your repertoire or recipe book of different French polishes by means of trial and error.

# PREPARATION

### THE TESTER

It is important for your first session of French polishing to practise upon a suitable piece of wood. Go to your D.I.Y. shop and buy an offcut of veneered chipboard or a piece of plywood, ideally between 12 and 18in (30 and 46cm) square. Henceforth this shall be referred to as a tester. When you have picked up the basics and are more confident, then you can transfer what you have learnt to your furniture. This 'tester' is an important part of your education and should be kept for future experiments with other French polishing techniques.

### OBTAINING THE MATERIALS

Next, you need some French polish. Today there are three types of French polish that are likely to be found upon the D.I.Y. shop shelf; they are button polish, white polish and French polish (*see* Fig 16.2). From the absolute beginner's point of view the only difference between these types of French polish is their colour.

White polish, as the name suggests, is a light creamy colour and is intended for use on light-coloured wood. Button polish is an orangey-brown colour meant for light brown or orange-toned woods, and French polish is a dark brown colour, for use on dark woods.

**Fig 16.2** LEFT: **The three types of French polish.**

**Fig 16.3** ABOVE: **Always ensure you have fresh French polish. Anything over a year old be suspicious of; and if you have problems, particularly with the drying time, question the age of your polish.**

Old polish is undesirable partly because it takes a long time to dry. Try to make sure that the polish that you buy is fresh and has not been sitting on the shop's shelf for too long. The telltale signs are dust and cobwebs covering the bottle, old price stickers which say 2/6d, or if it is sold in a stoneware jug. For the same reason do not use the stuff that 'Uncle George' has had cluttering up the potting shed since the coronation, because 'one day it might come in handy' (see Fig 16.3).

Next, you will need four pieces of 100 per cent cotton cloth between 9 and 12in (23 and 30cm) square. I prefer curtain lining, but old handkerchiefs, old bedsheets and shirts are all possible sources. If you use old bedsheets or shirts, make sure you get clearance from the relevant authorities (preferably in writing) that they are not wanted. I shall not easily forget the face of one of my students when he was threatened with his clothes being burnt and instant divorce if the spare bed linen was not returned immediately.

You will also need a quantity of cotton wool, an eggcup of raw linseed oil, a wide-brimmed container with a screw top, some methylated spirit and some 600 grit wet-and-dry abrasive paper, and lastly, a clean piece of thick paper.

Before proceeding further, I shall describe the whole process in brief, to give you an overview. Then I shall describe each step in detail.

The rubber is the tool with which we apply the polish. First I will show you how to make one. Then I will show you how to load the rubber with the polish. After that I shall describe to you how to make a pass, which is the method for applying a single coat of polish with the rubber. There are three different passes you will need to learn.

I shall then show you how these passes build up over three sessions to a high-gloss finish. These sessions are spread over three days. The first session is on day one, and will lay the foundations of the polish. Typically this will consist of between 12 and 25 passes of polish, depending on the type of wood. The second session is on day two, and will build up the polish above the surface of the wood. In this session the number of passes is unlimited but typically you can apply 20 to 40 passes. The third session, which should be left until day three, is known as 'spiriting off' and it is here that the classic high-gloss French polish finish develops.

At the end I shall outline for you some other methods of application. These you can experiment with once you have mastered the absolute beginner's method. They are intended to extend your mastery of the technique and give you a deeper understanding of the procedures involved.

## THE FRENCH POLISHER'S RUBBER

**MAKING A RUBBER** First we must make a rubber. This is a traditional French polisher's tool that we make from cotton material and cotton wool. It is used to apply the French polish in thin, even coats. Organize your workspace. Use the thick piece of clean paper to cover your bench so you have somewhere clinically clean to make and fill your rubber.

Take one piece of cotton material and fold it into a pad about 5in (13cm) square (see Fig 16.4). Take enough cotton wool in your hand so that when you squeeze the ball in your fist your fingertips just touch the palm of your hand (see Fig 16.5). Place this wad of cotton wool in the middle of the 5in (13cm) square of cotton material and mould it roughly into an egg shape (see Fig 16.6). Now wrap this egg shape as tightly as you can in the 5in (13cm) pad by drawing in the pad's four corners. Hold all the corners tightly in the middle with one finger (see Fig 16.7). This is called a fad and should be the shape of a diamond. You may need to adjust the size of the pad or the size of the egg to make a tight package.

Take another piece of cotton material and lay it flat on the clean scrap of wood or paper. Place the fad in the centre of the outer material with the top of the diamond pointing into one corner; now move it 1in (25mm) closer towards that corner (see Fig 16.8). Starting with the sides closest to the corner, pull the cotton material tightly up around the four sides of the diamond-shaped fad (see Fig 16.9) and gather any loose material above the fad and twist the loose material a number of times to hold everything in place (see Fig 16.10). You have now made your rubber which hopefully will look something like the one in Fig 16.11 and will feel very firm to the touch. You may need to do this a number of times before you get the hang of it and are able to translate my words into your actions. You will find it a lot easier if you make the whole thing wet with

# Making a rubber

**Fig 16.4** A B O V E : **5in (13cm) square cotton pad.**

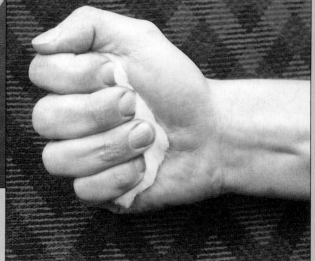

**Fig 16.5** A B O V E : **Squeezing the cotton wool ball.**

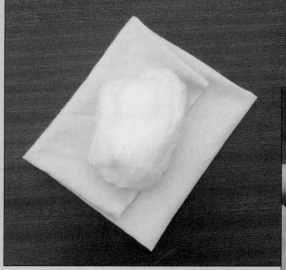

**Fig 16.6** A B O V E : **Cotton wool egg sitting on pad.**

**Fig 16.7** A B O V E : **A fad.**

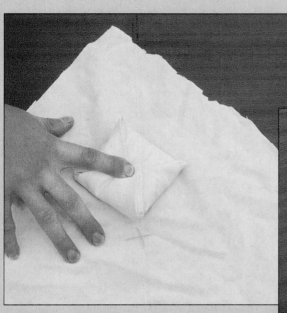

**Fig 16.8** A B O V E : **Fad placed on outer material 1in (25mm) from centre ('X' marks centre).**

**Fig 16.9** A B O V E : **Pulling up sides of outer material around the fad.**

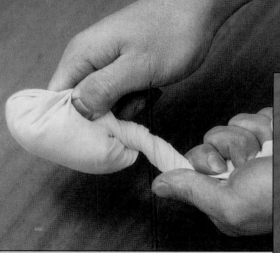

**Fig 16.10** A B O V E : **Twisting the loose material above the fad.**

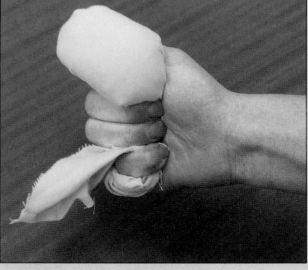

**Fig 16.11** A B O V E : **The finished rubber, held correctly.**

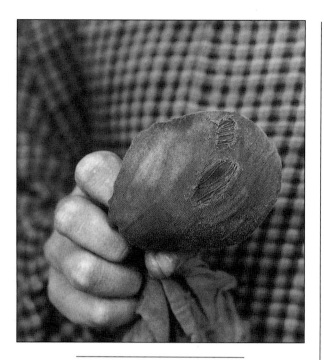

**Fig 16.12** A B O V E : **It is to be expected that your rubber will at some point wear out. Inspect the sole regularly and move the outer cloth as soon as a hole is found.**

methylated spirit; this will stop the rubber from springing open all the time.

The completed rubber is commonly referred to as a 'shoe', due to its shape. This is a useful description for us because it helps when describing the various parts of the rubber. It is from the sole of the rubber that the French polish is delivered, so it is important that there are no creases or bits of dirt attaching themselves to that area (*see* Fig 16.12). The rubber should be checked after each pass, the presence of any 'foreign body' could damage a French polish finish. In the first stages of French polishing the rubber may wear out quickly due to the roughness of the bare wood. If this happens, reposition the fad to another corner of the outer material.

You are now a fully qualified rubber maker. Rubbers can be made as small as your fingertip to get into all those nooks and crannies, or as large as your hand for the boardroom dining table. You can also use the toe of the shoe to reach awkward areas At other times you may need to make two rubbers – a big one for large flat areas, and a smaller one for the difficult-to-get-to regions; whatever the size, the method of construction remains the same.

**HOW TO HOLD THE RUBBER** It is important that you hold the rubber firmly in your hand so that it cannot 'rock and roll' on the surface of the wood. Grip it tightly at the base of the twisted gathered material (*see* Fig 16.11).

The rubber is the secret ingredient of French polishing; it enables the French polisher to perform amazing feats. First, it filters the polish so that no foreign bodies find their way to the sole and scratch the surface or become embedded in the finish. Second, it applies the thinnest of coats of polish to the wood. Thirdly, the abrasive quality of the cotton cloth will burnish every coat of polish as it is applied, not just the final coat as we do with rubbing compounds on other coating finishes. It is these three qualities, attributable to the rubber, that make French polishing unique in wood finishing.

## APPLICATION

Mix some polish (colour of your choosing) and some meths in equal quantities in a container, so you have a thin 50/50 mixture of French polish. Open the rubber up and pour a liberal quantity of polish into the cotton wool. Do not overdo it, but at the same time it takes a fair amount of polish to soak into the cotton wool and then into the outer cloth (*see* Fig 16.13).

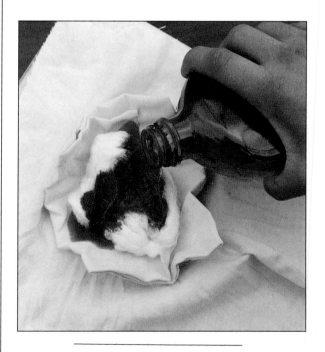

**Fig 16.13** A B O V E : **Charging the rubber.**

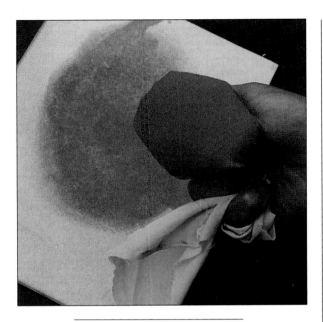

**Fig 16.14** A B O V E : **The ideal distribution of polish on the rubber.**

Wrap the rubber up again and squeeze it so that the French polish oozes through the cotton covering. You can rub this around on your clean scrap of wood to distribute it around the sole of the rubber. The ideal state is an even distribution of polish oozing from the sole of the rubber, with no dry spots and no areas that are too wet. Squeeze it on to the scrap of wood to test it. If necessary, put some more polish in. If it is too wet, rub it around on your thick piece of paper or a scrap of wood to dry it out a bit (*see* Fig 16.14).

When you are more experienced, you will realize that a rubber that is wet needs only a slight downward pressure to release a thin coating of polish. As the rubber becomes drier, more pressure is required, until eventually, a lot of pressure is necessary to release an almost non-existent film of polish.

This is the ideal process you are trying to achieve: you start off with a wet rubber which applies the polish but does not need much pressure, then as the rubber dries out, you have to apply downward pressure to release more polish; in so doing you burnish the polish that has already been applied with the abrasive quality of the cotton cloth.

It is this interplay between the application of very thin films of polish, and the burnishing of the previously deposited polish, that is the essence of good French polishing. It is this that gives the tradi-tional French polish finish its unique and unsurpassed quality, making it the cherished finish of craftsmen and connoisseurs for nearly two centuries.

*Please note:* The temperature and moisture content of the air when polishing is extremely important. If you French polish in a damp environment, the polish will take in some of the moisture in the air, resulting in a cloudy-white discoloration of the polish. If it is not warm enough, the polish will take too long to dry and be difficult to work. Ideally, the conditions should be warm and dry.

The wood you are working upon should also be warm and dry. Do not bring your project in from a cold and damp garage or outhouse and work on it straight away. Leave it overnight to 'acclimatize'. If you French polish cold wood in warm surroundings, the minute quantities of air contained in the wood will eventually expand underneath the finish and cause tiny unwanted bubbles in the surface of the wood.

## HOW TO MAKE A PASS

You are now ready to start polishing. Starting in a top corner, polish the rubber over the wood in small circular motions, moving it along in the same direction as the grain. When you get to the other end, move the rubber down a couple of inches and, still with small circular motions and without stopping, move back in the other direction (*see* Fig 16.15). Try not to touch the area of polish that you have just deposited on the wood, as it will be starting to dry and getting tacky. Continue on in the same pattern that a farmer would plough a field, moving up and down until the whole piece of wood has received an even coating of polish. You have just completed your first pass with a rubber. It may not be perfect, but do not worry, you have got plenty of opportunities to improve. Remember your goal, you are trying to apply a very thin coat of polish on to the wood as evenly as possible. Often the wood will slide around when you are polishing. Obviously this will not happen when you come to polish the grand piano or dining table, but it can be a problem with smaller items. With a table or chair you can usually find a place to hold with one hand while you polish with the other. A common problem with this method is that the hand becomes

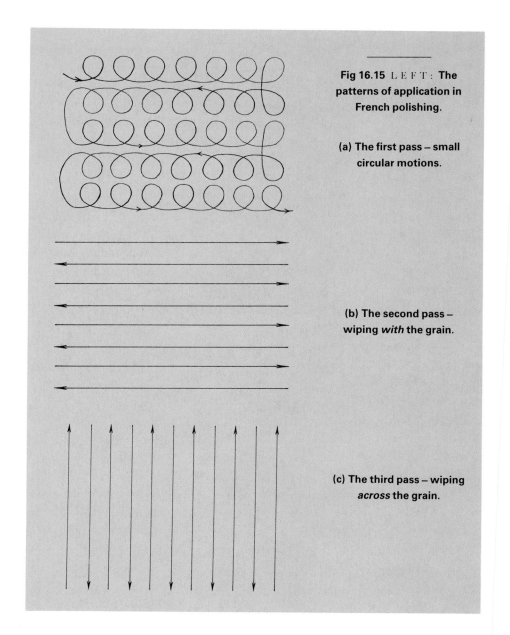

**Fig 16.15** L E F T : **The patterns of application in French polishing.**

**(a) The first pass – small circular motions.**

**(b) The second pass – wiping *with* the grain.**

**(c) The third pass – wiping *across* the grain.**

stuck or leaves deep fingerprints in the semi-hard polish you are clutching. The only answer to this is vigilance. For very small items such as boxes and your tester, you may have to clamp them to the table top, or you could place sticky tabs or plasticine under the project.

When making a pass, do not, under any circumstances, stop the rubber on the surface. When you lift the rubber off the surface, the rubber has to be moving and likewise, when you put the rubber down on the surface, it has to be in motion. Get into the habit of making a swiping action when you start and when you finish your pass. If you stop on the surface, the rubber will redissolve the finish and you will blemish the polish.

**THE SECOND PASS** Wait for the first pass to dry (about 30 seconds), then carry out pass number two. This is made in a wiping action moving with the grain, starting at a top corner. Wipe the rubber over the surface. Start your wiping action a few inches beyond the wood and then lower it down to land on the edge of the tester, just like a child pretending to land a toy aeroplane. This will ensure that the rubber is never stationary on the surface. When you reach the other end of the tester, you can 'lift off'. If you wish, you can also make the noise of a jumbo jet taking off, but don't let anyone catch you or they will think you have been at the meths.

Now repeat the same action. This time try to get the wipe as close to the previous one as possible without touching it. Keep repeating this all the way down the wood until the whole surface is covered. If you miss a bit do not go back and redo it – the rubber will stick to the polish and the pass will be ruined. Just make a mental note to cover it with the next pass. A common tendency with absolute beginners is to 'take off' too soon and 'land' too late, leaving dry patches near the edges. The answer to this is to slap your wrist and try harder. If it becomes a problem, sneak in some 'rogue' passes (when the previous pass is dry) that just cover the patches you have missed.

**THE THIRD PASS** Wait for the second pass to dry before proceeding with the next one. The third pass is made in exactly the same way as the second pass, except that it is made going across the grain instead of with the grain. You may well be asking at this stage, 'Why do I have to keep changing the way in which I make the passes?' The answer is simple: imagine you made just one type of pass, for instance wiping up and down in the direction of the grain. If you were to build up a complete finish like this then the finish is likely to start looking streaky and stripey in appearance. Alternating between the different passes ensures that a smooth and even surface develops. If you happen to make a bad pass in one direction and leave a noticeable pattern in the finish, you may find it useful to miss out that particular pass for the next couple of goes.

The fourth pass is made in exactly the same way as the first pass, and so the cycle continues. After about six passes you will see a shine developing. The degree of shine will be dependent upon the type of wood and the thickness of the polish used. After approximately 12 to 24 passes you should have built up enough polish on the surface of the wood to create a shine. It will also start to become a little bit sticky, so making it harder for the rubber to glide over the surface. At this point you should stop. The first session is complete.

Leave the polish to dry overnight. This will allow it to penetrate into the fibres of the wood and become hard, creating a firm foundation for the next session of polishing. Do not worry if some of the shine has disappeared. This is normal.

## THE SECOND SESSION

If you wish, you can stop completely at this stage. What you have completed is a recipe for what can variously be called a low-key, open-grained, low-lustre, sealer-type French polish finish. This recipe produces a very quick and effective finish.

If you want to continue with the main, high-gloss recipe, take 600 grit wet-and-dry abrasive paper and gently stroke the surface to remove any roughness. You may not perceive any roughness but if you were to rub one side of your tester with wet-and-dry, then rub your hand over both surfaces, the difference will be noticeable.

**Fig 16.16** R I G H T : **Flicking raw linseed oil on to the surface of the wood.**

Wipe off any dust with a clean rag and repeat the first day's session. Work through the various passes in sequence and watch the shine build up. The more you polish the more it will shine. (You can stop at any time and you will have achieved a French polish finish.) After more passes you will find that the surface becomes a little bit sticky; this is a dangerous situation. It could become so sticky that you actually stop. If you were to stop even for a second, the meths in the rubber would dissolve and remove the freshly applied polish.

This is to the French polisher what a shower of rain is to the pavement artist, or a late frost to the gardener. If it happens, this is what you do. Allow it to dry overnight, then rub the surface down with wet-and-dry abrasive paper until the blemish cannot be seen; you can then resume work as before.

To avoid this happening in the first place, you should stop when it gets sticky (in which case leave overnight before continuing). Otherwise, dip your forefinger into some raw linseed oil and flick the oil on to the surface of the wood (*see* Fig 16.16). Repeat this a few times and then wipe any excess from your finger on to the sole of the rubber. This will act as a lubricant for the rubber and will allow you to carry on polishing. Often it will allow you to polish even harder than normal, so increasing the burnishing action and the shine. Sometimes it may look a little smeary and lose a little of the shine, but this disappears as you continue to polish.

This second session of polishing can be repeated as often as you wish. How many times you repeat the second session depends on the quality of the wood and the depth of shine you are looking for.

## SPIRITING OFF

The second session or sessions should be allowed to dry overnight, before the final polishing process begins. This needs a brand new rubber which is then charged with a small quantity of methylated spirit. Pour it into the cotton wool and squeeze the rubber so that the sole of the rubber becomes almost dry to the touch. If it leaves a wet patch when squeezed hard against a dry piece of paper, then it is too wet. If it leaves a damp patch when squeezed hard, it is about right.

Dip your forefinger into the linseed oil and flick it over the polished surface. Wipe the excess from your finger on the sole of the rubber. Do this twice. Hover above the wood practising your circular motion in mid-air, then lower the rubber down until you reach the wood, and apply light pressure, rubbing in a circular motion in the same way that you did when you applied the first pass. It will take a little time before the meths starts to soften the polish, then the abrasive quality of the cloth will start to burnish the polish. As the shine begins to develop and the oil gets spread around, increase the pressure and the speed. This is the most strenuous part of the process and is best carried out in short bursts of energy. This is when the shine really starts to appear. Like the sun slowly rising over the distant horizon, the glory will appear before your eyes. The more you polish, the brighter it will become. This spiriting off technique is really an abrasive process. If you have any slight blemishes, it is possible to rub them out of the polish with this technique. But beware: if the finish is too thin, it is possible to rub right through the finish to the wood.

The finishing touch is a light application of thin wax which is buffed to a superlative shine. Although the polish is dry to the touch, it will be at least a week before it goes rock hard. If you place anything heavy on the surface before the seven days are up, it is liable to leave a mark. If you have to apply large areas of French polish, then break the surface into manageable sections and complete them one pass at a time.

You should expect to face some problems. French polishing is rarely perfect first time. If it is, it only goes to show what a superb book this is and you should rush out and buy a few dozen copies for your friends.

## COMMON PROBLEMS

There are a number of problems that can occur with this type of finish. Here are some of the common ones encountered by absolute beginners, and their remedies:

- The polish is made too thick and therefore cannot be applied thinly enough or evenly enough: thin the polish with meths.

- There is too much polish in the rubber, resulting in thin lines being laid down on the surface. These can vary in size and in how noticeable they are. Allow to dry and rub back with wet-and-dry. In future, adjust the amount of polish in the rubber, or the amount of downward pressure applied to the rubber.

- Not enough polish is applied to the edges and corners. Either concentrate more upon the edges, make a small rubber specifically for these areas, or make some rogue passes.

- Rough patches are caused by the rubber going over freshly applied polish and sticking to it, or by stopping on the polish and redissolving the polish underneath. This is a very common problem; try not to get so close when butting up against the previous row of polish, and whatever else you do, don't stop the rubber when it is on the surface.

- The rubber is not gripped close enough to the foot, allowing the foot to 'rock and roll' (*see* Fig 16.17). This causes the sides of the rubber, where thick French polish builds up, to come in contact with the surface, spoiling the finish.

- Dirt, grit or a tear is allowed to stay on the sole of the rubber, consequently scratching the finish. Check the sole of the rubber frequently. If necessary, change rubbers.

- The polish is not allowed to dry fully before sitting in the chair or putting the vase on the table. Get a friend to pull you out of the chair and take a hammer and cold chisel to the vase, then strip and refinish.

- The furniture or wood is held tightly with one hand while the other hand polishes, causing the supporting hand to become inadvertently stuck to the furniture. Call the fire brigade with your free hand.

- Somebody puts a hot cup of tea on the table within days of completion. Remove the mark with rubbing compound or spirit off.

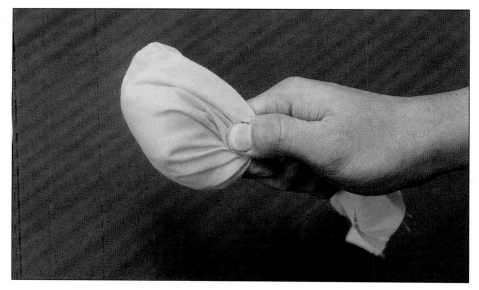

**Fig 16.17** R I G H T : **How not to hold the rubber. Grip the rubber close to the base of the 'twist', otherwise it will 'rock and roll'.**

## RULES FOR MAKING A PASS

1. Never, never, never stop the rubber on the surface.
2. Look after the edges and the middle will look after itself.
3. If you make a mistake, wait until it has dried and then rub back the offending area with wet-and-dry paper. As you gain in experience, this operation will become increasingly rare.
4. The rubber must be moving when it starts an application and when it finishes an application.
5. Work in a warm and dry environment, and on warm, dry projects.
6. Remember the basic principle of French polishing: you are trying to deposit lots of very thin and even coats of polish.
7. Check the face of the rubber frequently for dirt, holes and creases.
8. Alternate between the three passes. When you are more confident, make up your own passes in response to the way the finish is evolving and the shape of the furniture you are polishing (e.g. diagonal passes, figures of eight etc.).
9. Store a rubber between sessions in a tight-lidded container with a splash of meths.

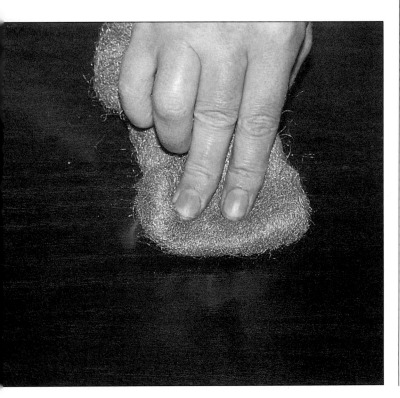

## APPLYING NON-GLOSS FINISHES

If you would like a satin finish then, after the second session of building up, instead of spiriting off, you should stroke the surface of the finish with fine-grade wire wool and thin wax (*see* Fig 16.18). Make sure you only stroke *with* the grain; do not under any circumstance scrub the finish as this will produce arc-shaped scratches in the finish and ruin the effect. If you are looking for a matt finish, rub in the same way, but use a little more pressure and experiment with a coarser grade wire wool.

## FURTHER INFORMATION

For further advice on French polishing, see the following:

- Chapter 7 on how to strip antique furniture sympathetically and then repolish.

- Chapters 8 (page 58) and 12 (page 106) on how to repair minor blemishes in French polish finishes.

- Chapter 12 (page 98) on how to fill the grain on coarse-grained woods with French polish as a base for a glossy French polish finish.

- Chapter 17 on how to apply French polish with a brush.

One last plea: once you have learnt these age-old skills of the master craftsman – the coveted mystery of generations – and you emit the glow of the self-satisfied know-it-all, then please, if anyone asks, don't tell them how it's done. Just send them straight out to buy this book. After all, writing is an impossibly skilled craft that takes many years of obsessive practice to master . . .

**Fig 16.18** L E F T : **Stroke the surface with wire wool for a satin or matt effect.**

# CHAPTER 17

# FRENCH POLISHING
## —— WITH A BRUSH ——

*In this chapter I describe a very simple and relatively quick method of achieving a French polish finish on furniture. It is often used by the commercial French polisher as a 'cheat' to speed up the more time-consuming and superior 'rubber' process. It would be beneficial to have read the preceding chapter before embarking on this one.*

Since this finish is so useful and easy it always amazes me how many people have never heard of it before. Because of its simplicity there are very few problems, and it is an ideal finish for the absolute beginner.

Before a very clever French person developed the technique of applying French polish with a rubber, which we now know as French polishing, the same liquid was called shellac and was applied with a brush. This brushing technique has been known by many cultures for thousands of years in one form or another. It is the quickest way to achieve a finish with French polish. The nice thing about this technique is that it can be combined with the traditional French polishing techniques described in Chapter 16 to speed up the traditional 'rubber' processes.

## PREPARATION

The brush is important. This finish can be applied with an ordinary decorator's brush but it will be improved and made easier if you use a special French polishing brush. The correct brush for the job is known to me as a 'flatty', though it may have other names in different parts of the world. These brushes are designed especially for applying very quick-drying finishes.

The difference between the ordinary decorator's brush and a flatty is best illustrated by viewing the two brushes from the side (*see* Fig 17.1). The flatty brush is about three times thinner in this side dimension. Unfortunately, these brushes are not commonly available in the average D.I.Y. store. However, they can be found in some model and

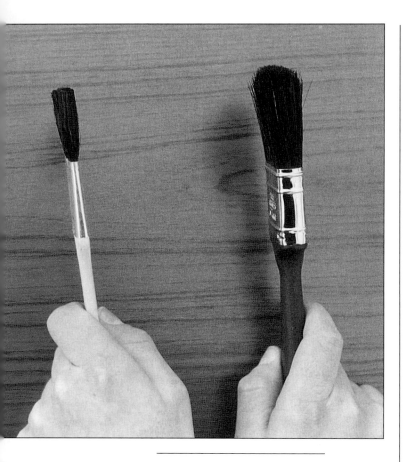

Fig 17.1 ABOVE: **Showing the difference between a traditional decorator's brush (right) – designed to be used with slow-drying finishes such as oil paints and polyurethane varnishes – and a 'flatty', designed for use with quick-drying finishes such as French polish.**

craft shops, so it may be worth ringing around. If not, you can buy one mail order from trade supply houses (ask for a brush to apply French polish), or you may wish to have a go with a normal decorator's brush. Many of my students have used a decorator's brush to very good effect with this technique.

As with French polishing with a rubber it is important that you do not attempt to apply this finish in damp, cold or draughty surroundings, so do not try it in the potting shed on a November morning unless you live in Australia or the Nevada desert.

Next you will need some French polish, colour of your choosing (*see* Chapter 16). This you should thin down with meths to a 50/50 mix.

Fig 17.2 RIGHT: **Applying the polish.**

## APPLICATION

Take your brush and dip just the first 25 per cent of the brush hair into the mix. If you are using a decorator's brush then just dip the first 10 per cent.

Now this is where the skill comes in: you should apply the polish in quick, even strokes as briskly as possible (*see* Fig 17.2) but without splashing it all over yourself, the new wallpaper etc. You should work around the furniture systematically like this:
1. Dip the brush.
2. Apply the polish.
3. Brush out any drips or runs.
4. Move on.

Do not spend hours lovingly stroking the finish out. The polish will dry quickly (depending on temperature) and as soon as it starts to dry the brush will stick to the freshly applied polish leaving a drag mark, which is not what we want. Only let the tips of the brush hair come into contact with the surface.

Just as in applying French polish with a rubber, the aim is to apply lots of very thin coats of polish as evenly as possible. Leave for 15 minutes to dry, then lightly rub down with wet-and-dry paper before repeating the process. Subsequent coats will go on much more easily and will quickly build up into a shine. After about four or five coats, allow the polish to dry overnight.

Rub down the following day, then continue in the same way as the first day. Do not forget to rub down lightly between coats. When rubbing down,

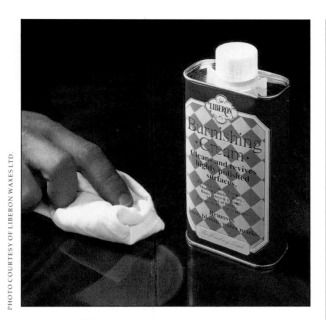

Fig 17.3 A B O V E : **Burnishing cream.**

beware of the edges of wood where it may be possible to rub away the polish completely.

The more you brush, the more you will get the hang of it. If you make a mistake and miss a drip or leave a drag mark in the polish, do not worry, just allow it to dry hard and rub it out with the wet-and-dry. Remember, the more polish you apply, the shinier it will become. As soon as you have built up what you consider to be a suitable finish you can stop. If you would like to get an even higher polish on the furniture, you can achieve it in one of the following ways:

The first way is the simplest; allow the polish to dry for about seven days, then, using a damp rag, rub burnishing cream into the polished finish (see Fig 17.3). Make sure that you do not overdo it, particularly on edges and corners, as this substance is slightly abrasive. Very soon you will see a high polish develop. This will also remove some of the garish quality that is sometimes associated with brushed French polish. Continue over the rest of the furniture, then take a small brush, dip it in some white spirit and brush out any white powder deposits that the rubbing compound leaves behind in small crevices etc. Finally, wipe over with a coat of liquid wax and buff (see Chapter 14).

The next technique for achieving a higher shine is the same process that is employed in the final stages of traditional French polishing and is called

spiriting off (see page 142). Instructions for a satin or matt finish can be found on page 144.

It's as simple as that. If you are lucky, the wood is with you and the drying conditions are good, you can achieve a brushed French polish finish within a couple of hours.

This technique is often used to polish areas and places that are difficult to polish with the traditional rubber methods, such as carved and fretted areas. Sometimes table tops will be finished using a rubber and the less visible legs of the table will be finished with a brush (see Fig 17.4).

As has been stated earlier, French polish is not very durable; it is softened and removed by alcohol and will be damaged by damp and heat. So choose where you place your French-polished furniture with care.

If you wish to colour the finish you can add a spirit stain to the brushing mix. In this way you can get a black (ebony) finish, a red (mahogany) finish, or any other coloured finish you desire (see Chapter 13 on stains and Chapter 21 on ebonizing).

This technique of applying French polish with a brush can also be employed alongside the more traditional French polishing with a rubber. Once you have mastered the absolute beginner's method of French polishing (see Chapter 16), you can experiment with the recipes detailed below.

Fig 17.4 A B O V E : **Pencil brush used to apply polish in crevices.**

## OTHER RECIPES

### THE QUICK AND EASY RECIPE

First fill the grain of the wood as described on page 98, then build up a thick coating of polish with a brush as described in this chapter. Apply the second session with a rubber, as described in Chapter 16, and finish by spiriting off. This recipe is often used on legs and the less visual parts of furniture, as well as on carvings and mouldings.

### THE CRAFTSPERSON'S RECIPE

For the perfect finish, when you have no concern for time or toil – all coats are applied with a rubber – apply the first coats of polish undiluted. Rub down between each session with wet-and-dry and as the finish builds up, thin the polish down, first 50/50 (50 per cent polish mixed with 50 per cent meths), then 60/40, 70/30, 80/20, 90/10, and finally spirit off with 100 per cent meths. If you want to be really fussy, you can substitute some of the rubbing down with wet-and-dry with spiriting off.

### THE BODGER'S RECIPE

Apply all the coats with a brush as described in this chapter. If you are doing this commercially, don't forget to charge for the craftsman's recipe (*see* Fig 17.5).

### MAKING UP YOUR OWN RECIPE

The thickness of the polish, the colour of the polish, the way the rubber is made, how the rubber is charged, how the wood is filled, how many coats to apply, how to spirit off – the list of variables that can make up a French polish recipe is endless. Consequently, so is the number of recipes. They all have their place, and as you become deeply involved in the craft you will undoubtedly collect some more recipes and hopefully make some up for yourself. Whichever recipe you use, you will soon come to realize that every recipe obeys the same principles. Once you have mastered these, the world of French polishing is your oyster.

**Fig 17.5** A B O V E : **Bill Bodger's invoice.**

# CHAPTER 18

# POLYURETHANE
## VARNISHES

PHOTO COURTESY OF RUSTIN'S LTD.

*Polyurethane varnish has the unenviable distinction of being the most maligned finish ever invented by man. It is therefore odd that it is probably the best-selling and most easily available type of finish on the market today. Every D.I.Y. shop, hardware store and ironmongers in the land will carry a selection of polyurethane varnishes.*

## WHAT IS IT?

Because the choice of polyurethane varnish is so vast, with a host of varieties and makes, I will try to define what I am about to talk about by describing the elements that are common to all in this vast range of finishes. It should be said at this stage that although the number of manufacturers of polyurethane finishes is large the method of application for all of them is the same, no matter what name is on the can.

Polyurethane varnish is normally supplied in the same sort of can that decorators' paint is supplied in. It is applied with an ordinary decorators' brush and each coat can take anything between four and 12 hours to dry. All polyurethane varnishes will emit a paint-type smell that will last for as long as the varnish takes to dry. On bare wood it is expected that three coats should be applied. The uncoloured, clear varnish is usually the colour of golden treacle (*see* Fig 18.2). The varnish is thinned, and the brushes are cleaned with white spirit. You can buy the varnish in gloss, satin or matt finish.

The matt finish has no shine at all, being the opposite of gloss which is shiny; satin could be described as having a dull sheen coming halfway between the two. Some polyurethane varnishes are designed for outdoor use. Some varnishes have had a stain added to them, thus a varnish with walnut stain added to it would be called a walnut varnish.

**Fig 18.1** A B O V E : **A can of polyurethane varnish.**

Fig 18.2 A B O V E : **The thickness of polyurethane varnishes vary, but this gluey consistency is typical, and makes it more difficult to obtain a good-looking finish. True, it will cover the wood quicker, but our goal is quality, not speed – so thin it down with white spirit.**

As I have said, polyurethane varnish has to be the most maligned finish ever created. The reason for this is clear: in 99.5 per cent of cases it is very badly applied, resulting in a poor and often ugly finish. Much of this is due to the poor instructions issued to the user by the manufacturers. This is a great pity because it can be applied very easily and can result in a finish that is extremely beautiful.

## PROS AND CONS

Polyurethane varnish has many positive aspects. Firstly, it is very hard-wearing – it is scratch-resistant, it will not be marked by heat or by water, nor will it be damaged by alcohol. It is not brittle like some other hard finishes and so is less likely to be damaged by knocks or bangs, and will 'move' with the wood when the wood expands and contracts according to seasonal changes in humidity. It is ideal for homes with children and for items destined for the kitchen or the bathroom, and it is much used on coffee tables and dining-room tables. The gloss finish is capable of achieving a flawless mirror-like shine if treated in the manner which I shall

soon explain. If an outdoor varnish is used, it can be applied to garden furniture, outdoor toys, windowsills and doors in the greenhouse, as well as on woodwork in the bathroom.

The drawback to this type of finish is that if it is poorly applied it looks terrible. It has a thick, treacly consistency and has a tendency to run, to pick up dirt and dust, and during the long drying process it becomes the most effective insect trap known to man. If gloss finish is badly applied the effect can look very much like a toffee-apple. Polyurethane varnish also tends to flake off if there is inadequate preparation or if it is poorly applied (*see* Fig 18.3)

The coloured polyurethane varnishes which have had a stain added to them are not recommended. If you wish to colour the bare wood then use a separate stain applied directly to the wood: the effect will be far superior. Coloured varnishes have a tendency to obscure the wood under the varnish and to have a very muddied look to them. The more coats of coloured varnish you apply, the muddier it will become and the more the natural wood will be hidden.

Fig 18.3 A B O V E : **The effects of the elements on polyurethane varnish.**

## HOW TO APPLY A GLOSS VARNISH

I will now explain the technique of applying a gloss varnish to achieve a mirror-like shine.

### PREPARATION

The biggest problem to overcome with poly-urethane varnish is the length of the drying time. Because it takes hours to dry, a hundred different things can go wrong. We must try and limit these. The first thing to ensure is that you have an area that is warm and dry, so turn the heating on if necessary. This will speed up the drying process. If you have a choice, do not varnish on days when the local population of midges, daddy-long-legs and gnats have decided to hatch, match and dispatch. If it is a windy day, take this into account; bear in mind that you will have to have some windows open for a free flow of air to aid drying and to release fumes. If the free flow of air is a

force nine blowing off the Atlantic Ocean then it would be wise to postpone varnishing until the storm has blown over. Pin a 'do not disturb' notice to your door so that the vicar does not pop by unexpectedly and try to talk you into becoming a missionary in the Upper Zambezi, or worse still, take charge of the tombola at the summer fête, while you should be concentrating on looking for drips and runs.

If you are doing this in a shed, garage or similar place, sweep the floor and dust the shelves etc. at least 24 hours before you start, to allow the dust that you have disturbed to settle back down again. If you can use a vacuum cleaner, this would be preferable. Lay some dust sheets or old newspaper down to protect the floor as well as keep any floor dust at bay.

Use a clean brush. I shall repeat that: use a clean brush! I am constantly amazed at the sorry specimens that surface during my classes. Do not use a brush that has previously been used for painting,

**Fig 18.4** A B O V E : **Avoid varnishing on days when the local population of midges, daddy-long-legs and gnats have decided to hatch, match and dispatch.**

or for that matter, basting the Sunday joint, cleaning your teeth, or washing down the engine of your car, all of which have been proffered by students as suitable erstwhile jobs for varnishing brushes. No matter how well you have cleaned it, there will always remain some dirt and dust in the base of the bristles. If you do not have one then buy a new brush and keep it specially for varnishing and nothing else. For most jobs a 1½ or 2in (38 or 50mm) brush will do. You do not have to spend lots of money, but at the same time the cheapest is usually a bad buy. Before using a new brush for the first time, give it a clean in some warm water and washing up liquid to remove dust and hairs, then dry it on a clean cloth and varnish a scrap of clean cardboard or wood. Keep brushing until the varnish becomes a bit sticky. The stickiness will remove the loose hairs that inevitably reside in any new brush. Finally, clean the brush in white spirit, shake out the excess white spirit from the bristles, wrap some clingfilm or aluminium cooking foil around the bristles and store in a dust-free environment until ready for use.

All of this may sound as if I am a bit paranoid about dust; it is entirely possible that you can get by without going to these extremes or by short-cutting. Having said that, these efforts will provide you with the perfect finish. Every time!

The other items that you will need are a pot or jar with a neck wide enough to accept your brush, some white spirit, your chosen gloss varnish and some wet-and-dry abrasive paper. You will also need some rubbing compound, some old rags and some wax polish (*see* Fig 18.5).

A word of warning: do not use varnish that has been half-used and then kept in the garden shed or under the sink for a couple of years. Uncle George will often have a vast selection of these varnishes just waiting to be foisted on to the un-suspecting absolute beginner with disastrous re-sults. Varnishes deteriorate with time and often will not dry as well as they ought to. Also, if it has been half-used, a skin will have formed over the top of the varnish which, when removed, will almost certainly leave behind bits of semi-dried varnish, and these are definitely unwelcome. How-

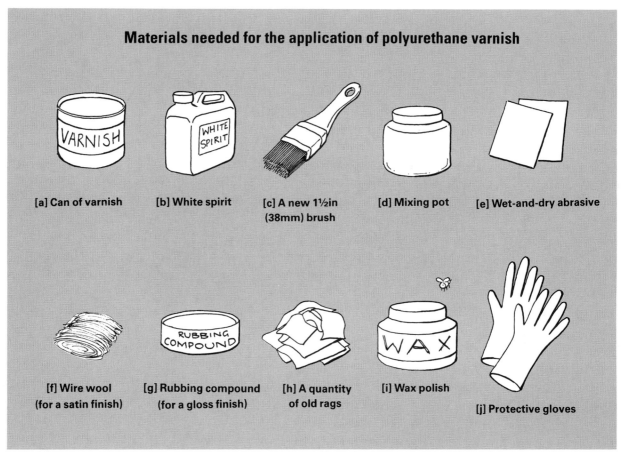

**Materials needed for the application of polyurethane varnish**

[a] Can of varnish   [b] White spirit   [c] A new 1½in (38mm) brush   [d] Mixing pot   [e] Wet-and-dry abrasive

[f] Wire wool (for a satin finish)   [g] Rubbing compound (for a gloss finish)   [h] A quantity of old rags   [i] Wax polish   [j] Protective gloves

**Fig 18.5**

ever, keep this old varnish as I have a recipe that this can be used for (*see* pages 129–30).

In the meantime, nip down to the shops and get some fresh new varnish. If the time and trouble you have spent so far is of any value, it's worth the investment. As the saying goes, 'There be no point spoiling the ship for a ha'pennyworth of tar'.

Before you start, consider raising the furniture off the ground so that you do not have to bend over. This will make working much easier, less tiring and therefore more enjoyable. This will always show in the work that you do. Remember, prepare!

## APPLICATION

Here we go! Stir your chosen varnish slowly with a clean stick or suitable implement for 60 seconds; do not shake it or stir vigorously as we do not want any small air bubbles getting trapped in the varnish (a very common problem).

Pour some of the varnish into your wide-brimmed pot, filling it to halfway. Now thin the varnish with the white spirit, between 10 and 30 per cent depending upon the thickness of the varnish. The varnish should run off the brush with ease; something like the consistency of milk is a good target to head for. Do not worry if it is too thin. It is far better for it to be too thin than too thick.

A new development in varnishes is the non-drip variety, which should not be thinned in the above-mentioned way. However, you can ease your path by dipping the first 25 per cent of your brush in a jar of white spirit, shaking off the excess before dipping it into the non-drip varnish.

Apply the first coat of varnish, working systematically around the furniture. Do not flit from one section to another. If you work to a system you will be less likely to miss a bit. Only dip the first 25 per cent of the bristles into the varnish (*see* Fig 18.6). This will prevent you picking up too much varnish and dripping it all over the floor, your hands and the cat etc.

Once you have deposited your brushful of varnish on to the bare wood you can brush the varnish out, spreading it as far as it will go. The more you spread the varnish, the less chance there will be of it dripping or sagging as it dries. Pay particular

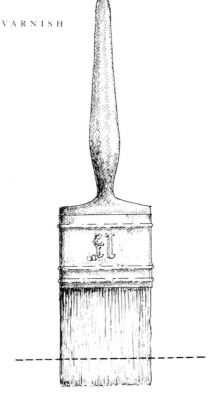

Fig 18.6 A B O V E : **Only dip the first 25 per cent of the bristles into the varnish.**

attention to carved areas; do not let the varnish build up too thickly. When you think you have completed the first coat, you are ready to practise a most important aspect of the art of the furniture restorer.

**THE VARNISH APPLICATOR'S DIP** This is a centuries-old ritual dance performed by craftspeople the world over. Essential though it is to fine varnish application, it can not be learnt, only absorbed. I shall attempt to describe.

The dance is performed at the end of each application of varnish and its purpose is to ensure that there are no drips, runs, sags or sections of furniture that have been missed. With a brush in one hand and a half-filled pot of varnish in the other, you screw your eyes up into a most unhealthy squint. Then, like some demented feline creature eyeing its prey, you slowly circle around your furniture, darting in upon a suspect area and flicking it with a deft brush of varnish, before retreating momentarily, your head cocked to one side, to continue your dance. This is interspersed with frequent dips of the knee and constant peering, before finally dropping to the floor to compete the second phase of the dance. This consists of a repeat of the first part, only now you shuffle around the floor on your knees in a third-rate impersonation of Toulouse Lautrec, prowling around the underside of the furniture where some of the worst drips have been known to lurk. Not until you find yourself doing this can you consider yourself a member of the Brotherhood of Varnish Applicators.

What I am trying to say in a very roundabout way is that once you have applied the varnish, you still have to patrol around the piece for a short while, keeping an eye open for drips, runs and missed sections, particularly in the areas that are easily missed, such as underneath.

If your project has been stained, on the first coat the brush will inevitably pick up some of the coloured stain from the wood. This is undesirable as the varnish gets muddied by the stain, so the first coat of varnish applied over a stain is always applied with the minimum of brushing out. Be quick and decisive. Put the varnish on with the brush and then leave it. Do not spend hours brushing it around as this will shift the stain from the wood. By employing this technique, the wood and the stain become sealed in, and the stain will not be picked up in the next coat of varnish.

Leave the first coat to dry overnight in a warm environment. The next morning it should be ready for 'denibbing'. This is a process of lightly rubbing with fine abrasive paper to remove all roughness from the surface of the finish. At this stage the finish may not look rough, but if you were to compare the denibbed surface with an untreated surface by running the palm of your hand over it, the difference would become obvious. Do not rub on corners and edges of the furniture as this will very quickly rub through to the wood. If you discover any drips or other blemishes you can simply remove them at this stage by rubbing them down with the abrasive paper. Wipe away any dust from the denibbing with a clean rag dampened with white spirit. Now you are ready to start all over again, only this time the varnish will not soak in as readily and you can make a brushful of varnish cover a lot more wood. Also, the subsequent coats will dry more quickly.

As each coat is applied the shine will develop. Do not forget to denib lightly between each coat. You can apply as many coats as it takes to obtain the thickness of finish you require. If you have thinned down as I have directed and you want to go for the mirror-like shine, I would suggest a minimum of five coats, but it will depend upon the thickness of the varnish and the type of wood that you are working with.

Hopefully, there are no runs, no drips, no hairs from the brush, no bubbles in the varnish and no insects or other small creatures entombed in your varnish like prehistoric fleas in amber. Now here comes the best bit! You have got your furniture coated with sufficient varnish. It is very glossy, but it is not a very nice gloss; it is too garish, too much like a toffee-apple. This is because you haven't quite finished yet – there is still one last stage. First you must allow the varnish to set really hard. To be on the safe side I would suggest seven days in a warm room.

Whilst you are waiting you can nip down to the car accessory shop and ask for some rubbing compound. Like many things that the furniture restorer uses, it will come in a number of different proprietary makes. Don't let this worry you; for our purposes, they are all the same.

Rubbing compound is a fine abrasive paste very similar to metal polish. Car owners use it on a clean cloth to rub down the paintwork of old cars to bring back the original colour and remove engrained dirt etc. Furniture restorers find a variety of uses for it. Use it to polish your varnished furniture and the effect is amazing. It will start to shine and reflect like a mirror. The more you polish, the more it will shine. It will also take away that toffee-apple look that is so disliked by professional wood finishers.

One word of warning: do not rub too hard at edges or corners. Remember, it is an abrasive and will go right through to the wood if used excessively.

When you have finished, some of the white rubbing compound powder will inevitably remain in the nooks and crannies. This can be removed by washing it away with a brushful of white spirit.

The finishing touch is provided by a rub over with a thin wax polish. Give the whole piece a thin coating of wax (*see* Chapter 14) and then polish up with a clean duster. Finally, sit down and reap the benefits by staring at length at a job well done.

## HOW TO APPLY A NON-GLOSS VARNISH

If you prefer a less shiny appearance, a satin finish may be to your liking. There are two ways that this can be achieved. First you could apply a gloss finish as described above, except that you do not finish off with the rubbing compound or have to wait seven days for it to go completely hard. Instead, leave for two days, then go to work with some medium- or fine-grade wire wool and some bees-wax. Rub the wax into the varnish with the wire wool, stroking with the grain of the wood, then finish off with a light waxing. The more you stroke with the wire wool, the duller it will become. The trick with this finish is to make sure you do not scrub the wire wool backwards and forwards but stroke the wire wool using the same action as you would to stroke a dog (*see* Fig 18.7). N.B. If you find yourself wanting to take your furniture for long walks, take a break. You are working too hard.

The second way of achieving a satin finish is to use a satin varnish. Apply this using exactly the same method as the gloss, only this time you will not need to use rubbing compound or wire wool as the varnish will be left with a satin finish after the last coat without need for any further treatment. This is obviously a lot easier than the gloss method, though many say it is not as beautiful.

If you desire a matt finish then use a matt varnish and apply exactly as has been described for the gloss, except there is no need for rubbing compound or wax.

If you want to colour polyurethane varnishes for patching in faded or worn areas and for colouring fillers, then add oil stain or artists' oil colour (*see* Chapter 13).

Most problems occur with polyurethane varnish when it is applied too thickly. The secret is to apply many thin coats, each one being allowed to dry and then rubbed down with fine-grade sandpaper or wet-and-dry abrasive paper before the application of the next thin coat. The success of this method is due to the fact that a thin coat dries a lot quicker than a thick coat; it is sticky for a much shorter time, so less dust settles on it and bugs do not get trapped in the gluey film. There is also less chance for runs and drips to develop. Remember,

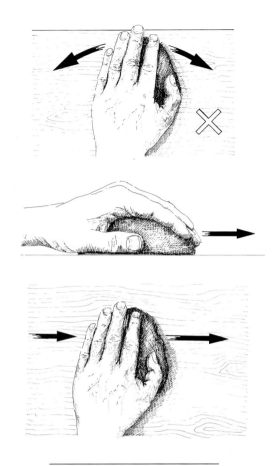

**Fig 18.7** A B O V E : **Do not stroke the wire wool backwards and forwards – only with the grain.**

the thicker the varnish, the longer it will take to dry and the more potential there is for problems to occur. The thinner the varnish, the quicker it will take to dry and the less potential for problems to occur.

A common problem with some outdoor polyurethane varnishes is that, after prolonged exposure to the elements, they can eventually break down and flake off, leaving bare wood. This bare wood is then bleached by the sun and becomes most unsightly and difficult to repair. If you have this experience then remove all the deteriorated finish with sandpaper and patch up with Danish oil, thinned polyurethane varnish or oil from another country (*see* Chapter 15). This will protect the bare wood until you decide to strip and refinish.

If you intend to store varnish for any length of time then push the lid firmly into place and stand the can upside down for 30 minutes (check for leaks after two minutes). This will seal the lid in place and prevent a skin forming.

# CHAPTER 19

# MODERN
# MASS-PRODUCTION
## —— LACQUERS ——

PHOTO COURTESY OF BINKS-BULLOWS LTD.

*There are a number of finishes used in the production of mass-produced furniture.*
*These include nitro-cellulose lacquer, cellulose lacquer, polyester lacquer, synthetic*
*lacquer, two-part lacquer, acid-cured lacquer, pre-catalysed lacquer and melamine*
*lacquer.*

It is not strictly fair of me to lump all the above finishes together into one group and call them 'modern lacquers'. To the specialist factory wood finisher, they differ in some significant and important ways. However, from the novice furniture restorer's point of view, and for the purposes of this book, they display a number of similarities.

As a rule, most mass-produced furniture made since 1945 will have some form of modern lacquered finish: televisions, toilet-roll holders, desk tops, bunkbeds, fire surrounds, kitchen cabinets, coffins, toys and of course furniture. You name it, if it is wooden and produced for profit in quantity, then it will be finished with a modern lacquer. It is also worth noting that the finishes sprayed on to cars are similar to the ones used for furniture.

These finishes are designed with mass production and the mass-producer in mind. If you had the job of producing 30,000 kitchen stools, each with a heat- and damp-resistant, hard-wearing finish and wanted to show a healthy profit, then you would appreciate that French polishing, hand

---

**Fig 19.1** A B O V E: **Water-washed spray booth.**

waxing or polyurethane varnishing are not really on the cards.

To the mass-producer, cheapness and speed are paramount, and this is what modern finishes are designed for: to be sprayed on to the finished item by skilled craftspeople in modern factory units, and to dry very quickly (often in specially designed drying booths), so the product can be packaged and delivered to the stores ready for sale.

From the consumer's point of view, this is a mixed blessing. The consumer gets reasonably priced furniture with a finish that is tough, hard-wearing and easy to care for. The problems occur when the furniture starts getting a little old and tatty. Restoration of this finish is difficult.

Manufacturers would argue that this is one of its benefits. After all, they make no profit from you restoring furniture and getting another 25 years' wear out of it. No, the manufacturers, in line with the twentieth-century practice of built-in obsolescence, are relying on the fact that when your furniture is 'past its best', you will throw it away and buy some more, ideally from the same place where you bought the last lot. This makes fine business sense. However, as is often the case, fine business sense does not mean fine environmental sense. Or fine for the potential restorer.

The next obvious question is, what use is this type of finish to the novice furniture restorer? Although this family of finishes is primarily de-signed for mass production, some finish manufac-turers supply a limited range of 'modern finishes' for the D.I.Y. market and for the use of smaller woodworking businesses.

## ADVANTAGES

For the furniture restorer and woodworker this kind of finish has a number of benefits: it is very fast-drying – a thin coat can be touch-dry in a few minutes; it has a high level of solids and therefore it builds up very quickly to a thick finish – much faster than any comparable finish. It is a very durable and hard-wearing finish, suitable for table tops, kitchen cupboards and the like. For this reason it is also recommended for households with young children, misbehaving pets, inconsiderate teenagers, absent-minded pensioners, wild party

throwers and parents who do not want to scream themselves hoarse every time someone puts a hot cup on the coffee table.

It is available in gloss, satin and matt finishes. The gloss finish can be burnished to an incredible, flawless mirror-like shine by using burnishing cream (*see* Fig 19.2). The satin finish can be used as a single-coat sealer before waxing to give a hybrid 'ancient and modern' finish. Because of its hard-wearing qualities and the fact that it dries quickly,

**Fig 19.2** A B O V E : **The high-gloss finish found on many guitars and pianos is often achieved by spraying them with a modern lacquer.**

it is highly suitable for use on floors and staircases. Some manufacturers make a formula just for this purpose.

It is heat-, alcohol-, scratch- and wear-resistant, so is often used on bar tops and in food preparation areas. It will resist wet and dampness, however I would not recommend it in areas that are permanently damp such as showers, because the water will eventually find its way underneath the finish and it will start to flake.

The colour can vary from crystal-clear to a yellow straw colour. Some of the cellulose finishes can start to yellow within weeks, so beware of this with lighter-coloured woods, and question your supplier on this point.

It is possible to obtain tinted and coloured versions of these finishes but again I would advise consulting individual suppliers for advice. In the past I have tinted lacquers with oil stains and spirit stains. If you wish to try a coloured finish the only advice I have for you is experiment. Usually slight changes in colour (tinting) are no problem, but be wary of adding too much colour, as this may have adverse effects.

## DISADVANTAGES

With all these outstanding attributes I feel sure that many of you will be rubbing your hands with glee and searching for the phone book to find your nearest supplier. Hold tight. There are always a number of drawbacks to every finish and this one is no exception. The biggest problem with this type of finish can be summed up in one word – smell.

This finish is *not* absolute beginner-friendly; in fact it is not anybody-friendly. To achieve all those quick-drying, hard-as-nails, cheap-spraying attributes, it is necessary to use some very powerful chemical solvents. These are usually highly volatile, pungent and flammable chemicals. Cosmetic nail varnish is a variety of this modern wood finish. The solvents used in wood finishes are similar, so if you are thinking of trying a modern lacquer take a tentative whiff of the average nail polish to see what you are letting yourself in for. Do not forget the quantities involved. The surface area that you are to cover is going to be far greater than the average fingernail, and therefore the smell is going to be that much stronger. If you are using this in the home then the smell will permeate everything for at least 12 hours. This is fine if you are expecting unwelcome visitors. Otherwise, I suggest you only use this in a workshop or out of doors.

On a more serious note, some of the solvents used in modern finishes can be very dangerous. Take note of the instructions on the package. Be over-generous with the safety preparations. Do not use in enclosed areas or if you have medical problems with your lungs, eyes, nose, skin or stomach. If you are anxious, consult your doctor. In a factory situation, where these chemicals are being used all day long, the solvents and smells can be safely dealt with by using extraction fans, special spraying booths and safety clothing that would make a deep-sea diver look overdressed (*see* Fig 19.1).

For the above reasons, many manufacturers have removed a lot of the chemical smells associated with these finishes. These improved types are labelled as low-odour formulas. If you have a choice, use them. However, these improvements only lessen the problem, they do not eradicate it. If you are worried, ask the manufacturer or retailer about the smell. If you speak to them very nicely they may even take the top off and let you have a whiff, but this is a dubious pleasure.

Do not think that you can avoid these problems by wearing an ordinary dust mask. You will need a sophisticated and expensive mask to solve this problem. In my experience, the best place to apply these finishes is out of doors when there is a very light breeze and, ideally, a little sunshine too. I hate to sound as if I am putting people off attempting new techniques, but as I say in Chapter 3, ignorance is the biggest threat to your health. With that in mind, I'll tell you of the other problem with this type of finish: inflammability. The same volatile chemicals that cause the smell are also highly inflammable. Do not smoke, beware of naked flames, door-to-door barbeque salesmen and itinerant fire eaters.

Another disadvantage of modern lacquers is their unsuitability for use out of doors or on garden furniture. This is because they dry very hard and brittle, and are therefore not flexible enough to withstand the constant expansion and contraction of timber from wet to dry.

This brittleness leads to another problem encountered with this type of finish, particularly when used in the thick build-up, high-gloss situations best characterized by modern piano and guitar finishes. That is the problem of chipping. If the finish is knocked or dropped, it is quite likely to chip.

Lastly, it should go without saying that this finish is not environmentally friendly, due to the evaporation of solvents into the atmosphere.

**Fig 19.3** B E L O W : **Suction- or siphon-fed gun.**

PHOTO COURTESY OF BINKS-BULLOWS LTD.

## SUPPLIERS

Now you know the positive and the negative sides, you can decide yourself if you want to use it. If you decide to give it a go, the next problem is where to get supplies. First, try the local D.I.Y. store or craft and specialist wood suppliers. If they do not stock it they will often know of a suitable finish and order it specially for you. Ask.

If you have problems, you can contact one of the trade supply houses listed on page 188. Many suppliers only sell large quantities; five litres (one gallon) is normal, although some suppliers do sell smaller quantities. Ask their information department what type of finish they recommend for your particular project or projects. Do not forget to tell them you will be applying it with a brush and that you are an absolute beginner. It is worth noting that although the quantities sold in these establishments are probably excessive to your requirements, the price per litre will usually be very keen. If nothing else, you will have a lifetime supply of clear nail polish at a very good price.

## APPLICATION

A good-quality brush is essential for this job. Always use a new brush for the very good reason that, no matter how well you have cleaned the brush from the last job, there will always, I repeat, always be some left over paint in the roots of the bristles. It may have been there for weeks, it may have been there for years, but one thing is certain: when the old brush comes into contact with the solvents used in modern lacquers, that old paint is going to redissolve and, just like your life flashing before your eyes, you will see every shade of paint that you have ever applied with that brush flow effortlessly out, smearing the project that you have spent the best weeks of your life on.

If possible, use a brush that is designed specifically for use with modern lacquers. These are not commonly available, but if your supplier stocks modern lacquers they should also stock special brushes. These brushes have no paint on the handle which could be dissolved by the solvent fumes. Also, the bristles are held in place by non-dissolving glue.

First strip the furniture back to bare wood. If you have stained the wood, the first coat of lacquer is liable to pick up some of the stain on the brush and redeposit it elsewhere. Avoid this by applying the first coat as thinly and quickly as possible, with a minimum of brushing out.

For this first coat on stained wood, it is advisable to decant a small quantity of the lacquer into a jar so that the stain is not transferred to the main supply of lacquer. This first coat can then be easily thinned down with 10 per cent of the appropriate thinners.

Thinners is a special liquid used for thinning the finish so that it becomes more liquid and flows more easily; it is also used for cleaning brushes and cleaning up splashes and spillages. Ideally this is purchased at the same time as the lacquer. Take advice from your supplier about suitable thinners.

Do not dip the brush too deeply into the lacquer. No more than the first 25 per cent of the brush should be immersed. Work around the project methodically, lacquering one section completely before moving on to the next. The first coat will usually be absorbed into the fibres of the wood. Allow this to dry.

Adhere to the suggested drying and recoating times displayed on the lacquer container. Rub down between each coat with fine-grade wet-and-dry abrasive paper. Remove any dust, loose brush hairs and anything else that may have become embedded in the lacquer, and repeat the process. Depending on the type of wood you are applying it to, the thickness and make of lacquer, and the finish that you are trying to achieve, between two and five coats will be sufficient.

Personally I use this type of finish in one of two ways. Firstly, to provide a very quick-and-easy, low-key, hard-wearing finish, I apply two coats of matt or satin finish. This finish can be completed in 30 minutes if the conditions are right. Or, for the full-blooded, over-the-top, get-the-sunglasses-out, turn-the-lights-down, mirror-finish, high-gloss shine (*see* Fig 19.4), I have a slightly more elaborate method. The finish can comprise any number of applications (until it's right), rubbed down between coats with 600 grit wet-and-dry, and allowed to dry for 24 hours. Then I apply rubbing compound with a damp rag and rub until the shine becomes unbearable, and you can read this book in the reflection. Finally, finish off with the thinnest of wax polish to clean off any surplus burnishing cream.

Subsequent care consists of a wipe over with a damp rag, and buffing with a soft cloth. Do not use spray waxes or any other sort of wax in the cleaning of the surface finish, as they will just leave a wax deposit on the surface, and make it smeary.

## RESTORATION

From the absolute beginner's point of view, there are a number of restoration techniques that you can try out on modern-finished furniture. The first and most obvious is to strip the furniture back to bare wood and start again (as detailed in Chapter 6). This is recommended for furniture that needs a lot of repair. It can then be refinished with another modern lacquer finish, or one of the other types of finish detailed in other chapters. Any other attempt at repair has to be done with fingers crossed and reference to Chapter 8.

Taking everything into consideration, I would not advise the absolute beginner to use this type of finish until they have experienced some of the other finishes detailed in this book.

If you are determined, try to find one of the finishes specially made for the amateur D.I.Y. person. Some companies supply complete starter kits that include everything the beginner is going to need; these will typically comprise a lacquer, hardener, thinners, burnishing cream and full instructions (*see* page 188 for information on suppliers).

# CHAPTER 20

# WATER-BASED
# VARNISHES

PHOTO COURTESY OF CUPRINOL.

*If you have never been involved in using wood finishes before, you may now be thinking that all wood-finishing preparations are either very smelly, hazardous to your health, or a fire risk, and in some cases all of these. If you object to the user-unfriendliness of the finishes so far described, you are now in for a treat.*

Water-based finishes are a relatively new innovation on the D.I.Y. furniture restoration scene. They are becoming much easier to find in the stores and are quickly growing in their popularity. This popularity is largely due to their environmentally friendly properties and their ease of use.

Most wood finishes consist of a solid which is made liquid by the addition of a solvent. When the finish is spread thinly on a piece of wood the solvent evaporates and the liquified solids return to their former solid state. When the solvent evaporates, it 'disappears' into the atmosphere. French polish has meths as a solvent, wax has turpentine, polyurethane varnishes have white spirit, and so on. With water-based finishes the solvent is harmless water. This fact itself is a good enough reason for anyone to become familiar with these finishes.

## ADVANTAGES

Apart from these environmental considerations, this family of finishes contains other benefits. They are quick drying – between 10 and 30 minutes depending upon make and ambient conditions. They are easily applied with an ordinary decorator's brush; they dry to a crystal-clear film and will not yellow with age (a very important quality when dealing with light-coloured woods); the smell during application is a very pleasant, clean, detergent-type smell, which makes a change from some of the more overpowering and dangerous odours that some finishes emit.

If you are a chain-smoker, this is the only finish in this book that does not contain some sort of fire

**Fig 20.1** ABOVE: **A can of water-based varnish.**

risk. If you used to be a chain-smoker or suffer from a lung disorder, this finish will not aggravate any breathing problems. It is an ideal finish to use if you are restoring furniture and you would like the kids to help, or kids and pets are likely to be around.

It is hard wearing and will withstand assault by boiling water and alcohol-based products, but most manufacturers warn against cleaning with harsh chemicals or abrasive cleaners. Having said that, at this moment I am wearing a pair of jeans that eight months ago had some coloured water-based finish accidentally spilt on them; the jeans have subsequently faded with numerous washings, but the water-based finish is stubbornly staying put (*see* Fig 20.2). (Clean off splashes and spillages whilst still wet!)

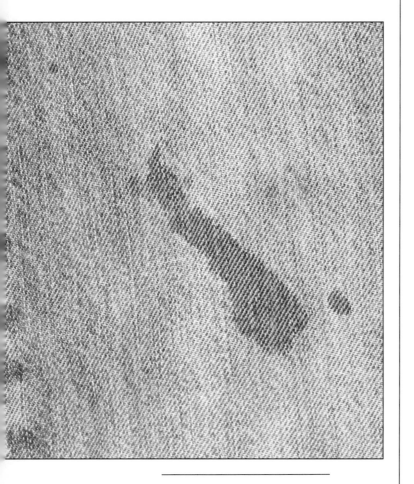

Fig 20.2 A B O V E : **This water-based stain has remained on my jeans through several washes, in spite of manufacturer's advice that the finish will not survive harsh washing.**

## DISADVANTAGES

All in all it sounds like every D.I.Y. furniture restorer's dream. However, nothing is perfect. As with anything new, there will always be some people who are against it, simply because it is not traditional. This argument is all well and good when the furniture requiring a finish is an antique; however, if we were to extend these sentiments to other walks of life, you would be reading this information from half a ton of stone tablets. Besides, once this finish is applied, most of us would not be able to tell the difference between this and many other types of finish.

Perhaps the biggest drawback with water-based finishes is the fact that they can raise the grain of the wood. This can be a big problem if you are looking for perfect, marble-smooth surfaces. There are two ways in which you can deal with this problem. First, you can wet the grain of the bare wood prior to finishing, thereby raising it. Then allow the wood to dry thoroughly and sand down with fine-grade abrasive paper. When the wood is made wet again the grain will now stay flat. Problem solved. However, do not try this technique on veneered surfaces as you are liable to damage the veneer.

The following method is far more suitable for veneers, but you should still guard against overwetting. Apply a thin coat of varnish, allow to dry and then rub down. On solid wood you can use both of these methods in tandem to get a perfectly smooth surface.

There is one other method of getting around the problem that should be considered; that is, using the natural decorative qualities of raised grain. It works very well on nicely figured woods, particularly pine, oak and elm. Raise the grain of the wood by wetting as described above; for best effect you may have to wet it a number of times. When dry, varnish over the top. I have seen this used to great effect on doors and other architectural fittings with a clear satin water-based finish and also with water-based paints. It results in a natural 'textured' surface that can look quite stunning. It should be said, however, that its success is dependent on the type of wood used, and a little luck.

## PREPARATION

**Fig 20.3** A B O V E : **Water-based finished are a milky-white colour when liquid.**

Different manufacturers will provide different instructions for the use of their individual products. However, I have compiled some general guidelines to give you some idea of what is involved and how to get the best results.

The thinners for this finish is ordinary tap water; if you are a perfectionist you could use bottled mineral water, but personally I can't tell the difference. Some manufacturers warn against thinning the varnish too much as it can cause the finish to become cloudy. If the container does not make this clear, contact the manufacturer. Do not presume you should thin it with water.

Use a new brush to apply the finish. Before using it, clean it in warm soapy water and dry thoroughly. If you were to use an old brush, the crystal-clear finish would highlight any dirt, hairs or colour left in the brush, especially on light woods.

When liquid, the water-based finishes are a milky-white colour, but don't worry – they dry clear (*see* Fig 20.3). If you shop around, you can

find water-based finishes for both indoor and outdoor use, as well as a special flooring quality finish (*see* Fig 20.4). All manufacturers will carry gloss, satin and matt formulations; some will also supply water-based stains, tints and paints (*see* page 188).

As with many other finishes, the ambient conditions are important. Water-based finishes should not be applied in cold, damp, dusty or windy conditions, nor should they be applied during periods of high humidity. All of these conditions will adversely affect the finish. Also, because these finishes are very quick drying, avoid direct sunlight or heat during application, otherwise the finish will become sticky, the brush will drag and the final finish will be spoiled.

**Fig 20.4** A B O V E : **A can of water-based floor varnish.**

## APPLICATION

Apply the first coat as thinly as possible to the bare wood and brush out quickly before it becomes tacky (*see* Fig 20.5). Allow to dry, then rub down any raised grain. Wipe off any dust with a damp cloth. From now on you should not experience any further raised grain. Further coats are applied in the same way. Just rub over with fine abrasive to remove any imperfections in the finish between coats. Stop when you have a good build-up of varnish (*see* Fig 20.6). In places of high wear, such as table tops, you can apply an extra coat or two to aid durability.

The gloss finish can be burnished seven days after application with a rubbing compound to provide a mirror-like finish in the same way as polyurethane varnishes (*see* pages 151–4). If you feel the need to improve the look of the satin and matt finishes, they can be treated with wire wool and wax (*see* page 155).

You can use any of the different types of water-based finish as a sealer before waxing, but allow the varnish to dry hard before applying the wax.

Cleaning of brushes could not be simpler; just run the brush under warm soapy water, then dry with a cloth. Do not allow the brush to harden between coats; either wash out between applications as described, or keep the brush in a tumbler of water. The cheapness and the convenience of the thinners and brush wash should be taken into account when judging the cost of these finishes.

## RESTORATION

When the finish eventually deteriorates through old age or wear and tear, it is a simple job to repair; just rub down with a fine abrasive paper and re-coat. If it is a well-used piece of furniture, clean down the surface with some white spirit to remove grease, dirt and wax before rubbing down and recoating.

If the project has been stained, you will have to be careful, as the brush will 'pick up' this stain and muddy the finish. One way around this is to use a cheap trigger-operated garden spray, the type commonly used for spraying insecticide (*see* Fig 20.7). Spray methodically, giving a good spray

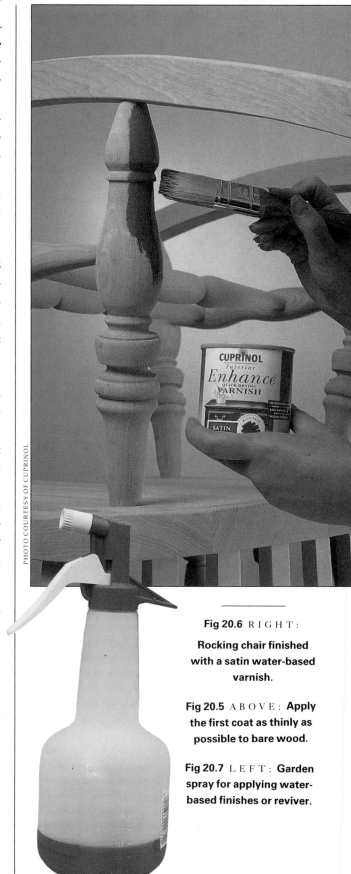

PHOTO COURTESY OF CUPRINOL

**Fig 20.6** RIGHT:
**Rocking chair finished with a satin water-based varnish.**

**Fig 20.5** ABOVE: **Apply the first coat as thinly as possible to bare wood.**

**Fig 20.7** LEFT: **Garden spray for applying water-based finishes or reviver.**

coating of finish to one area at a time. Wipe off any excess or drips straight away with a cotton cloth without interfering too much with the stained surface. Then move on to the next part of your furniture. It usually takes two or three coats from the spray before the stain is fully sealed in. If you wish, you can complete the finishing process by applying the final coats in the same way.

If you are forced by necessity to do your furniture restoration in the house, then you will find the low odour, zero fire risk and high safety factor of these finishes irresistible. Additionally, it is quick drying, a must for light-coloured timber, and so environmentally friendly you could almost varnish a beagle with it. I recommend every absolute beginner to give water-based varnishes a try.

# CHAPTER 21

# EBONIZING

PHOTO COURTESY OF BUCKINGHAMSHIRE COLLEGE.

*For the uninitiated, ebonizing is the craft of making ordinary, run-of-the-mill wood look like ebony. This is the furniture restorer's equivalent of the medieval sorcerer transforming lead into gold.*

## WHY EBONIZE?

Ebony is a magnificent and exotic timber which has one large drawback: it is fiendishly expensive. However, it is also fiendishly beautiful. Put the two together and you get a very high demand, with a prohibitively priced supply. Add a few hundred years of craftspersons' ingenuity and you will find at least a dozen recipes for faking, copying and reproducing the look of ebony. If you then add another few hundred years of Uncle Georges having a go, you will have another half a dozen bodges.

This sharply characterizes the two classes of ebonizing. First, the highly skilled efforts of the true craftsperson who endeavours to copy exactly the look of the finest-grade ebony cabinetwork. And second, Uncle George's method, which should more properly be called staining the wood jet black. Whatever it is called, Uncle George's method is still a very useful and, when done with skill, beautiful finish. It is a little easier to accomplish than the orthodox method, simply because this process is not so concerned with the finer details of ebonizing, such as copying the grain structure of ebony, or disguising the true nature of the wood.

**Fig 21.1** A B O V E : **Ebonized wood cabinet (1871).**

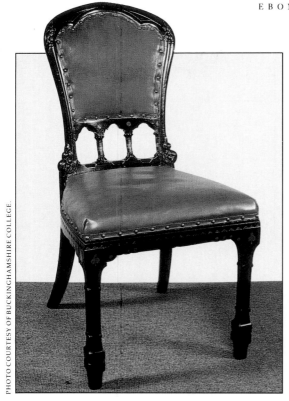

**Fig 21.2** A B O V E : **Ebonized birch chair (1865).**

**Fig 21.3** A B O V E : **Ebonized chair.**

**Fig 21.4** A B O V E : **Ebonized chair and sideboard,
designed by E W Godwin.**

## A LIFESAVER FINISH

The description that I will give encompasses both types of finish. I shall let you decide which is best for your project. From the furniture restorer's point of view these finishes are invaluable. They have three marvellous and important properties. First, they look very exotic and beautiful; second, the look is very easy to achieve; third, they are what I have come to refer to as a 'lifesaver finish.'

A lifesaver finish is exactly what the name implies – when you have had to use half a ton of filler to rebuild the back of a carved chair; when you have had to replace the mahogany table top with plywood because that's all you can afford; when you decide that the environmental implications of using three litres of bleach to remove the ink stain from your finest writing desk are too much to bear; when you tried to stain the sideboard a light oak effect and you picked up the wrong container and stained it peacock blue; when you tried to burn the paint off the chair with a blow torch and had to call the fire brigade to finish the job – it's in these instances that the furniture restorer really appreciates the value of the ebony lifesaver finish. In short it does not matter what you, nature, your

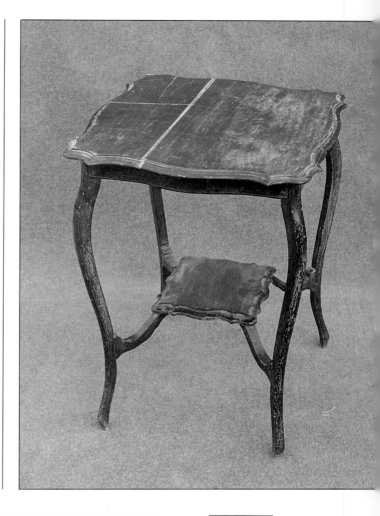

**Fig 21.6** ABOVE: **This elegant table is an ideal candidate for ebonizing.**

**Fig 21.5** LEFT: **Sometimes the music can get too hot! In which case try an ebonized finish.**

children, or past generations have done to the furniture; all of the most obscene blemishes imaginable will disappear quickly and forever beneath the ebonized finish (*see* Fig 21.5).

But all of this damage limitation talk ignores the other important attribute of the ebonized finish; it is, as I have said, extremely beautiful. If you have never experienced ebony, the easiest way to get a feel of it is to look at the black keys of an old piano keyboard. This is ebony; very smooth, very hard, very satiny, close grained and jet black.

It has to be said at this stage that an ebony finish will not always look right on every piece of furniture. To the tutored eye, true ebony furniture is usually slender, fragile and elegant in style. This style is a reflection of its rarity and the small sections that it is naturally available in (*see* Fig 21.6). If the furniture you apply this finish to is of a rugged, large, robust style, it may look slightly 'wrong', but I should not let such details deter you from using this finish. These are just 'awareness guides' to help you understand the finish's finer points.

The finish that I am about to describe to you is the traditional Victorian craftsman's ebonizing technique. In essence this is a satin, black French polish finish. Therefore, it will have the same negative and positive characteristics as any other French polish, except that it will not show as many discoloration marks, e.g. ink stains, and, as it is a satin finish, smaller scratches will not be so noticeable.

## PREPARATION

The first essential for proper ebonizing is a close-grained wood. The old-time fakers – sorry, craftsmen – used to employ a variety of different types of wood to copy the ebony look. However, since you are not making the furniture, only restoring it, this aspect is beyond your control. But it is worth knowing that of the common furniture-making woods, beech, close-grained mahogany, and fruit woods such as apple, lime and pear are very good for this job.

If you have a very open-grained wood, you could always fill the grain (*see* Chapter 12). Without a filler, open-grained woods will not pass muster as an ebonized finish, but they will still look very attractive with jet-black finishes.

You will need some black spirit stain, some French polish and some methylated spirit, as well as a French polishing brush (*see* Chapter 17). Black spirit stain is best bought in powder form and mixed to your own strength using methylated spirit. You can buy spirit stain in liquid form, but often this is not strong enough to turn the wood jet black. For something of the size of a chair, you will need approximately a teaspoonful of powder. To this add ¾ of a pint (0.426 litre) of meths. Test this on the wood by painting the stain on with a brush. It should totally obliterate the colour of the wood and turn it charcoal black. If the mix is too strong then a black powder will be left on the surface of the wood; if it is too weak then the colour of the wood will not be completely obscured and it will look a greyish blue. When you have achieved the correct strength, paint the rest of the project with the stain. Try not to handle the furniture too much at this stage, as you are very soon likely to end up looking like an overworked chimney sweep.

Now you have to mix some black French polish. This you do by pouring the required amount of French polish into a wide-brimmed jar and adding the same quantity of black spirit stain.

## APPLICATION

Apply three coats of this finish as described in Chapter 17. Rub down very lightly between coats, being careful not to rub away stain at corners and edges. If you do remove stain, then apply some neat stain to the area with an artist's brush and polish over the top.

The crucial test of a good coating of stain is to view the project in bright sunlight. So when you have put your first coat of polish on, take it out of doors at midday for an inspection. Better still, take the day off, put in in the back of the car and take it to the park – the rest will do you good. You may be surprised at how much is disclosed by pure sunlight, and how much is hidden by artificial lighting.

When you have built up a thick enough surface and it is looking glossy, leave it overnight to dry. Next morning, stroke the surface over with fine-grade wire wool and a liquid wax (*see* Chapter 14).

Be sure to stroke the surface *with* the grain and keep the stroking action straight. Do not scrub in a windscreen wiper motion, as this will lead to curved scratches that will ruin the ebony grain effect.

When you think you have finished, buff with a soft rag. Often after you have buffed, you will spot areas you have missed and that are too shiny; go back and rub with the wire wool some more. Beware of rubbing too heavily over edges, corners, carved and moulded areas. If you do, touch in with some black French polish. All the while you are involved in this process, try to keep in mind the type of finish you are trying to achieve: very satiny, very hard and very black. If this job is done properly, it is almost impossible to tell the difference between the real thing and your copy. There are always other ways to produce similar effects, but this one is the orthodox Victorian method and to my mind is still the best.

If you prefer a harder-wearing finish, you may like to try staining the wood with the same spirit dyes, and then adding the remaining stain to some satin finish cellulose lacquer. This will provide a similar but much tougher finish.

## STAINING BLACK WITHOUT EBONIZING

If you just want to stain the project black and then coat with a finish, you can choose any of the finishes so far described in this book. One very good method that I have used before is to rub black gloss oil paint into the wood (thinned with a little white spirit first) (*see* Fig 21.7) and then overcoat with some satin polyurethane varnish. The care and maintenance of this black finish depends on the type of finish you apply over the stain. However, if you happen to chip, scratch or in any other way damage the finish, so that the base, lighter wood shows through, then you can repair the blemish very effectively with a black spirit marker pen by simply rubbing it over the offending area (*see* Fig 21.8). Scratches can be filled with black wax or black French polish.

**Fig 21.7** A B O V E : **By rubbing black paint into the wood you can create a rich deep black stain. (Incidentally, this can be done with any colour paint, so if you can't find the correct colour stain, experiment with rubbing paints into the wood.)**

**Fig 21.8** A B O V E : **You can easily patch up ebonized furniture with a black marker pen.**

# CHAPTER 22

# PAINTED FINISHES

PHOTO COURTESY OF ICI PAINTS LTD.

*Today, the most commonly applied finish for wooden surfaces is undoubtedly paint. Doors, skirting boards, picture frames, shelves, window sills, doorsteps, gates, garage doors, window frames, staircases, bannisters, handrails – paint, paint everywhere, but never, it seems, on furniture.*

This is a pity as paint is the perfect way to transform a piece of drab old woody-toned furniture into a sparkling, effervescent, interior-coordinated, any-colour-of-the-rainbow, modern, easy-to-care-for, conversation piece. If you are fed up with me waffling on about grain structures, the natural beauty of the wood and patinas, then have a go with this finish.

## STYLES OF PAINTED FINISH

There are dozens of recipes for the application of paint, from prehistoric cave painting through to the Sistine chapel, Henry Ford's cars and hand-painted ties – the list is endless. As far as painted furniture is concerned, there are two distinct classes. Firstly, there are those which require a little practice and perhaps the ability to paint in a realistic manner; included in this class are trompe l'oeil, marbling, graining and the imitation of all sorts of weird, wonderful and sometimes doubtful materials.

Secondly, there are those painting skills that just need some good instruction and are easily managed by the absolute beginner. These are called broken colour techniques. It is these simple forms of painted decoration using just two colours that will be described in this chapter.

From the absolute beginner's point of view, these basic recipes will be sufficient to keep the novice furniture restorer occupied for an unlimited number of projects. With this information you can then create painted furniture to your heart's delight, and with the addition of a little experience and artistry you can create unique works of art. Applying broken colour technique involves painting a base coat on to the furniture in one colour and then highlighting various features of the furniture with another colour.

## PAINTED FURNITURE IN THE HOME

Contrary to popular belief, painted furniture is not a modern-day fad. A large part of the furniture of the past, going right back to Egyptian times, was in some manner or degree, painted (*see* Figs 22.2 and 22.3). In recent years there has been a revival of interest in this form of furniture finishing.

However, in my classes I often find a reluctance amongst my students to experiment with paint. 'Why,' I ask them, 'when every style magazine in the country is advocating its use?' It appears that painted furniture will look out of place in many homes because it has a somewhat 'arty', modern look to it – the lime green sideboard with yellow mouldings looks magnificent, but exactly what room do you put it in, once you have finished it? Much painted furniture will stick out like a candle on a cake in the average conservatively furnished home. So, although painted furniture is much vaunted in the arty style magazines, it is viewed with a little trepidation by owners of the more functional households.

**Fig 22.2**

RIGHT AND BELOW: **Egyptian painted boxes (1550–1296 BC).**

**Fig 22.3**

PHOTOS COURTESY OF BUCKINGHAMSHIRE COLLEGE.

However, even in the more conservative households there are many rooms where this kind of finish will work extremely well. The nursery is an obvious place to have brightly painted furniture and fixtures (*see* Fig 22.4). Here you may like to try some of the more brightly coloured schemes and techniques. In this environment it is important that you only use paints that are clearly labelled as non-toxic and safe for toys.

Another place that painted furniture works well is in the bathroom. Here the other practical attributes of painted furniture come to the fore; paint provides extremely good protection to wood from damp and water. Then there is the conservatory or

garden furniture; for the same reason, painted furniture has many practical benefits in these settings. In recent years there has been an explosion of interest in exotically painted wooden fixtures and fittings for the kitchen (*see* Fig 22.5). Lastly, there is the bedroom – usually the most private of rooms. Here you are free to indulge your most creative whims on fantasy furniture, without the fear of an unfavourable review from the neighbourhood 'style guru'.

**Fig 22.5** B E L O W : **A kitchen with wooden areas painted in Do It All own brand colours: Oxford Blue and Cornfield liquid gloss.**

**Fig 22.4** A B O V E : **A chair for the nursery.**

Apart from these aesthetic reasons for choosing a painted finish, there is another very practical reason why it is an essential part of every furniture restorer's reportoire. Along with ebonizing (*see* Chapter 21), paint is a 'lifesaver finish'. When all else fails and you are just about to douse the furniture with petrol and end it all, try painting it. Every blemish known to man, no matter how bizarre, can be obliterated under a beautiful coat of artistically applied paint.

There is one last reason for using paint: it allows you free rein to express any artistic leanings in a very practical way. You can turn the most plain and ordinary piece of furniture into a real conversation piece. What better way to impress the vicar than sitting him in a chair which has been hand-painted by you to depict your impression of the 'Rape of the Sabines', or your copy of Picasso's 'Guernica'. If you are the least bit capable with paint and brush you can simply use the furniture as a three-dimensional canvas (*see* Figs 22.6 and 22.7). You can use artists' oil colours, designers' craft colours or whichever paint type you are used to.

## CHOOSING THE COLOUR

One of the biggest problems with this type of finish is choosing the colour scheme. Colour is notoriously difficult to choose. Whether you are choosing an outfit for a wedding or the colour of your curtains, it takes a lot of head scratching.

I hope to make this easy for you. For the broken colour technique you will need to buy two colours; one of them is white (that's half the problem solved). The colour of the other pot of paint depends on the colour scheme of the room where the furniture is going to be placed. Choose a colour that is the same as one of the major colours in that room. Look at the colour of the carpets, the curtains, the walls, the ceiling, the rest of the furniture, and decide on a fitting colour (*see* Fig 22.8). If you like, take some colour swatches (available wherever you buy paint) to the room and sit there for a while contemplating. Take stock of what is already there and make a match. Try to imagine your furniture

**Fig 22.6** B E L O W : **Amsterdam cabinet with painted interior.**

**Fig 22.7** L E F T : **Painted wardrobe from Germany.**

painted in your chosen colour. If you think you may have found a colour but are still not sure, go out and buy a small pot of it, apply it to a sheet of card or hardboard and stand it in the room for perusal.

Sometimes you will not know where the furniture is to end up, so you are free to indulge your most creative whims. After all, if you don't like the end result, you can always paint over it! Total freedom is yours. Let yourself go. Enjoy it.

If you have trouble with these colour-choosing methods, or you are looking for something a bit more radical, try this method of finding two matching colours: look through some magazines and find a colour scheme that you like. This does not have to be in features on home decoration; it could just as easily be in an advertisement for baby food or for lawnmowers. The point is, every image in a colour magazine will have been carefully thought about in terms of its colour balance. The designer has spent a lot of time, energy and experience matching colours that work well together. Why waste their hard work? When you find a colour combination that you think is suitable, quite simply copy it.

For the purpose of this chapter I shall presume that you have chosen navy blue as your colour to add to your pot of white paint.

**Fig 22.9** R I G H T : **White and the chosen colour paint decanted into jars prior to mixing.**

**Fig 22.8** A B O V E : **Green bedroom.**

## CHOOSE YOUR PAINT

Decorators' oil paint is recognized by the fact that it is slow drying and the thinners and brush cleaner is white spirit. It is the standard housepainters' paint and so should be obtainable from any D.I.Y. store. When you go to the store to buy your paint you will have a choice of gloss, satin or matt; any of these types will be suitable.

There are many different manufacturers of paints, and some stores only carry a limited number, so it is worthwhile looking at other stores to see if they have the colours you want. If you can't buy the colour you want off the shelf, some stores will mix the colour for you.

## MIXING PAINT

Here is how you make your perfect colour match. Decant half of the white paint into a screw-top container, then add a teaspoon of the blue and stir thoroughly; this could take three or four minutes of vigorous stirring (*see* Fig 22.9).

This will produce a light blue that will match perfectly with the dark blue. The lighter colour is the one that you are going to apply first and is going to cover all parts of the furniture, so make sure you mix enough. The darker, stronger colour is going to be applied to create the 'decoration'.

The same principle of mixing a colour with white to produce a lighter shade of the colour produces a good colour combination every time – yellow and light yellow, green and light green, red and light red etc. It does not matter what the main colour is; if you mix it with white and produce a lighter shade, the two colours will work perfectly together.

## APPLICATION

First strip the furniture back to the bare wood as described in Chapter 6. If it is cabinet furniture, i.e. it has drawers or cupboard space, you can decide at this stage if you want to paint the inside of these areas. If you do want to paint them (and some stunning results can occur if you decide to do so by using a contrasting colour inside), then you will need to strip these areas as well. When finished, fill any holes and mend any broken bits, rub the wood down with medium-grade sandpaper to leave a smooth surface, and then you are ready to start.

The first coat is thinned down with 10 per cent white spirits and applied to the project, working methodically round the furniture (*see* Fig 22.10). This coat is intended to soak deep into the wood and grip the surface of the wood so that the paint sticks well. Fifteen minutes after you have finished, check the finish for drips and runs. Wipe these off

**Fig 22.10** R I G H T : **This little cabinet was found in a skip. I have stripped it, replaced the damaged top with some plywood and added some wooden knobs.**

with a cloth dampened with white spirit and leave to dry overnight.

It would be helpful for you to think of paint as polyurethane varnish with pigments added, and read Chapter 18 on this subject. It describes some of the finer points of paint application, which will save me from repeating them here.

The first thing to be noticed by anybody who uses paint is that smudges and blobs of paint will find their way to every conceivable part of your anatomy. If you use the paint thinly as I suggest, it is easily flicked off the end of the bristles and could end up anywhere within a five-mile radius. So the first thing to do is prepare for the inevitable by protecting surfaces such as floors and walls. Then protect yourself by wearing old clothes. Have some white spirits and cloths handy to clean off paint that gets on to your hands, face, hair, feet, ears, nose and throat. Stay clean by following these instructions:

- Only dip the tip of the paintbrush into the paint.

- Keep the handle of the brush scrupulously clean.

- Keep hands clean.

- Wipe up spills, drips and runs as they occur.

- Decant the paint into a shallow container so that it is no more than ½in (12mm) deep. This will stop the brush sinking into the paint and coating the handle as well as the bristles. It will also save you wiping the bristles on the rim of the can, causing drips to run down the outside.

If you stick to these rules, then the paint will stay firmly where you want it, and will not travel anywhere unintended.

Leave the first coat to dry overnight, then rub down with wet-and-dry abrasive paper. The next coat can be applied in a similar fashion. The secret ingredient of this type of finish is the rubbing down. Many people presume that a good finish is achieved by applying the paint well; this is wrong. A good coat of paint is achieved by rubbing down the previous coat well with abrasives. Three or four coats should suffice.

If you follow my colour scheme you should now have a light blue piece of furniture. This is a lovely colour and you may choose to leave it just like that (*see* Fig 22.11). But by applying a coat of the darker blue colour you can really make the furniture come alive.

In my project I have decided to limit my darker colour to some well-defined areas. I drew a border in pencil around the doors and top of the furniture and filled them with navy blue paint using an artist's brush (*see* Fig 22.12).

For the cloudy-looking areas I have used a technique called 'ragging on' (*see* Fig 22.13). This involves screwing up a rag of cotton cloth, then using the texture and the folds of the cloth to print the mid-blue colour over the light blue (*see* Figs 22.14 and 22.15). Test your print on a piece of paper first to establish how hard you have to push and how much paint you need to use (*see* Fig 22.16). It will take a little experimenting before you get the right mix of paint and pressure. When you think it is about right, transfer to the furniture. Protect with newspaper any areas you do not want painted and start printing.

Once the first coat has dried you can apply another one on top, so building up the depth of the decoration. If you overdo it, just rag on a little of the lighter blue to mingle with the mid-blue and break up some of the darker colour. You can fiddle about with the two colours, applying one and then the other to your heart's content.

When you are happy with your handiwork, allow it to dry overnight, then give your handiwork a protective top coat to seal everything in. If you have used a light colour scheme, as in my example, then I suggest you use two or three coats of white French polish or satin water-based varnish as these finishes do not discolour with age.

The other type of finish to use as a sealer is satin polyurethane varnish, but I only use this with darker colour schemes or yellow- and brown-toned paint as this tends to yellow with age.

There are many ways in which paint can be used to enliven furniture, so if you enjoy the look and the process of this finish, I suggest you use this chapter as a springboard for research and experiment into other colour schemes and techniques.

## The broken colour technique applied to a small cabinet

**Fig 22.11** L E F T : **The cabinet, now with two coats of light blue paint.**

**Fig 22.12** R I G H T : **I then applied some decorative borders with the dark blue paint. The knobs were painted gold on the instructions of Alice, my five-year-old daughter.**

**Fig 22.13** L E F T : **The final stage is the application of the ragged effect, achieved by printing with the rolled up cloth dipped in a mid-blue paint. This colour has been made by adding an extra teaspoon of dark blue to the white.**

## Ragging on

**Fig 22.14, Fig 22.15** A B O V E : **To make the pad for rag rolling, fold and roll up the cotton cloth into a rose-like shape until you have a pad that leaves a satisfactory print.**

**Fig 22.16** A B O V E : **Test the pad on a spare sheet of paper before applying it to the furniture.**

# CHAPTER 23

# DISTRESSING AND
## —— PATINA ——

*So, you have finished the project. The furniture is looking as good as new — no unsightly stains, no scratches, no dents, no wobbly bits. Everything is looking just dandy, except for one problem . . . It looks just a little bit too new.*

Now, if you are one of those people who are restoring their furniture so that it can become a functional and useful piece of furniture again, you may well wonder what on earth can be the problem with a piece of furniture that looks too new. The answer is, of course, there is nothing wrong. However, some furniture, particularly older, antique furniture, can look odd if it is sporting a brand-new finish and looks as if it has just been delivered from the store. Often the fact that the piece is so obviously old will jar visually with the fact that the finish is so obviously new.

If this is how you feel about your finished project, then there is a particular range of 'restoration' techniques that you can employ to remedy the problem. This is known in furniture restoration circles as 'distressing'. This is a particularly interesting aspect of furniture restoration, but it has to be said that most newcomers to the craft rarely have the nerve to take part in it wholeheartedly, especially when they have spent so many long hours lovingly trying to achieve a state of newness. If you are worried about some of the following techniques and think that you may ruin an otherwise good job, then practise some of these techniques on a spare piece of finished timber or board.

## WHAT IS DISTRESSING?

A very simple definition of the term distressing is 'to make something that is new look old'. When this technique is done badly, it is little short of vandalism. When done well with skill and sympathy, then it is an art in its own right. When done with intent to deceive a potential buyer, it comes under the heading of fraud, but that is an issue of conscience that I shall leave the reader to wrestle with.

In the more orthodox world of furniture restoration, distressing is employed when a missing piece of furniture is replaced. Usually the new wood will need 'ageing' to blend in with the older portion of furniture. For example, a restorer or cabinetmaker may need to make a new leg for a Queen Anne chair. Once made and finished the repair would have to be distressed to match the original condition and patina of the rest of the chair.

## WHAT IS PATINA?

Before progressing to some of the techniques of distressing, I should like to clarify the meaning of the word patina. There are two different types of patina: patina of the wood and patina of the finish. Patina of the wood is the surface discoloration of wood that occurs over a period of time. This can be caused by a number of different elements. Sunlight can affect the colour of wood by either darkening or bleaching. Over a period of time, depending on the type of finish employed, dirt can become embedded in the wood. Also, finishes such as waxes and oils can oxidize (change chemically) and darken the wood. Likewise, wood colour can be affected by reactions between chemicals in the wood and chemicals in the air, water, and cleaning agents. These changes can continue to have an effect on the colour of wood many years after the furniture was made.

Patina of the finish is caused by the accumulated build-up of wax, dirt, scratches and worn patches – in other words, wear and tear. This is known as either character or damage depending on whether you are selling or buying.

Both of these patina types – patina of the wood and patina of the finish – will indicate the      of a

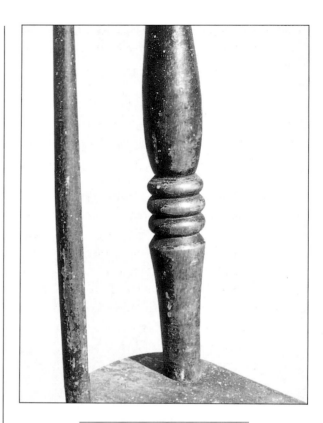

**Fig 23.1** A B O V E : **Example of an original distressed finish.**

piece of furniture. If the furniture has a value because of its age, the absence of these indicators will adversely affect the price. More importantly from the restorer's point of view are the aesthetics involved in patina. If patina is removed during restoration, the furniture can lose a lot of its character and look 'wrong'. If you would like to replace some of that patina and character to a restored piece of furniture, then read on . . .

## GOOD AND BAD DISTRESSING

If you have no experience of this type of technique or the notion of patina, character, and dirt, the first thing to do is to look at some old furniture. Take a trip to an antique shop and view the furniture there. Look for any marks or blemishes that give the furniture character and are attractive, then try to find a way of copying them (*see* Fig 23.1).

To an experienced eye, a piece of furniture that has been badly distressed is as obvious as a flag in a breeze; this is because the distressing has been done without thought or consideration for what makes up an original distressed finish. If you stop to consider that an original finish is an accumulation of many decades, or centuries, of wear and tear, it would be foolish to think that you could emulate this by applying a dark stain and indulging in half an hour of 'stress relief' with a bicycle chain. The best and most convincing distressing is achieved over as long a period of time as possible, and with as many different weapons as possible.

If you try to invent the features that make a piece look old, you will be far too logical. Look at an old piece of furniture; often it is the marks that are not readily understood which are the most intriguing, and give it character. The marks left by Aunt Ada's high heels when she got a little drunk and danced on the sideboard with cousin Kevin; the burn marks that Grandad left by tapping his pipe out on the corner of the kitchen table; the knife marks that young Brian left in his bedside cabinet when he tried to teach himself how to gut fish. These marks and scratches act as a diary of events in the life of the furniture and give it character. (On the other hand, they may remind you just how disgusting your relatives are, and are therefore best removed.)

## HOW TO DISTRESS YOUR FURNITURE

Distressing is not an exact science, as you may have guessed, and each distresser will invent and compose a number of different techniques and recipes. I shall try to list the ones that I have used or heard about and allow you to choose the ones that most suit you and your furniture. Feel free to experiment with other methods that you think may be successful.

If you are intending to distress your furniture then the earlier you make the decision the easier the job will be. It's an obvious waste of time to spend weeks removing the tiniest of scratches only to decide that you want to spend weeks putting them all back again. However, these decisions take a little experience and so are difficult for a novice to make. Ideally, you would decide whether you are going to distress a piece *before* you actually start work on it. Often this is not the first thing on your mind.

I shall work through some of the distressing techniques that can be employed in the same order as you would work on a piece of furniture, starting with stripping. Perhaps the most useful and time-consuming device is to read Chapter 7 on the sympathetic stripping of old French-polished furniture known as antiquikstrip. This technique will allow you to strip the finish without disturbing the wood or many of the original surface scratches.

Before stripping it is worth making a few notes just to remind you of the areas of the furniture that have shown the most wear and tear. You may also like to take a photograph. This may give you a few clues if you decide to replace some of the character you remove by stripping. If you strip back to the bare wood, the first consideration is the stain to be used on the furniture. If you are intent on distressing, the correct colour is most important – usually the darker the better – achievable with any of the stains mentioned in Chapter 13.

After staining, consider wiping off some of the stain in areas that show wear or the bleaching effect of the sun. This would typically be places like the rails of chairs where feet tend to be rested. Conversely, at the base of kitchen furniture you will often find black marks caused by accumulated knocks, grease and the effects of frequent sluicing down of stone floors and mopping or scrubbing. This you may wish to copy with a dark stain at the bottom of chair and table legs etc. It is also common to splash writing ink on to writing furniture (*see* page 53).

With pine furniture there is a technique of painting on malt vinegar to emulate the effect of ageing. This can be followed by a wax finish. Otherwise you can just apply an off-the-shelf 'old pine' stain.

Alternatively, there is a well-known technique for ageing wood which relies on the fumes given off by ammonia. This technique will give certain woods, such as mahogany and oak, an old, grey, weathered look. However, these fumes can be dangerous. If you wish to try it, obtain some ammonia from the chemist or D.I.Y. shop. Always use this chemical out of doors and keep well away from your face. Wearing gloves, pour some of the ammonia into a dish, place the item to be fumed over or next to the dish, then cover the whole lot with a sheet of plastic arranged in a way that holds

in all the ammonia fumes. Cut an inspection flap in the sheet of plastic and tape it back up. Leave for two hours or longer, depending on the size of item and strength of ammonia and check every 45 minutes; the longer you leave it under, the darker it will become (*see* Fig 23.2).

The under edge of country chairs and tables, which are usually unfinished, are often coloured with dark finger marks (*see* Fig 23.3). This can be copied with a combination of grease from the car engine, plus dark brown stain, mixed with a little wax. Apply this concoction with the fingers and allow to dry before cleaning with some clean wax. If you are fussy or a dentist by profession you can wear a pair of gloves.

**Fig 23.2** A B O V E : **Arrangement for fuming using ammonia. Always perform this operation out of doors.**

If you are back to the bare wood, you may wish to consider not filling some of the less noticeable dents and gouges, but only removing the more visually annoying problems. Dents in the wood can be emulated with any number of weapons, but beware of making too many marks with the same weapon. If you beat the furniture mercilessly with a baseball bat with old nails in it, then it is going to look like someone has beaten it mercilessly with a baseball bat with old nails in it. Try a little subtlety.

If you want to give some wear and tear to a top, rolling half a house brick around yields some good results, as does dropped cutlery, or beatings with various lengths of chain (*see* Fig 23.4).

If you intend to wax the furniture, you may wish to make up your own antique wax (*see* page 127). If you are using a French polish finish, you can apply some layers of ordinary polish, followed by a layer of darker-toned French polish. This is made up by mixing some spirit stain with some French polish, so producing dark brown French polish (*see* pages 116–7). This can be applied with a brush to the nooks and crannies. When dry you can rub this back to soften the effect with some fine wire wool until you are satisfied with the results, before continuing with the standard-coloured French polish. When this is complete, you can finish off with your home-made antique wax (*see* Chapter 14 for the recipe).

You may wish to consider leaving the unfinished furniture outside on a warm day and allowing it to be caught in a shower of rain. Sun will cause wood to colour naturally and the shower of rain will age the wood. This technique can also split the end grain, so beware.

Some craftspeople have been known to place the stripped furniture in a horse's stable or pigsty for a couple of weeks. Here the animals rub up against the wood and knock into it, causing rub

**Fig 23.3** ABOVE: **The black fingermarks around the edge of the underside of this chair are found on all old furniture.**

**Fig 23.4** RIGHT: **Just some of the weapons used to distress newly finished furniture to give it that 'antique' look: blowtorch, wire brush, loose change, the bottom of stoneware jugs or pots, fine-grade sand or salt, nuts and bolts, bricks, wire wool.**

**Fig 23.5** A B O V E : **An example of the wear, tear and patina encountered around small knobs and clasps.**

marks and dents, the ammonia contained in the animal urine will colour the wood, and the legs of the furniture will stand in 'nature's own colouring matter', recreating the effect of decades of kitchen floors.

Once you have applied the finish, there are a number of things that can be done to make furniture look less than new. You can emulate the wear that is commonly found around the lower reaches of chairs and the bottom of legs and stretchers, with sandpaper. Rub back to the bare wood and refinish with more polish.

Places where hands are commonly placed, such as handles and knobs, will be highly polished in some areas and grubby in others. Often the polish will be removed by fingernails when the fingers clasp a small handle or knob (*see* Fig 23.5).

If a French polish finish is looking too bright, try wafting a blowtorch over the surface; this will deteriorate it, removing any freshness, and will emulate a few scorching hot summers by the window (*see* Fig 23.6). This can be followed up with medium-grade wire wool and antique wax rubbed into the surface as gently as you possibly can.

If you wish to copy some of the scratches often found on the top of furniture, select some loose

change, nuts and bolts, a little fine-grade sand, and anything else that springs to mind. Move them around the surface of the table, picking them up and putting them down over a period of a couple of days, then rub in some antique wax, and finally, buff gently.

You can use rubbing compound to polish the well-used parts of furniture that have a satin finish. This can be used on chairs which have been given a brush-applied French polish. Old chairs will be highly polished on the seat, back and arm rests (sometimes the finish is worn away completely). On the underside of the arms, between slats, and on the legs, the finish will be very dull and dirty.

If you employ all of the above techniques you will end up with a piece of furniture that looks exactly the same as the project that you started off with. So what better excuse do you need to turn to the front of the book and start all over again.

**Fig 23.6** A B O V E : **To emulate the damage caused by hot summers by the window, and winters too close to the open fire, waft a blowtorch over the fresh polish to age it.**

# GLOSSARY

**ANILINE DYES**  Variation on spirit dyes.

**BITE**  The ability of a stain to penetrate the wood.

**BURNISHING CREAM**  Paste used to polish hard substances.

**CABINET FURNITURE**  Furniture with drawers and/or doors.

**CABRIOLE LEGS**  A type of curved leg design much used in old furniture.

**CAR RUBBING COMPOUND**  Burnishing cream prepared specifically for use on cars.

**CHIPBOARD**  Man-made wood composed of compressed wood chips.

**CHIPPENDALE**  Famous 18th-century master cabinetmaker.

**CLAW HAMMER**  Special type of hammer incorporating device for removing nails.

**COMMODE**  A chair with a hinged flap concealing a chamberpot.

**DENIB**  Smooth with abrasive paper to remove roughness in a finish.

**DISCLOSER STAIN**  Thin stain used to highlight blemishes prior to use.

**DOWELS**  Rods made of wood.

**EMULSION PAINT**  Water-based paint much used in home decoration.

**FORMICA**  Man-made plastic veneer often used in food preparation areas.

**FRETWORK**  Decorative technique of cutting through thin wooden sections of wood to create a pattern.

**GRAINING**  Imitation of various wood grains using paint.

**HACKSAW**  Saw with very fine teeth used to cut metals.

**HARDBOARD**  Thin man-made board composed of compressed wood dust.

**HOSE CLIPS**  Clips designed to secure pipes and hoses.

**HUMIDIFIERS**  Device hung on radiators to put moisture into the air.

**LEACH OUT**  Drain out slowly.

**LIGHT FAST**  Something that will not fade in strong light.

**LIPPINGS**  Solid wood often used around the edge of veneered wood.

**MARBLING**  Imitation of marble using paint.

**OAK PANELLING**  Wall decoration composed of squares of oak wood.

**PATERA**  Round wooden low-relief decorations used to decorate furniture.

**PIGMENT**  Powders used to colour paint (amongst other things).

**PLANING**  The smoothing and squaring of timber with a plane.

**PLASTER OF PARIS**  White powder that hardens when mixed with water.

**PLASTICINE**  A clay substitute used by artists and craftspeople.

**PLYWOOD**  Layers of veneer stuck together to make a board.

**QUADRANT**  Wooden moulding shaped in cross section like quarter of a circle.

**ROGUE PASSES**  Unscheduled passes in French polishing, intended to fill in where scheduled passes miss.

**SHAKERS**  American religious sect renowned for their crafts.

**SIDEBOARD**  Piece of furniture traditionally used to store cutlery.

**SOLID WOOD**  Wood in its natural state, i.e. not veneered or man-made.

**SPIRIT MARKER PEN**  Pen with fibre tip and spirit-based ink.

**STABLE WOOD**  Wood that is known for its ability not to warp or move.

**STAY**  Hinge used to stop lids of boxes opening too far.

**SUEDE BRUSH**  Small wire brush.

**SWAG**  Crescent-shaped area of wood that is usually carved.

**TROMPE L'OEIL**  Painted effect designed to deceive the eye.

**UNCLE GEORGE**  Person who gives questionable advice on matters of furniture restoration.

**WADDING**  Cotton wool-based material used to upholster furniture.

# SUPPLIERS

## GENERAL

Craft Supplies Ltd, *The Mill, Millers Dale, Buxton, SK17 8SN*

Rustins Ltd, *Waterloo Rd, London NW2 7TX*

W S Jenkins & Co. Ltd, *Jeco Works, Tariff Rd, London N17 0EN*

John Myland Ltd, *80 Norwood High St, West Norwood, London SE27 9NW*

House of Harbru, *101 Crostons Rd, Elton, Bury, Lancashire BL8 1AL*

Liberon Waxes Ltd, *Learoyd Rd, New Romney, Kent TN28 8XU*

Restoration Materials, *Proctor St, Bury, Lancashire BL8 2NY*

Cuprinol Ltd, *Adderwell, Frome, Somerset BA11 1NL*

Sterling Roncraft, *15 Churchfield Court, Barnsley, South Yorkshire*

John Boddy's Mail Order Catalogue, *Riverside Sawmills, Boroughbridge, North Yorkshire YO5 9LJ*

F T Morrell and Co. Ltd, *214 Acton Lane, London NW10 7NH (and branches)*

## HARDWARE

Martin & Co., *119 Camden St, Birmingham B1 3DJ*

Romany Tyzack, *52–56 Camden High St, London NW1 0LT*

Suffolk Brass, *Thurston, Bury St Edmunds, Suffolk IP31 3SN*

## LEATHER AND DYES

Artisan Products, *4 The Parade, Valley Drive, Brighton, East Sussex*

J T Batchelor Ltd, *10 Culford Mews, London N1 4DZ*

## VENEERS

The Art Veneer Co. Ltd, *Mildenhall, Suffolk IP28 7AY*

J Crispins & Sons, *92–96 Curtain Rd, London EC2A 3AA*

Transworld Veneer Co. Ltd, *55 The Avenue, Luton, Bedfordshire LU4 9AF*

## WATER-BASED PAINTS

Maestro Craft Colours, *7 Stephen Gray Rd, Mold, Clwyd CH7 1JR*

## WATER-BASED FINISHES

West Country Finishes, *The Paint Factory, Pottery Rd, Bovey Tracey, Devon TQ13 9DS*

## USA SUPPLIERS

Sutherland Welles, *113 W. Main St, Carrboro, NC 27570*

Vartung Coatings, *Box 1042, Picayne, MS 39466*

H Behlen & Bros, *RT. 30N, Amsterdam, NY 12010 (write for the location of nearest distributor)*

Universal Shellac and Supply Co., *495 W. John St, Hicksville, NY 11801*

Mohawk Finishing Products, *RT 30N, Amsterdam, NY 12010*

Constantine, *2065 Eastchester Rd, Bronx, NY 10461*

Garett Wade Co., *161 Ave of the Americas, New York, NY 10013*

Star Chemical Co. Inc., *360 Shore Drive, Hinsdale, IL 60521*

Laurence McFadden Co., *7430 State Rd, Philadelphia, PA 19136*

James B Day & Co., *Day Lane, Carpentersville, IL 60110*

Woodcraft, *41 Atlantic Ave, Box 4000, Woburn, MA 01888*

Craftsman Wood Service Co., *1735 W. Cortland Court, Addison, IL 60101*

The Bartley Collection Ltd, *747 Oakwood Ave, Lake Forest, IL 60045*

Hughson Chemical Co., *Erie, PA 16512*

Flecto International, *1000–1002 45th St, Oakland, CA 94608*

Talas, *213 W. 35th St, New York, NY 10001–1996*

William Zinsser Co., *39 Belmont Drive, Somerset, NJ 08873*

Bix Process Systems, *Plumtrees Rd, Bethel, CT 06801*

# ABOUT THE
## AUTHOR

*Kevin Jan Bonner is an artist, designer,
craftsperson and teacher.
After studying sculpture at art college, Kevin
started his own craft/design workshop,
specializing in the design and manufacture of
award-winning, sculpted wooden toys. He has
also spent many years teaching art and craft
subjects at adult education institutes.
He lives in North London with Debbie, five
children, two dogs, a cat, seven rabbits (at last
count), three guinea pigs and a hamster.
His ambition is to take a holiday.*

# INDEX

# TITLES AVAILABLE FROM
# GMC Publications

## ━━ BOOKS ━━

### WOODTURNING

| | | | |
|---|---|---|---|
| Adventures in Woodturning | *David Springett* | Practical Tips for Turners & Carvers | *GMC Publications* |
| Bert Marsh: Woodturner | *Bert Marsh* | Practical Tips for Woodturners | *GMC Publications* |
| Bill Jones' Notes from the Turning Shop | *Bill Jones* | Spindle Turning | *GMC Publications* |
| Bill Jones' Further Notes from the Turning Shop | *Bill Jones* | Turning Miniatures in Wood | *John Sainsbury* |
| Carving on Turning | *Chris Pye* | Turning Wooden Toys | *Terry Lawrence* |
| Colouring Techniques for Woodturners | *Jan Sanders* | Understanding Woodturning | *Ann & Bob Phillips* |
| Decorative Techniques for Woodturners | *Hilary Bowen* | Useful Woodturning Projects | *GMC Publications* |
| Faceplate Turning: Features, Projects, Practice | *GMC Publications* | Woodturning: A Foundation Course | *Keith Rowley* |
| Green Woodwork | *Mike Abbott* | Woodturning Jewellery | *Hilary Bowen* |
| Illustrated Woodturning Techniques | *John Hunnex* | Woodturning Masterclass | *Tony Boase* |
| Keith Rowley's Woodturning Projects | *Keith Rowley* | Woodturning: A Source Book of Shapes | *John Hunnex* |
| Make Money from Woodturning | *Ann & Bob Phillips* | Woodturning Techniques | *GMC Publications* |
| Multi-Centre Woodturning | *Ray Hopper* | Woodturning Wizardry | *David Springett* |
| Pleasure & Profit from Woodturning | *Reg Sherwin* | | |

### WOODCARVING

| | | | |
|---|---|---|---|
| The Art of the Woodcarver | *GMC Publications* | Understanding Woodcarving | *GMC Publications* |
| Carving Birds & Beasts | *GMC Publications* | Wildfowl Carving Volume 1 | *Jim Pearce* |
| Carving Realistic Birds | *David Tippey* | Wildfowl Carving Volume 2 | *Jim Pearce* |
| Carving on Turning | *Chris Pye* | The Woodcarvers | *GMC Publications* |
| Decorative Woodcarving | *Jeremy Williams* | Woodcarving: A Complete Course | *Ron Butterfield* |
| Essential Woodcarving Techniques | *Dick Onians* | Woodcarving for Beginners: | |
| Lettercarving in Wood | *Chris Pye* | Projects, Techniques & Tools | *GMC Publications* |
| Practical Tips for Turners & Carvers | *GMC Publications* | Woodcarving Tools, Materials & Equipment | *Chris Pye* |

### PLANS, PROJECTS, TOOLS & THE WORKSHOP

| | | | |
|---|---|---|---|
| The Incredible Router | *Jeremy Broun* | Sharpening Pocket Reference Book | *Jim Kingshott* |
| Making & Modifying Woodworking Tools | *Jim Kingshott* | The Workshop | *Jim Kingshott* |
| Sharpening: The Complete Guide | *Jim Kingshott* | | |

### TOYS & MINIATURES

| | | | |
|---|---|---|---|
| Designing & Making Wooden Toys | *Terry Kelly* | Miniature Needlepoint Carpets | *Janet Granger* |
| Making Board, Peg & Dice Games | *Jeff & Jennie Loader* | Turning Miniatures in Wood | *John Sainsbury* |
| Making Little Boxes from Wood | *John Bennett* | Turning Wooden Toys | *Terry Lawrence* |
| Making Wooden Toys & Games | *Jeff & Jennie Loader* | | |

### CREATIVE CRAFTS

| | | | |
|---|---|---|---|
| Celtic Knotwork Designs | *Sheila Sturrock* | Creating Knitwear Designs | *Pat Ashforth & Steve Plummer* |
| Collage from Seeds, Leaves and Flowers | *Joan Carver* | Making Knitwear Fit | *Pat Ashforth & Steve Plummer* |
| The Complete Pyrography | *Stephen Poole* | Miniature Needlepoint Carpets | *Janet Granger* |
| Cross Stitch on Colour | *Sheena Rogers* | Tatting Collage: Adventurous Ideas for Tatters | *Lindsay Rogers* |
| Embroidery Tips & Hints | *Harold Hayes* | | |